National Reckonings

National Reckonings

*The Last Judgment and Literature
in Milton's England*

Ryan Hackenbracht

Cornell University Press
Ithaca and London

First published 2019 by Cornell University Press

Library of Congress Cataloging-in-Publication Data

Names: Hackenbracht, Ryan, author.
Title: National reckonings : the Last Judgment and literature in Milton's England / Ryan Hackenbracht.
Description: Ithaca : Cornell University Press, 2019. | Includes bibliographical references and index.
Identifiers: LCCN 2018034212 (print) | LCCN 2018047137 (ebook) | ISBN 9781501731082 (pdf) | ISBN 9781501731099 (ret) | ISBN 9781501731075 | ISBN 9781501731075 (cloth ; alk. paper)
Subjects: LCSH: English literature—Early modern, 1500–1700—History and criticism. | Judgment Day in literature. | Eschatology in literature. | Nationalism in literature. | Christianity and politics—England—History—17th century.
Classification: LCC PR438.J83 (ebook) | LCC PR438.J83 H33 2019 (print) | DDC 820.9/3581—dc23
LC record available at https://lccn.loc.gov/2018034212

For my grandmother, May Ukita

From first to last, and not merely in the epilogue, Christianity is eschatology.

    —Jürgen Moltmann, *Theology of Hope* (1965)

We hunger for ends and for crises. "Is this the promis'd end?" we ask with Kent in *Lear*; if not, we require that it be an image of it.

    —Frank Kermode, *The Sense of an Ending* (1966)

Now is our salvation nearer than when we believed.

    —Romans 13:11

CONTENTS

ILLUSTRATIONS

ACKNOWLEDGMENTS

I have accrued a great number of debts to people and institutions while researching and writing this book. I am indebted, first and foremost, to Laura L. Knoppers, who helped me craft the project in its early stages, read countless drafts of chapters, and gave guidance along the way. She has been the very best of teachers. The book has also benefitted from the insight of Garrett A. Sullivan, Jr., another inspiring mentor, who has given me keen advice and suggestions over the years. At Cornell University Press, Achsah Guibbory and another, anonymous reader provided me with detailed recommendations for revision, and I am deeply grateful for the care with which they read the manuscript. I am thankful, as well, to Mahinder Kingra, editor in chief at Cornell University Press, for selecting such thoughtful readers and for his enthusiastic support of the project. I also extend my gratitude to Production Editor Sara R. Ferguson for her exceptional work in bringing the manuscript to press. Paul Stevens generously read chapters and helped me refine my arguments on nationalism, while Patrick Cheney challenged me to think through the implications for literary form and genre, Philip Jenkins aided in the nuances of early modern theology, and Linda Woodbridge offered invaluable comments on early drafts. For training in historical methodology and archival resources, I am appreciative of the excellent instruction I received from Robert D. Hume. Reading multiple drafts of chapters (without complaining) is the mark of a true friend, and Giuseppina Iacono Lobo, Leah Orr, and Paul Zajac have proven among the truest; I am thankful for their perceptive comments on chapters in various stages of development. The delightful community of early modern scholars at Texas Tech University, particularly Matthew Hunter, Abigail L. Swingen, and Sarah Banschbach Valles, has been a terrific source of support and wisdom. I am also deeply grateful to my two medieval colleagues and mentors at Texas Tech, Julie Nelson Couch and Brian McFadden, for their advice and support of my work over the years. For their discerning feedback on chapters and general encouragement, I would also like to thank Katharine Cleland, Timothy M. Harrison, Rayna Kalas, Ivan Lupić, Ryan Netzley, Alan Rudrum, Chad Schrock, James R. Siemon, David V. Urban, Joseph Wittreich, and Keith Wrightson.

This project has been supported by fellowships and grants from several institutions. The William A. Ringler Fellowship at the Huntington Library in San Marino, CA, allowed me to carry out vital archival research in the summer of 2014, as did a seminar grant from the Folger Shakespeare Library in Washington, D.C., over the 2010–11 academic year. A faculty fellowship from the Humanities Center at Texas Tech University, directed by Dorothy Chansky, supplied me with the time to carry out revisions in the spring of 2016, while a subvention award covered the cost of image reproductions and permissions. In its early stages, the project was supported by a residency at the Institute for the Arts and Humanities at the Pennsylvania State University, directed by Michael Bérubé, in the summer of 2011, while a grant from the Research and Graduate Studies Office at Penn State (with additional support from Hellene S. Runtagh) enabled me to do research at the British Library and Cambridge University library that same summer. For assistance with archives and acquiring images, I am grateful to the staff at the libraries mentioned above, as well to those at the Bibliothèque Nationale de France, the British Museum, and the Southwest Collection/Special Collections Library at Texas Tech University.

I would also like to thank the audiences at conferences where I presented portions of the book. Paul Stevens very kindly invited me to speak at the 2016 Canada Milton Seminar, and I am grateful to my fellow Miltonists for the helpful comments and questions I received there. I am also thankful to the wonderful audiences at meetings of the Modern Language Association, the Renaissance Society of America, the Conference on John Milton, and the Sixteenth Century Society.

Part of chapter 1 first appeared in "Milton and the Parable of the Talents: Nationalism and the Prelacy Controversy in Revolutionary England," *Philological Quarterly* 94, nos. 1–2 (2015): 71–93. Part of chapter 2 first appeared in "Hobbes's Hebraism and the Last Judgment in *Leviathan*," in *Identities in Early Modern English Writing: Religion, Gender, Nation*, edited by Lorna Fitzsimmons (Brepols, 2014), 85–115. I appreciate *PQ* and Brepols allowing me to publish revised versions of this material.

Finally, I would like to thank my parents, Brent and Ruth Ann, for their support over the years, as well as Douglas Sugano, who read many essays on Milton and the end of the world and encouraged my initial interest in the subject.

A Note on Spelling, References, Abbreviations, and Translations

When citing from early modern texts, I have retained the original spelling with the exceptions of u/v and i/j, which have been modernized.

References to Milton's prose works are from *The Complete Prose Works of John Milton*, 8 vols., gen. ed. Don M. Wolfe (New Haven, CT: Yale University Press, 1953–82), abbreviated as *CPW* and followed by volume number and page number. References to scriptural text in English are from the King James Version (1611), reprinted as *The Holy Bible*, edited by Gordon Campbell (Oxford: Oxford University Press, 2010). References to scriptural text in Greek are from *The Greek New Testament*, fourth revised edition, edited by Kurt Aland et al. (Stuttgart: Deutsche Bibelgesellschaft, 2003). References to scriptural text in Latin are from *Biblia Sacra Vulgata*, edited by Roger Gryson and Robert Weber (Stuttgart: Deutsche Bibelgesellschaft, 2007).

Definitions of English words are from *The Oxford English Dictionary* (Oxford: Oxford University Press, 2018), online, abbreviated as *OED*. Definitions of Latin words are from *The Oxford Latin Dictionary*, edited by P. G. W. Glare (Oxford: Oxford University Press, 1982), abbreviated as *OLD*. Definitions of Greek words are from *A Greek-English Lexicon*, edited by Henry George Liddell, Robert Scott, and Henry Stuart Jones (Oxford: Clarendon, 1968), abbreviated as LSJ. *The Oxford Dictionary of National Biography* (Oxford: Oxford University Press, 2018), online, is abbreviated as *ODNB*.

All translations of Greek and Latin texts are my own.

National Reckonings

INTRODUCTION

In the mid-nineteenth century, the French artist Gustave Doré created two of his most memorable sets of engravings. The first set was for a folio edition of the Bible in French, known popularly as *La Grande Bible de Tours*, which was printed in Tours in 1866. The second set was for a folio edition of John Milton's English epic, *Paradise Lost*, which also appeared in 1866 and was printed in London.[1] The penultimate image in the Bible is an illustration of the Last Judgment, in which an angel holding a sword looks down upon a train of people, some of whom are falling to hell while others are billowing, like the clouds around them, up to Christ (see figure 1).[2] That same image appears in altered form as the second illustration in *Paradise Lost*, which depicts the fall of the rebel angels (see figure 2).[3] Doré, under pressure to meet deadlines, sometimes recycled ideas for illustrations.[4] In his engraving of the end of the world, with its vengeful angel, he found a fitting image for an event from the world's beginning, when Satan and his troops fell from heaven, cascading down like so many autumn leaves.

Figure 1. *Jugement Dernier*, by Gustave Doré (1866).

Smith Lesouef R-6284, Bibliothèque Nationale de France.

Figure 2. *The Fall of the Rebel Angels*, by Gustave Doré (1866).

The difference between the two images is telling, and in adapting the original engraving for *Paradise Lost*, Doré enlarged the action of the original scene. The falling figures (now angels) are almost spilling off the page, and the reader can see details obscured in the original image, such as the individual links of Satan's chain mail shirt. The perspective has also been altered, and instead of looking straight on at the central angel, the reader now looks up at him, as if he or she too is being judged.[5] Moreover, the heavenly figures, nearly lost in light in the first engraving but now quite visible, are noticeably larger and occupy a great deal more of the visual space. Brandishing spears and trumpets, their sudden encroachment compels the other angels to make room for them and heightens the tension between these two communities—the one perfect and glorious, the other spiraling into ruin. Doré has, in effect, brought judgment closer to the viewer, who is given a rare glimpse into the machinery of reckoning just before the rebel angels fall to hell—and we fall with them.

In revising the biblical engraving for the epic engraving, Doré mirrored a process taking place in *Paradise Lost* and other literary works of revolutionary England. Adapting scriptural narratives of the world's end to describe their own struggles, Milton and other writers drew the Last Judgment into the present in the minds of their readers, thereby forcing a confrontation between two communities: the nation and *ecclesia universalis* (the church universal). Confident their world was drawing to a close, and confident as well in the wondrous world to come, they looked with eager expectation for the arrival of this universal community, which the Bible describes as "a great multitude, which no man could number, of all nations, and kindreds, and people, & tongues" (Rev. 7:9). In Protestant theology, the Church consists of the faithful departed in heaven (*ecclesia triumphans*) and the faithful remnant upon Earth (*ecclesia militans*), who would join together to form the church universal (*ecclesia universalis*—hereafter, *ecclesia*) at the Last Judgment.[6]

As writers imagined the transition from this world to the next, how did a sense of impending judgment shape English identity? How did the expectation of a perfect and universal community put pressure on existing ideas of the nation—a community that was always falling short of *ecclesia*'s ideal? In his *Paradise Lost* engraving, Doré made room for a heavenly community by diminishing a flawed one, and in a similar fashion, Milton and other writers used the encroaching presence of *ecclesia* to reshape national community in revolutionary England.

This meant that for Milton and his contemporaries, nationalism was not only a horizontal affair between citizens but also a vertical one that pitted England against the shortly expected kingdom of God. The seventeenth century was a period of great political creativity, when many ideas of what the nation was and could become were disseminated in print. For Milton and other authors, writing the nation was hardly an ordered or systematic process, but rather a "conflicted, strained, and volatile" endeavor, as David Loewenstein and Paul Stevens observe.[7] Far from a fixed concept, the nation was marked by "strains and contradictions" even as it relied (ironically) upon an underlying logic of unity and cohesion.[8] However, this conflict has been overwhelmingly studied as a horizontal phenomenon, not a vertical one, which is due in part to the lasting influence of Benedict Anderson's model of the nation as a "deep, horizontal comradeship" between citizens.[9] And while scholars of course acknowledge religion's influence on ideas of the nation, the current book proposes to give a face to that religious influence (*ecclesia*), excavate its place in political imaginings, chart its points of contact with the nation, and trace the tension between them in period literature.[10]

To be sure, an awareness of the horizontal dimension of identity formation is essential to explaining nationalism in Milton's England, but it is inadequate to perform that task in and of itself. The illuminating work of John Kerrigan and Willy Maley shows that "Englishness was a contested resource" to which writers from Ireland, Scotland, and Wales laid claim.[11] Tension and paradox were central to the hybridity of Englishness, and national identity was reinforced at the local level even as it was being molded by "the pressures of impending plurality" from across the British archipelago.[12] Scholarly interest in the development of laws governing the relations between nations also benefits from scrutinizing the geographic interplay of political identities. Much attention is paid to the end of the Thirty Years War at the Peace of Westphalia in 1648—according to Jürgen Habermas it paved the way for the "postnational constellation" toward which modern globalization strives, while for Craig Calhoun it established "a principle of independent sovereignty and mutual recognition which became basic to the flourishing of nationalism," so that, centuries later, it is now impossible to live outside of nations.[13]

Geopolitical in their focus, these studies of archipelagic Englishness and of international law both demonstrate the importance of boundaries—namely, their permeability—in mediating expressions of the nation. But this prompts us to ask, what lies beyond those boundaries? For Kerrigan, Maley, Habermas, and Calhoun, as for Anderson before them, it is simply "other nations," but in Milton's England, there was another answer: *ecclesia*.[14] Nationalism was characterized by competition between the nation and *ecclesia*, and the Last Judgment was the site at which these two communities would meet.

Put another way, nationalism was a matter of measuring the conceptual and temporal distance between England and *ecclesia*; of navigating the horizontal and vertical axes of identity simultaneously; of balancing a particular community against a universal one; and of using the Last Judgment to pivot one's perspective on the nation. In Milton's England, eschatology—the theological last things of death, judgment, heaven, and hell—catalyzed new and radical ideas of the nation, and literature served as an arena within the imagination for witnessing the spectacular collisions between England and *ecclesia*. Those collisions reminded Englishmen that the Christian is "every where an Exile, because he is a Citizen of the Heavenly Jerusalem, and but *a Stranger and a Sojourner here*," as the philosopher Robert Boyle put it.[15] Of the period Bryan Ball notes, "Few things were more certain to them than that God had revealed quite definitely that every man, living or dead, must ultimately be brought to judgment."[16] A cultural imaginary of inestimable influence, the Last Judgment was both a near event on the horizon of history and a biblical narrative of comfort in times of political crisis.

As a heuristic for making sense of political events, the Last Judgment appealed to writers because it restructured existing communities according to the divine rule of reckoning, which was God's means of separating the faithful from the wicked.[17] It offered, that is, a logic of political organization backed by divine authority but enacted by a human writer, who could apply that logic to whomever he pleased. In Doré's engraving from *Paradise Lost*, for comparison, the only difference between the unfallen angels and the fallen ones is the fact of the latter's fall. A reflection of heavenly light is visible on the inside of Satan's shield and on his wings, which suggests his kinship with the angels above, as well as the arbitrary nature of the sudden distinction between them. Satan and his fellows are not demons but fallen angels, and the only difference between them and their heavenly brethren is that Doré has positioned them among the wicked, rather than among the faithful. In a similar manner, Milton and his contemporaries sought to locate and relocate the boundary between the nation and *ecclesia*. Membership in the former was complicated by membership in the latter, and the moment when those two communities would meet was fast approaching. "I will come neere to you in judgement" (Mal. 3:5), God promised in the Bible, and in revolutionary England, Milton and his contemporaries took comfort in that fact and sought to hasten the event.

The current book, then, is an account of how seventeenth-century writers appropriated biblical stories of judgment and put them to fascinating political uses. From the parables of Matthew to the *Chaoskampf* imagery of Revelation, the Bible supplied writers with a wide range of materials with which to imagine the Last Judgment—and with it, the nation. The chapters in this book show how authors accomplished this by coding their praise and criticism of the nation through the scriptural language and imagery of reckoning. Steeped in biblical knowledge and immersed in a rich religious culture, seventeenth-century readers were well positioned to receive such messages and imagine the workings of divine judgment in their own lives. But in our secularized societies of the twenty-first century, we lack many of the tools to do the same. We must labor, therefore, to reconstruct this "alphabet of Protestant belief," as Rosemond Tuve calls it, that was lost with the advent of Enlightenment rationalism.[18] To perform a labor of cultural excavation and recover, as fully as we might, the religious texture of early modern political thought, it is necessary to relearn the alpha and the omega of that alphabet.

"Thy Kingdom Come": Expecting Judgment in Seventeenth-Century England

One step toward relearning this religious alphabet is recognizing, quite simply, how belief in a world to come shaped political thinking in the early modern present. As Julia Reinhard Lupton points out, the early modern Englishman was a "citizen-saint," someone in the world but not of it, and thus a "centaur, a hybrid between sacred and secular forms of community and hence at home in neither."[19] Lupton anticipates the work of Charles Taylor, who proposes that the seventeenth century was the last age to espouse an "enchanted" worldview—in which the self was "porous" and seen as subject to the influence of external, supernatural powers—before the advent of secularism.[20] The studies of Taylor and Lupton are part of an important religious turn in recent scholarship on British intellectual history, which complements the Cambridge school's work on the revival of classical republicanism by uncovering the Judeo-Christian contours of early political theory.[21]

However, one problem with the arguments of Taylor and Lupton is that they tend to mystify, exoticize, and "other" pre-Enlightenment religion. As a result, the premise of religion's underlying strangeness becomes a precondition for its study, and belief in the God of Christianity is viewed as akin to a belief in pixies, aliens, bad luck, or fortune cookies.[22] The critical apparatus designed to help us understand early modern religion itself becomes an impediment to such understanding. Consequently, whether an enchanted being or a centaur, the early modern Christian is reduced to an enigma whose cognitive operations are shrouded in mystery and whose religious convictions can only be glimpsed obliquely—not on their own merits, that is, but in terms of how they differ from our own secular age.

By contrast, biblical literacy allows us to approach the religious beliefs of Milton and his contemporaries from the inside. Theirs was a Protestant society shaped in every way by diligent close reading of scripture, and only by immersing ourselves in the biblical narratives that gave rise to their ideas of politics and community can we comprehend the intellectual purchase the Last Judgment and *ecclesia* had on the minds of seventeenth-century writers.[23] Today, we might scoff at the notion that an invisible community of saints could compete in any real capacity with the nation-state as a historical fact and political reality—yet this is exactly what we find in *Paradise Lost, Leviathan, Silex Scintillans, The True Levellers Standard,* and other works of the period. The Last Judgment was a certain fact, quite simply, because the Bible told them so. Martin Luther went so far as to insist that "the sin which God considers the greatest sin of all, the one that he condones or tolerates less than any other, is the sin of his people not acknowledging his Day of Judgment."[24] As Luther saw it, the Bible presented the Last Judgment as a fundamental article of the faith, and consequently all Protestants had a duty to watch for its appearance and encourage their neighbors to do the same.[25]

To understand how the expectation of judgment underpinned Milton's society, we might consider three rituals: the Nicene Creed, communion, and the Lord's Prayer. Every Sunday, Englishmen gathered at their parish churches and recited the creed, which professes a belief in the Last Judgment and the wondrous world to come. "Hee shall come againe with glory," the Jacobean Book of Common Prayer reads, "to judge both the quicke and the dead: whose kingdome shall have no end."[26] This is the kingdom of God, of course, but the slippage in ownership hints that it is also the kingdom of the saints, where they would dwell in the New Heavens and New Earth for eternity (Rev. 21:1). The creed is followed by the Confession of Sin, during which the priest admonishes the people, "Judge therefore your selves (brethren) that yee be not judged of the Lord."[27] Communicants then partook of the Eucharist, a ritual that reminded them of their membership in the spiritual brotherhood of all Christians. "The Church, which is *Communio Sanctorum*, the Communion of Saints," wrote Lancelot Andrewes, bishop of Winchester, required the Eucharist as an outward sign of its inward grace.[28] Every Sunday in seventeenth-century England, Christians performed in ritual the motions they would soon perform at the Last Judgment, when they would join the saints from history in everlasting communion.

Like communion and the creed, the Lord's Prayer was a routine activity that galvanized the present with eschatological significance.[29] By reciting the words, "Forgive us our trespasses, as wee forgive them that trespasse against us," Protestants reminded themselves on a daily basis of the certainty of their ultimate reckoning with God.[30] (What English prayer books render as "trespasses" is *opheilēmata* or "debts" in the original [Matt. 6:12], which suggests a reckoning taking place.) They also willed the kingdom of God into the present when praying collectively, "Thy kingdome come."[31] John Donne, preaching to the Prince and Princess Palatine in Heidelberg, used the occasion of his visit to Germany in 1619 as an illustration of the unity all Christians have as members of *ecclesia*. At the arrival of the Last Judgment, Donne proclaimed, "We shal leave off all those petitions of *Adveniat regnum*, thy Kingdom come, for it shal be come in abundant power."[32] Until then, Protestants had a responsibility to pray every day for the arrival of that kingdom.

Appreciation for this everyday, eschatological approach is often missing from the scholarly conversation on ideas of the world's end, which focuses on radical forms of end-time expectation (namely apocalypticism, millenarianism, and chiliasm) and the radical sects that espoused them, such as the Fifth Monarchists.[33] The work of Nicholas McDowell and Loewenstein, which builds upon the seminal work of Christopher Hill, documents the important place of apocalypticism in mid-century discourses of sovereignty, liberty, and the nation.[34] But one unintended effect of this focus on apocalypticism and radical religion has been to forget that many people from many denominations believed the world was about to end, and that eschatological expectation was an orthodox practice by no means restricted to groups on the fringes of society. The intention of the current book is to present a more comprehensive range of end-time speculation by focusing on eschatology, which was far more pervasive in the period than apocalypticism, and which had quite a different influence on ideas of the nation.

Apocalypticism shows the faithful a world to come that is inherently foreign, but eschatology grows the world to come from *within* the faithful and from that which is familiar.[35] Apocalypticism imposes another world on top of this world, but eschatology builds the kingdom of God from the ground up, so to speak, and discovers eternity in the mundane. The faithful do not simply await a world to come but find it already blossoming among them in common activities like prayer, ritual, and worship. From Milton's concern for criminal justice to Hobbes's coopting of the Lord's Prayer, from Winstanley's love of dirt to Coppe's adoration of bodies, and from Thomas Vaughan's fascination with fire to his brother's fixation on the scythe—always, it is the ordinary and everyday things that reveal an eternal world that is both to come and, in a sense, already here.

As an example of the difference between eschatology and apocalypticism, we might compare the works of Anna Trapnel and John Milton. Apocalypse is a visionary genre of writing, and in *Strange and Wonderful Newes from White-Hall*, Trapnel has a vision of a strange world, in which there is "a glorious Throne with winged Angels flying before the throne, and crying, Holy holy, holy, unto the Lord."[36] "The great one," she proclaims, "is coming down with terror to the enemies."[37] Trapnel's vision is based on St. John's apocalyptic vision of the Last Judgment (Rev. 20), which also uses nonhuman creatures, cryptic symbols, and mysterious sayings to create an alien alterity. Milton, however, takes an eschatological approach to the world's end in *Paradise Lost*. After Adam eats the fruit, the experience of being judged by the Son is painful, but Adam soon learns from Eve that judgment is God's way of reconciling the faithful to himself.

Consequently, when Adam is later shown an awe-inspiring image of the Last Judgment, he rejoices not because it is strange but because it is deeply familiar: he has seen its like before. Looking past all its earth-shaking terrors, Adam welcomes the Last Judgment because he sees, in its midst, the familiar face of his redeemer.

The End is Now: Protestant Temporality

As they drew the Last Judgment into the present in the minds of readers, Milton and his contemporaries built upon a notion of temporality they inherited from the Reformation. Reading the struggle against Catholicism as the fulfillment of biblical prophecy, the reformers insisted that the Last Judgment was near and the faithful should prepare themselves, mentally and spiritually, for reckoning.[38] As they blurred the line between historical imminence and psychological immanence, the last things became present things.

Guided by Augustine's teachings, the reformers reminded the faithful that judgment, as something integral to the divine being, is coeternal with God and not limited to the *saeculum* of human experience. As Rome collapsed, Augustine comforted Christians by turning to judgment, writing, *Cum diem iudicii dei dicimus, addimus ultimum vel novissimum, quia et nunc iudicat et ab humani generis initio iudicavit dimittens de paradiso et a ligno vitae separans primos homines peccati magni perpetratores* (When we speak of the day of God's judgment, we add "ultimate" or "last," because God judges even now, and he has been judging since the beginning of the human race, when the first humans were expelled from paradise and separated from the tree of life as perpetrators of a great sin).[39] Like the Doré engravings, the Last Judgment at the world's end would be the same as God's judgment upon the angels at the world's beginning. Like Christ's declaration that he is "Alpha and Omega, the beginning and the end" (Rev. 22:13), Genesis and Revelation enclose two ends of the same divine action.

Led by this truth, the reformers encouraged the saints to read the future into the present. In the Middle Ages, only sects like the Franciscan Spirituals and the Flagellant Brethren did such a thing, but in the sixteenth century, the reformers made it respectable for all Protestants to imagine the Last Judgment dawning among them.[40] Luther preached to his congregations, "We must, therefore, not think of Judgment Day as coming in the distant future, but anticipate it every day."[41] He declared, "We have but a left-handed half-hold on this life, but with our right hand and open hearts we await the day that our Lord will come in glorious majesty and splendor."[42] Confident he was living in the final days of the world, Luther saw himself as part of the biblical *hupoleimma sōthēsetai*, the faithful remnant or "remnant that shall be saved," which was prophesied to endure trials and tribulations in the final days of the world and welcome in the Last Judgment at Christ's return (Mark 13:26, 1 Thess. 4:17; Rev. 12:17).[43] Referring fondly to Protestants as *ecclesiola* (the little Church), he reminded his followers that they would soon join *ecclesia*, and he preached that their current period of tribulation was, in fact, a period of grace.[44] In what little time remained, the faithful had been granted an opportunity to prove themselves worthy of the calling they had received.

Calvin, too, taught his congregations to imagine the Last Judgment arriving at every moment. "Let us place that Judge before our eyes," he advised, for "it should be the object of believers [. . .] with increasing cheerfulness and readiness, to meditate on the future and eternal life."[45] Calvin preached an eschatology of progressive renovation, wherein all nations would eventually follow Geneva's example and, becoming the New Jerusalem, witness Christ descend and rule among them.[46] "We undertake for every thing as though we were erecting for ourselves an immortality on earth," Calvin wrote, and by perfecting human institutions, "here we are in some measure prepared for the glory of the heavenly kingdom."[47] The endeavors of the faithful in this life, Calvin taught, prepared the way for the kingdom of God, which was already being revealed in their everyday activities like prayer, Bible study, and devotion.

In this regard, literature was uniquely suited for imagining the world to come, since it afforded writers an imaginative space wherein they might construct the Last Judgment and play out political fantasies of national reckoning. As Philip Sidney argued in the sixteenth century, what sets literature apart from history or philosophy is its ability to produce alternatives to reality—fictions—that are unhindered by fact or truth. Lifted up by the imagination, Sidney wrote, the writer is able to "growe in effect, another nature [. . .] better then Nature bringeth forth."[48] Literature also serves a heuristic purpose, and Frank Kermode notes that narrative allows us to "project ourselves [. . .] past the End, so as to see the structure whole, a thing we cannot do from our spot of time in the middle."[49] In this way, the end of the world suddenly becomes "a future with being in the present," as Ryan Netzley observes, and we are thus able to see "what it means for something to happen while we are still able to do something about it."[50] Paul Stevens points out that poetry "exercise[d] its readers" and "work[ed] by indirection, enabling them to enact or perform its moral lessons," often with the goal of inciting virtuous action.[51] Literature, then, did not simply inform the faithful that the end was near. Instead, it gave flesh to prophecy and drew the end of the world into the reader's present, thereby granting him or her the experience of reckoning while indicating that there was still time to alter its outcome.

Literature offered readers a special opportunity to participate in the cosmic drama unfolding on the page before them. Unlike history or philosophy, literature is personal, and it invites readers to identify with the speaking subject and turn fictional experiences of reckoning into their own experiences.[52] As an example, we might consider a copy of Richard Baxter's *The Saints Everlasting Rest*, currently housed at the British Library, on which a seventeenth-century reader inscribed, "Richard Kinnick. his Booke. 1667." In the text, Baxter describes *ecclesia* and says he has "endeavored to shew you a Glimpse of the approaching Glory," at which point Kinnick writes, "Read this not as a storie: But read it & practice it to / the glory of God: and the killinge of Sinne in o^r Lives."[53] In this short note, Kinnick gives us an idea of how early readers responded to a literary representation of judgment by personalizing the experience. Kinnick is not content with reading about the world to come; rather, he inserts himself into Baxter's narrative and finds his place among the saints of heaven. Internalizing Baxter's lesson that the kingdom of God is near and reminding himself to "read it & practice it," Kinnick has taken Baxter's "storie" of *ecclesia* and turned it into something far more: a reality.

Kinnick's marginal note exemplifies how early modern Protestants approached the Last Judgment with joy. Undoubtedly, this is the biggest difference between an early modern notion of judgment and a modern one: today, we imagine judgment as strictly punitive.[54] But it was not always so, and Luther wrote that far from imagining Christ as a "stern judge," Protestants should expect the Second Coming as the happy arrival of *ecclesia*.[55]

"Let the Judgment Day come when it will," he declared, "it cannot come too soon for me."[56] Calvin, as well, preached that reckoning was a prerequisite to immortality and therefore to be desired. "No man has made any good proficiency in the school of Christ," he wrote, "but he who joyfully expects both the day of death and that of the final resurrection."[57] The Last Judgment would be the joyous reunion of Christian brothers and sisters, and by it the faithful on Earth would "come nearer and nearer to the Communion of Saints in Heaven," as Donne preached.[58] Similarly, Luther promised his congregations, "You will not be set free until the world comes to an end," and in the tumultuous days of the English Revolution, Milton and others imagined they could see their freedom fast approaching.[59] Drawing the Last Judgment closer in literature, they awaited with eager expectation the moment in history when they no longer needed to pray, "Thy kingdom come," for then it would have come indeed.

National Reckoning and the Politics of *Ecclesia*

In Milton's time or any other, exploring one's identity as a Christian and therefore a member of *ecclesia* meant renegotiating one's political affiliations. *Ecclesia* is a hybrid community, both human and divine, which presumes to transcend the nation while assimilating its members in order to exist. As Giorgio Agamben notes, it "impart[s] to itself an organization distinct from the [national] community while pretending to coincide with it."[60] Tertullian, for instance, living in the third century, wrote with joy that the New Jerusalem had at last been sighted in the East. Each morning, it hung suspended in the sky above Jerusalem, as if beckoning to Christians in the earthly city, and then it disappeared as though it were a mist. In this way, Tertullian wrote, the faithful were reminded that *politeuma nostrum, id est municipatum, in caelis esse pronuntians* (our *politeuma*, or citizenship, is manifestly in heaven).[61] The mirroring of these two cities, as the Christians in Jerusalem looked up at their eternal home, epitomizes eschatology's ability to generate an alterity that disrupts one's current sense of political belonging. Whether in third-century Judea or revolutionary England, earthly states paled in comparison with the kingdom of God, and the faithful had to do what they could to guarantee that they were among the saved on the day of reckoning.

While Milton and his contemporaries knew very well which side they wanted to be on when the kingdom of God arrived, this rarely involved abandoning the nation; instead, they attempted to reconcile the often discordant measures of the nation with the perfect harmony of *ecclesia*. This was done by appropriating and reinventing scriptural narrative. As Achsah Guibbory shows, the Old Testament was a cornerstone of national identity in early modern England. In the service of Protestantism and the new identities it seemed to require, "the Jewish past was appropriated," Guibbory notes, and writers sought to connect themselves to Israel's history in such a way that would infuse their own political struggles with sacred meaning.[62] Within the Pentateuch, they found "not just political wisdom, but a political constitution," as Eric Nelson puts it.[63] The concept of *respublica Hebraeorum* came to dominate English republicanism, most notably in the works of Harrington and Milton, who saw their own moment in history as the "reenactment" of a sacred past.[64]

The flip side of that typological activity involved coopting biblical futures and writing the nation into scriptural prophecies of the world's end. In the Bible, prophecies of the end times are riddled with the language of national reckoning and repudiation, but at the same time, the Bible holds out hope that the nations might add their numbers to the saints of *ecclesia* on the last day. Isaiah says that at the world's end, God "shall judge among the nations, and shall rebuke many people" (Isa. 2:4), and Christ says that at Last Judgment, he will "separate [the nations] one from another, as a shepheard divideth his sheepe from his goats" (Matt. 25:32). "The nations were angry," Revelation adds, for God's "wrath is come, and the time of the dead that they should bee judged" (Rev. 11:18). In revolutionary England, the hermeneutic ambiguity of these prophecies invited new interpretations of the nation's role at the world's end and its fate at the Last Judgment. In this way, Milton, Hobbes, and other writers managed to imp their own damaged narratives of political turmoil and unrest onto *ecclesia*'s boundless wing as it alighted into the uppermost reaches of eternity.

One way of reconciling England with *ecclesia* was to turn to a third community, the faithful remnant.[65] In the Old Testament, the remnant was the part of Israel that survived exile or captivity, and in the New Testament, the remnant is a select body of Christians who persevere in obedience until Christ's return. Christ foretold that they would "see the

Sonne of man comming in the cloudes, with great power and glory"
(Mark 13:26), and Saint Paul anticipated the moment when "we which
are alive and remaine shalbe caught up together" (1 Thess. 4:17) with
the saints. In early modern England, the idea of the remnant assumed
political meaning with national implications. Amid the persecution of
godly ministers at the turn of the century, William Perkins advised, "we
ought to pray daily unto Christ [. . .] that the remnant of Gods elect may
bee gathered, and so we see an end of these miserable dayes wherein we
live," and Donne, looking upon the continental chaos that would become
the Thirty Years War, hoped that he might number among those who
"shall behold God, and never taste deaths woe."[66] As we shall see, the
remnant was also a useful tool for Milton and his contemporaries, who
learned that if the nation was at times difficult to reconcile with *ecclesia*,
then one option was to reshuffle the deck and deal a new set of political
configurations.

Another option was to eschew the nation altogether (or attempt to do
so), and the chapters in this book illustrate the variety of ways eschatology was used to challenge, reinvent, or deconstruct the nation. Chapters 1 and 2 show how two great intellectuals of the age, Milton and
Hobbes, reinvented the nation by reading it through the Last Judgment.
Bridging the gap between England and *ecclesia*, Milton experiments in
Lycidas, Sonnet 19 "When I Consider How My Light is Spent," and
other poems with different models of England as the faithful remnant.
For Milton, the remnant was a kind of Trojan horse for ushering the
nation into a community that would otherwise repulse it. For Hobbes,
writing in the aftermath of the civil wars, the answer to England's crisis
of sovereignty was Christ's unmatched authority at the Last Judgment.
The title page to *Leviathan*, with the sovereign appearing like Christ at
the Second Coming, suggests how the Last Judgment serves as sovereignty's ideal in Hobbes's political system. However, it is an ideal that
Hobbes labored to postpone in history, so that Christ's authority would
validate (but not infringe upon) the sovereign's absolute power in the
present.

Chapters 3 and 4 turn to counternationalism and document the conflicted nature of attempts to replace the nation with *ecclesia*. Counternationalism, like nationalism, was not without its paradoxes, and writers
often opened up avenues for the nation's salvation even as they labored to

dismantle it.[67] Chapter 3 shows how, as a response to the economic injustices of the 1640s, the radicals Gerrard Winstanley and Abiezer Coppe proclaimed that the Day of the Lord has arrived. Imagining reckoning as a tactile experience, the New Adams (the Diggers) excavated their salvation in the black dirt of St. George's Hill, while Coppe's Anointed (the Ranters) discovered *ecclesia* in the flesh of London's poor and destitute. Chapter 4 turns to Oxford and the ancient hamlets of Breconshire, where Thomas and Henry Vaughan crafted literary personas that enabled them to invoke a national reckoning. Imagining the Last Judgment as an alchemical process, Thomas cast himself as a modern Moses—a man of two nations— who would reconcile England and Wales and lead them in the recovery of hidden knowledge. By contrast, Henry, the Silurist, waged a one-man campaign against the Commonwealth. Politicizing the English devotional mode of his mentor, George Herbert, Henry presented *Silex Scintillans* as a voice piece for Welsh suffering and the liturgical center of an episcopalian remnant.

Chapter 5 returns to Milton and shows how *Paradise Lost* participates in Restoration debates over the infamous trial of Charles I. Milton's epic uses the memory of that event to theorize how responses to God's judgment might ruin or redeem a community, and the examples of the Son, Abdiel, and Eve teach readers that the nation might be saved yet through judgment and union with *ecclesia*. Chapter 5 thus reflects the book's larger claim that, in our assessments of early modern nationalism, we miss half the story if we neglect the vertical axis of identity. Rather, our labors toward the recovery of nationalist thought should take into account the two-dimensional nature of political imaginations in the period, as Milton and his contemporaries mapped the nation, *ecclesia*, and the spaces in between. We disadvantage ourselves, in other words, if we restrict our gaze to surveying the earthly city of Jerusalem and forget, all the while, the New Jerusalem that lies suspended above.

1

Milton and the Faithful Remnant

Locating the Nation in the Early Poetry

At the end of his first antiprelatical treatise, *Of Reformation Touching Church-Discipline in England*, Milton imagines England as the faithful remnant, those prophesied to "see the Sonne of man comming in the cloudes, with great power and glory" (Mark 13:26) at the end of the world.[1] In the treatise, Milton expresses his hope that

> this great and Warlike Nation [. . .] casting farre from her the *rags* of her old *vices* may presse on hard to that *high* and *happy* emulation to be found the *soberest*, *wisest*, and *most Christian People* at that day when thou the Eternall and shortly-expected King shalt open the Clouds to judge the severall Kingdomes of the World, and distributing *Nationall Honours* and *Rewards* to Religious and just *Common-wealths*, shalt put an end to all Earthly *Tyrannies*, proclaiming thy universal and milde *Monarchy* through Heaven and Earth.[2]

As we saw in this book's introduction, scripture foretells a reckoning of nations at the Last Judgment, when God would "sift the nations with the sieve of vanitie" (Isa. 30:28) and "separate them one from another, as a shepheard divideth his sheepe from the goats" (Matt. 25:32), after which the faithful would become part of *ecclesia*. Scripture has no room for the nation in the world to come, so in his own reworking of the Last Judgment, Milton makes room for it by furnishing England with an end-time identity that satisfies the demands of both patriotism and eschatology. Despite its shortcomings, for Milton, England was ever the leader of the Reformation and a "noble and puissant Nation" (*CPW* 2:558) about to rouse itself to some great feat in God's service. But to imagine England as the remnant receiving *"Nationall Honours* and *Rewards"* at Christ's hand is no easy task. As he anticipates the Last Judgment appearing to his generation, Milton is faced with the difficult job of reconciling the nation with the nationless community that would succeed it.

As Paul Stevens observes, Milton's nationalism is characterized by a Janus-faced oscillation between a projected ideal and a disappointing reality, and I would like to suggest that such tensions are at their most fraught when Milton compares an imperfect England to a perfect *ecclesia*.[3] To close the distance between these two communities, Milton turns to a third community, the remnant, which allows him to welcome in the kingdom of God while ensuring that England would not be swallowed up in that totality. The remnant allows him, that is, to guarantee that his own nation would retain its identity at the moment of reckoning, when all other nations would lose theirs. The faithful remnant is thus for Milton a kind of Trojan horse that ushers England into the ranks of *ecclesia* and opens up a space for the nation amid a community that would otherwise reject or overwhelm it.

Feeling his way around the temporal and spatial edges of the nation allows Milton to better understand the nature of the community that lies inside, as well as to stretch the nation this way, or pull it that way, to bring it into alignment with *ecclesia*. From *In Quintum Novembris* to Sonnet 19 "When I Consider How My Light is Spent," Milton experiments with different situations in which the nation might be reconciled to those "sweet Societies" of heaven and the "thousands" who at God's bidding speed.[4] Milton is "as regular a traverser as a reinforcer of national boundaries," as Elizabeth Sauer notes, and as we move from one model of England-as-remnant to the next, the nation becomes increasingly unmoored from its geographic foundations, as Milton theorizes how the nation might reside in a single citizen.[5] The nation's place in time changes as well, and as its rate of acceleration toward the Last Judgment increases, so too does the reader's burden to act grow heavier. Within Milton's cooperative view of history, the faithful have a responsibility to aid the plans of providence and the fulfillment of biblical prophecy.[6] Their godly labors serve an eternal good, Milton reminds them, but frustratingly, the nation seems to require more and more time to get the job done. Both past and future meet in the labors of the present, as the faithful work to hasten the coming of *ecclesia* but, in doing so, simultaneously set themselves apart from that universal community.[7]

Gens hæc mihi sola rebellis: The Pious English of *In Quintum Novembris*

Milton composed the miniature epic *In Quintum Novembris* (On the fifth of November) in 1626 to celebrate the failure of the Gunpowder Plot of 1605, when Guy Fawkes and other Catholic conspirators tried to set off thirty-two hundredweight of gunpowder beneath the Parliament House. The plot was the subject of numerous neo-Latin epics.[8] *In Quintum Novembris* employs recurring epic phrases from Homer, Virgil, and Ovid and takes as its heroic subject the conflict of two great civilizations. But instead of positioning that conflict in a mythic past, Milton reads the Gunpowder Plot through the future as foretold in Revelation. In doing so, Milton synthesizes the classical concern for *patria* with the Protestant expectation of *ecclesia*. Borrowing from Luther, who saw the faithful's persecution in "these evil latter days" as signs of the end, Milton depicts the plot as an end-time struggle between the people of God and the people of Antichrist.[9] In that struggle, Satan recruits Pope Paul V, the *antistes Babylonius* (156, Babylonian high priest), to help destroy the English.

As Milton's epic about the world's end, *In Quintum Novembris* casts the nation as the faithful remnant on Earth. Revelation prophesies that in the last days, the faithful would be persecuted by the Whore of Babylon and her minions (Rev. 18:4), and in *In Quintum Novembris*, England proves its virtue by resisting Babylon, the Catholic Church. As Satan travels

to and fro across the Earth, he pauses to consider England's seaside cliffs
and white fields:

At simul hanc opibusque & festâ pace beatam
Aspicit, & pingues donis Cerealibus agros,
Quodque magis doluit, venerantem numina veri
Sancta Dei populum, tandem suspiria rupit
Tartareos ignes & luridum olentia sulphur.
Qualia Trinacriâ trux ab Jove clausus in Ætna
Efflat tabifico monstrosus ab ore Tiphœus.
Ignescunt oculi, stridetque adamantinus ordo
Dentis, ut armorum fragor, ictaque cuspide cuspis.
Atque pererrato solum hoc lacrymabile mundo
Inveni, dixit, gens hæc mihi sola rebellis,
Contremtrixque jugi, nostrâque potentior arte.
Illa tamen, mea si quicquam tentamina possunt,
Non feret hoc impune diu, non ibit inulta.

[But as soon as he gazes upon this country, blessed with riches
And festive peace, and the fields fertile with the gifts of Ceres—
What grieved him more, a people worshipping
The sacred divinity of the true God—he broke away
With sighs smelling of Tartarean fires and lurid sulfur.
Sighs such as this the wild and monstrous Typhoeus, shut up
Beneath Sicilian Aetna, expels from his devouring mouth.
Satan's eyes inflamed, his row of teeth—as hard as steel—
Grind as if the clash of weapons, or spear striking spear.
"Having wandered through the world," he said,
"This is my only sadness: this people alone is defiant of me,
Contemptuous of my yoke, stronger than our stratagems.
Yet if my efforts are able to do something, that people
Shall not carry on any longer without impunity, or go unpunished."]
(31–44)

England's singular virtue as the remnant, Milton suggests, is its steadfast
adherence to the reformed faith. After traveling throughout the world,
Satan notes with irritation that England is the sole obstacle to his plan of
world domination. He declares, *Gens hæc mihi sola rebellis* (This people

alone is defiant of me), and he complains that the English alone are *venerantem numina veri / Sancta Dei populum* (a people worshipping the holy divinity of the true God). The English are "the only righteous in a World perverse," as Milton would later write of another remnant, and like Enoch, they alone persevere amid widespread apostasy.[10]

In Quintum Novembris also anticipates *Paradise Lost* by conflating beginnings and endings. Specifically, Milton sutures together a scriptural narrative of the world's end with a classical narrative of the nation's origin. Four times, Milton describes the English as pious, and twice, he refers to the noble lineage of the English through Brutus, grandson of Aeneas, who first settled the island of Britain. Consequently, the piety of the English, the sole people worshipping God, has been inherited from *pius* Aeneas, the greatest of the Trojan princes. Milton connects his miniature epic to Virgil's *Aeneid* at the opening of *In Quintum Novembris*, which describes England's great prince, *pius Jäcobus* (pious James):

> Jam pius extremâ veniens Jäcobus ab arcto
> Teucrigenas populos, latéque patentia regna
> Albionum tenuit, jamque inviolabile fœdus
> Sceptra Caledoniis conjunxerat Anglica Scotis:
> Pacificusque novo felix divesque sedebat
> In solio, occultique doli securus & hostis.

> [Now pious James, coming from the far north,
> Took command of the Trojan-born people and their
> Wide ranging realms, having already joined in sacrosanct league
> The scepters of England and the Caledonian Scots.
> The peace-making king sat on a new throne, happy
> And wealthy, untroubled by hidden treachery and enemies.]

(1–6)

James's coming, like the coming of Aeneas, is to found a great realm, which consists here of the union of England and Scotland. However, at the very moment when Milton expands England's spatial identity by locating its origins in Rome, he delimits the same by cutting Scotland out of the picture and anglicizing James. Having fulfilled its purpose by linking James to Aeneas, Scotland receives no further mention in the poem, and Milton instead casts England as God's champion at the world's end and the sole heir of Trojan *pietas*. Building upon Virgilian epic, *In Quintum Novembris* compares England's struggle against Babylon with the Trojans' struggle against the Rutulians, who endeavored in a similar manner to weaken a pious nation and vanquish its people. England's virtue as the remnant, then, is inherited from its heroic prehistory.[11] A scriptural narrative of England's future fuses with a classical narrative of the nation's past to equip England with a new identity as the pious remnant in the historical present of Stuart England.

Milton's project of reading England as the remnant involves reading Satan and the pope as the figureheads of a wicked cosmopolitanism that is opposed to nationalism. Satan is described as wandering throughout the world, wherein *sceleris socios, vernasque fideles* (10, the associates of wickedness, his faithful slaves) do his bidding across his earthly kingdom. The pope is designated *regum domitor* (74, vanquisher of kings), and Milton writes that *præeunt summisso poplite reges* (57, kings went before him kneeling). When responding to Satan's plan, the pope rallies his fighters from across Europe and tells them, *Finibus occiduis circumfusum incolit æquor / Gens exosa mihi, prudens natura negavit / Indignam penitùs nostro conjungere mundo* (157–59, At the world's western edge, a people detestable to me lives surrounded by the ocean, an unworthy people, whom Nature, in her wisdom, refuses to connect to our world). He commands, *Tartareoque leves difflentur pulvere in auras* (161, Blow them into air with Tartarean powder). As the remnant, England represents the interests of nationalism against an aggressive Catholic cosmopolitanism that has devoured the other nations of the world. The Gunpowder Plot, consequently, is an attack not only on England as the remnant but also on the idea of nations in general. The Gunpowder Plot revived old fears that England's boundaries had been penetrated, and in response, Milton presents an image of national integrity and celebrates England's ability to repel a nation-consuming force.[12]

As it approaches its epic conflict, *In Quintum Novembris* invokes the Last Judgment and draws England toward a national reckoning. Improving upon the classical epic formula, Milton portrays the final conflict as a fight between God and Antichrist, rather than between men. Like Zeus favoring the Greeks, *populi miserescit ab alto / Æthereus pater, & crudelibus obstitit ausis / Papicolûm* (220–22, the heavenly Father has compassion on his people from on high and opposes the cruel crimes of the papists). In a reworking of the Last Judgment, Milton writes that the papists are dragged off to painful punishments, while the remnant remains *pia thura Deo, & grati solvuntur honores* (223, paying back pious incense and grateful honors to God). Here, *pia thura* correlates with the *pius* English and suggests that at the end of the world, England is justified by the *pietas* it inherited at its epic beginning. The same religious devotion that shaped the nation's identity on the first day of its founding finds it worthy on its final day of reckoning.

In *Quintum Novembris* concludes with a temporal shift that draws both the past victory over the Catholic conspirators and England's future triumph at the Last Judgment into the present. Epic is a genre that celebrates life in the present.[13] When the young men and women of *In Quintum Novembris* dance and light bonfires in the streets, Milton's miniature epic transforms the nation's victory in 1605 into the nation's victory in 1626 and for every year to come. Milton concludes, *Quintoque Novembris / Nulla Dies toto occurrit celebratior anno* (225–26, In all the year, there will be no day more celebrated than the fifth of November), and as the reader participates in the celebration, the past is resurrected to new life.

In this regard, *In Quintum Novembris* illustrates nationalism's tendency to defy historical fixedness and yet, ironically, rely on nationalized interpretations of time as a condition of its survival. Nationalism thrives, we might say, on the illusion that by participating in culture in a single spatiotemporal moment, one has access to the whole of that collective identity. In Milton's miniature epic, the fortunes of Christianity's faithful remnant are one and the same as those of England, and the survival of a universal community depends upon nationalizing the past and future to bolster the English faithful in the present.

The New Heavens and New Earth in Elegy III
In Obitum Præsulis Wintoniensis

Near the same time as *In Quintum Novembris*, Milton composed Elegy III *In Obitum Præsulis Wintoniensis*, which also characterizes England as the remnant awaiting the Last Judgment. The poem mourns the loss of England's famous minister Lancelot Andrewes, who died on September 25,

1626. Celebrating the nation synecdochically through a celebration of Andrewes, Milton praises England for its commitment to true religion, as he did in *In Quintum Novembris*. But unlike in the miniature epic, England's singularity in Elegy III lies not in its exclusive claims to virtue but in leading the European Reformation. As he had done with Rome in *In Quintum Novembris*, and as he would do with the Waldensians in Sonnet 18 "On the Late Massacher in Piemont," Milton locates the English nation in Elegy III by means of a European correlative. England is privileged with uniting Protestants across the world as no other nation could—a fitting subject for an elegy on an English divine who, in his own life, united Protestants everywhere in the principles of reformed religion. Neo-Latin elegies were ritualistic poems designed to be read in public, and in Elegy III, Milton offers his countrymen an opportunity to celebrate England's leadership of an international community by mourning together the loss of a national figure, Lancelot Andrewes.[14]

In Elegy III, Milton presents the dual threats of the 1625–26 plague and the Thirty Years War as tokens of the end of the world. Revelation prophesies that in the last days, the moon would grow red like blood and the earth would quake, and after all these tumults, the remnant would emerge clothed in white robes as "they which came out of the great tribulation" (Rev. 7:14). As a kind of everyman, the speaker offers Milton's readers an opportunity to imagine their own labors on behalf of true religion, as England shepherds the world's faithful through tribulations in the final days of the world. Sitting alone and without a companion, Milton's poetic speaker sees *funestæ cladis imago / Fecit in Angliaco quam Libitina solo* (3–4, an image of the deadly destruction that Libitina brought forth on English soil), and he remembers *clarique ducis, fratrisque verendi / Intempestivis ossa cremata rogis* (9–10, the famous general, and his awe-inspiring brother, their bones cremated on ill-timed funeral pyres). From 1625–26, England endured a severe outbreak of plague, represented here as Libitina, Italian goddess of corpses. Her association with Rome connects her to England's second crisis.

For Protestants and Catholics alike, the Thirty Years War was a conflict to determine the fate of reformed religion in Europe. Recalling two great heroes of the conflict—likely, James I of England (d. March 27, 1625) and his *frater* in the Protestant cause, Maurice of Orange (d. April 23, 1625)—Milton again reads England's great king in relation to a European counterpart who serves to highlight England's special leadership role. James was outspoken throughout his reign about his ecumenical plans to unite Christianity around the fundamental doctrines of the faith, and Elegy III accordingly depicts him as a leader of singular virtue who honors England by honoring Protestants everywhere.[15] James's recent death was a devastating blow to English Protestantism, and in Milton's poem, the outbreak of plague across the country mirrors the nation's suffering in the absence of its king.

To mitigate England's loss of its beloved king and its beautiful countryside, Milton constructs a mirror world, the New Heavens and New Earth, in which Lancelot Andrewes illuminates the nation's path homeward and to its true self, much as Michael the archangel would later do in *Lycidas*. The plague radically reconfigured how people conceived of public spaces, and during an outbreak, bodies often littered the ground, making travel across London hazardous and rendering dangerous those locations which had previously been sites of communal identity formation.[16] In Elegy III, the diseased English soil (*Angliaco solo*), which bears the scars of Libitina's abuses, is replaced with *florea terra* (58, flowery earth), and *pellucentes locos* (52, shining lands). The fell air, too, which was believed to spread plague and is figured here as the *afflata* (19, poisonous breath) of Death, is replaced in the New Heavens and New Earth with *serpit odoriferas per opes levis aura Favoni* (47, the light breath of Favonius, which glides through the fragrant opulence) of this second Eden.[17]

Most important, the speaker's initial isolation—which mirrored the nation's isolation from European Protestants after the death of James—is replaced with the godly fellowship of *ecclesia*. At the poem's beginning, the speaker sits *nullo comitante* (1, without a companion), but in the new world being unveiled before his eyes, *quisque novum amplexu comitem cantuque salutat* (61, everyone greets his new companion with a hug and a song). In the speaker's first vision of the deaths of James and Maurice, Protestant community is fractured and England much diminished, but in his second vision of the New Heavens and New Earth, *ecclesia* has arrived and the saints from all times enjoy one another's company for eternity.

At the head of that universal community is Lancelot Andrewes, whose messianic appearance evokes the Second Coming of Christ.[18] Like the faithful remnant in Revelation, who "came out of great tribulation, and have washed their robes, and made them white in the blood of the Lambe"

(Rev. 7:14), Andrewes is clothed in *vestis candida* (55, a robe of shining white), and like Christ, he is the gateway from a world of trouble to one of peace:

> Ecce mihi subito pæsul Wintonius astat,
> Sydereum nitido fulsit in ore jubar;
> Vestis ad auratos defluxit candida talos,
> Infula divinum cinxerat alba caput.
> Dumque senex tali incedit venerandus amictu,
> Intremuit læto florea terra sono.
> Agmina gemmatis plaudunt cælestia pennis,
> Pura triumphali personat æthra tubâ.
> Quisque novum amplexu comitem cantuque salutat,
> Hosque aliquis placido misit ab ore sonos;
> Nate veni, & patrii felix cape gaudia regni,
> Semper ab hinc duro, nate, labore vaca.

> [Behold, suddenly the bishop of Winchester stood before me,
> and the heavenly light of the stars shone in his bright face;
> His bright robes flowed to his golden ankles,
> And a white fillet encircled his divine head.
> Dressed in such finery, the old man then came forward,
> And the flowery ground resonated with a cheerful sound.
> The heavenly host clapped their jeweled wings,
> And the clear air resounded with a triumphal trumpet.
> Everyone greeted his new companion with a song and an embrace,
> And one of them spoke these words from his peaceful mouth:
> "Come, son, and happily seize the joys of your father's kingdom;
> Henceforth rest, son, from your hard labor forever."]
>
> 　　　　　　　　　　　　　　　　　(53–64)

The heavenly saint welcomes the speaker just as Christ was prophesied to welcome the remnant, when those "which are alive, and remaine, shalbe caught up together with them in the clouds, to meet the Lord in the aire" (1 Thess. 4:17). Milton imagines Christ's coming by means of a scriptural parable of judgment that would become one of his favorite tools for envisioning reckoning, and which he would employ again in Sonnet 19 "When I Consider How My Light is Spent." In the parable of the talents, a lord goes on a journey and imparts to one servant five talents, to another two, and to a third one. After a long time, he returns to reckon with his servants. The first two servants have put their talents to good use and doubled the amounts they were given, and they receive the commendation, "Well done, good and faithfull servant [. . .] enter thou into the joy of thy lord" (Matt. 25:23). In Elegy III, a saint welcomes the poetic speaker into *ecclesia* with the words, *Nate veni, & patrii felix cape gaudia regni, / Semper ab hinc duro, nate, labore vaca* (Come, son, and happily seize the joys of your father's kingdom; henceforth rest, son, from your hard labor forever). As he appropriates the parable to offer England hope amid its crises, Milton skips over reckoning, and the speaker discovers to his delight that he has already been justified in God's sight. Through the speaker, Milton's readers too learn that despite the crises that have befallen them, the nation has shown itself approved unto God and a workman who need not be ashamed.

Elegy III builds upon the reformers' teachings that knowledge of the end times was given "for our comfort," as Luther put it, so the faithful would know of their future justification at the Last Judgment.[19] Yet at the crucial moment in Elegy III, when the speaker is invited to join the saints, Milton collapses the vision he has constructed and denies him entry into *ecclesia*. The dawn suddenly arrives, and weeping for the beautiful place and glorious future he has lost, the speaker echoes Ovid's *Amores* and cries out, *Talia contingant somnia sæpe mihi* (68, May such dreams often befall me!).[20] About to enjoy a boundless community and an eternal world, the speaker finds himself bounded again by time and space, in which the memory of James's death is still painfully close and the fetid stink of corpses pollutes England's capital. But the speaker is not the same person he was at the poem's beginning, for he now possesses the virtues he initially lacked: patience and hope. Through an encounter with the Last Judgment, he has learned that he and his countrymen are already justified in God's sight. All that is required of him now is to do what the remnant does best, which is to stand and wait for the return of Christ and the wondrous community that would accompany him.

With its concluding temporal shift, Elegy III reforms a classical elegiac convention, in which the final turn from past to present is an occasion for the poetic speaker to gain self-knowledge. In Elegy III, the turn from future to present offers knowledge not about the speaker but about the nation in relation to *ecclesia*. The arrival of the dawn is England's opportunity to make up the distance between the future and the present and prove itself fit company for *ecclesia*. The return of time is Milton's boon to the nation, since while England stands and waits for the Last Judgment, it has a chance to accrue "*Nationall Honours* and *Rewards*" in the days before *ecclesia* arrives. The return to time and place in Elegy III, moreover, sets the stage for a similar moment of national self-discovery in another elegy, when Milton would again withdraw from *ecclesia* to offer his readers time and space for labor—the hope of a tomorrow filled with fresh woods and pastures new.

"Where Ere Thy Bones are Hurld": *Lycidas* and Triangulated Nationalism

While scholars observe that *Lycidas* engages nationalist concerns of the 1630s, they have not noted the triangulated structure of nationalism in the poem, nor that Milton imports this structure from an earlier poem, Elegy I *Ad Carolum Diodatum*.[21] *Lycidas* borrows from Elegy I politically and aesthetically and rethinks, in the context of another friendship, how place informs identity. Milton composed Elegy I from his home on Bread Street, London, in the spring of 1626, after having been suspended from Christ's College, Cambridge, as a result of an argument with his tutor.[22] Addressed to Charles Diodati, then a student at Trinity College, Oxford, Elegy I uses geographic space to map out the friendship between the two men and measure the distance between them. In a period of juvenile liminality, when both men were in constant transition between the university and their family homes, Milton discovers that human relationships are perpetually subject to motion and change and that the search for a friend is the narcissistic search for one's own place in time and space.

In Elegy I, Milton uses geographic triangulation to understand who he is by means of where he is. Like a navigator with compass, Milton takes a bearing of three points on the horizon—the Irish Sea, Cambridge, and London—to pinpoint his own location on the map. The first bearing is the Irish Sea, a barbaric other that contrasts with the familiarity of London.[23] At the poem's beginning, the speaker describes Diodati (who was at the time in Chester, where the River Dee flows into the Irish Sea) as residing in *tellus longinqua* (7, a distant land) within *terras remotas* (5, the remote regions) of the world. Measuring the geographic and emotional spaces between them, the speaker laments Diodati's remoteness and wonders when they would be reconciled. The speaker's concern for the strangeness of Diodati's abode at the edge of civilization hints at fears that Diodati too has been changed into something alien.

The disturbing foreignness of the Irish Sea is soon remedied by a shift to a more comfortable residence, as Milton takes his second bearing and alights on a new location. Suddenly, Diodati's abode by the Irish Sea is all the more deplorable because it is not London, the *mœnia fausta* (86, the fortunate city), wherein *Virginibus Britannis* (71, the young women of Britain) outshine the maidens of Troy and Rome. Throughout the poem, the speaker reads England through London and praises the nation by means of its major city. He celebrates London as *urbs Dardanniis [. . .] structa colonis* (73, the city built by Trojan colonists), which harbors within its walls *quicquid formosi pendulus orbis habet* (76, whatever beauty the pendant world holds). In Milton's adolescent mind, London was ever the *patria dulcis* (10, dear native city). Resorting to the beloved metropolis renews his sense of English identity after his disconcerting encounter with the foreignness of the Irish Sea. Shielded by London's walls and invigorated by its rich culture, the speaker takes comfort in the fact that he is part of an urban community whose members date back to antiquity.

But Milton is not done, and he soon takes a third bearing and shifts focus to Cambridge, which further enhances his understanding of himself as an Englishman. As with the move from the Irish Sea to London, antithesis through juxtaposition elucidates Milton's differing attitudes toward each location. The speaker complains, *Stat quoque juncosas Cami remeare paludes* (89, It has been decided as well that I am to return to the reedy marshes of the Cam River). Though this place is familiar like London, it calls up no warm thoughts—quite the opposite, in fact.[24] In his later writings, Milton was highly critical of the education he received at Cambridge, and in Elegy I, Cambridge is an unkind place.[25] Instead of beauty and wisdom, Cambridge produces harsh tutors who terrorize their pupils. The speaker complains,

> Jam nec arundiferum mihi cura revisere Camum,
> Nec dudum vetiti me laris angit amor.
> Nuda nec arva placent, umbrasque negantia molles,

Quàm male Phœbicolis convenit ille locus!
Nec duri libet usque minas perferre magistri
Cæteraque ingenio non subeunda meo.

[Right now, I do not care to revisit the reedy Cam,
Nor am I bothered by homesickness for my forbidden residence.
The bare fields—denying any relaxing shade—do not give me pleasure;
How poorly agreeable that place is to worshippers of Phoebus!
Nor is it pleasing to suffer, at every moment, the threats of a hard tutor
And other things unbearable to my spirit.]

(11–16)

London is an urban metropolis *structa coloniis* (built by Trojan colonists) but Cambridge is a national wasteland, and its reedy swamps symbolize the intellectual and aesthetic stagnation of the place. In London, the speaker enjoys *suburbani nobilis umbra loci* (50, outstanding shade in a place just outside the city walls), but at Cambridge, he finds only barren fields that offer no reprieve from the sun. As metaphors for intellectual activity (or the lack thereof), the barren fields of Cambridge are as wretched as the sweet shades of London's suburbs are wonderful. If Diodati's place by the Irish Sea represents everything in Britain that is un-English, unrefined, and alien, then Cambridge is England gone wrong. If London is the glory of England, then Cambridge is England ruined, the excess of its glory obscured—it is London without its beauty, charms, and learning. The Irish Sea reminded Milton that it is a fabulous thing to be a Londoner and to walk its streets, feeling the history and beauty of the city beneath one's feet, but Cambridge teaches Milton that such moments are fleeting, and that he must enjoy them while they last.

In *Lycidas*, Milton recycles his method of triangulated nationalism and puts it to new use, as he reads his friendship with Edward King through his friendship with Charles Diodati.[26] The historical allusions in *Lycidas* to the dispute over King's fellowship at Christ's College complicate its representation of nationalism. In the spring of 1630, Andrew Sandelands resigned his fellowship at Cambridge, and King—as a lesser pensioner of exceptional promise in the classical languages—was appointed to fill his position. But King's Irish identity, and thus his eligibility for the fellowship, were contested. King was a Yorkshire man, some claimed, since his family had lived there before his father became vice-treasurer of Ireland,

and someone else already held the fellowship reserved for Yorkshire. King Charles settled the dispute by decreeing that Edward King would take Sandelands's place "notwithstanding any statute."[27] Despite the favorable outcome, King's nationality had been thrown into question, and he was seen as a man of two nations—or none. *Lycidas* responds to the dispute by turning the accusations of King's detractors to the young man's advantage. Praising King as a man who transcends all nations, the poem claims for him a Christian identity fit only for the holy company of *ecclesia*.

As it moves across the sea and from one shore to another, the dead body of Lycidas is in constant motion and flux. Its lack of fixedness mirrors King's own life, as a man who flittered between England and Ireland. As in Elegy I, in *Lycidas* the Irish Sea is an alien place signifying barbarism and monstrosity.[28] Unlike the shadowed haunts that appear in both Elegy I and *Lycidas*, where the poetic speaker finds refuge, the Irish Sea is a place of exposure, where Lycidas's body "flote[s] upon his watry bear [. . .] and welter[s] to the parching wind" (12–13). In *Lycidas*, the Irish Sea is a deconstructive force that sets itself against the reconstructive powers of elegy. Instead of remembering Lycidas, as the Swain does, the sea dismembers him, "wash[ing] far away" the body of the deceased and "hurl[ing]" his bones from the Hebrides to Spain (155). In Elegy I, the Irish Sea was a marker of distance, but in *Lycidas*, it is a force for oblivion and erasure of the self. Elegiac recollection reaches new poetic heights in *Lycidas*, as the Swain uses poetry to shape scattered limbs into an image of the man he knew, while the Irish Sea undoes his work, scattering that which the Swain tries desperately to recollect.[29]

From the Irish Sea, Milton turns to Cambridge, and while scholars have tended to romanticize the appearance of Camus, god of the River Cam, the poem gives no indication that this is a happy event.[30] On the contrary, the appearance of Camus in *Lycidas* recalls Milton's complaint in Elegy I about his *durus magister* (hard tutor) and his reluctance to return to life at the university. The Swain says,

> Next *Camus*, reverend Sire, went footing slow,
> His Mantle hairy, and his Bonnet sedge,
> Inwrought with figures dim, and on the edge
> Like to that sanguine flower inscrib'd with woe.
> Ah! Who hath reft (quoth he) my dearest pledge?
> (103–7)

Lycidas offers two competing versions of a university experience. One, cited above, depicts a feeble old man whose appearance is comical—an inside joke, perhaps, among King's friends, referring to their aged and slow-minded teachers. As in Elegy I, the tutors of Cambridge do not prick the imagination but stifle it. This image jars with the second representation of university life in *Lycidas*, in which Milton and King "drove a field" (27) and welcomed the dawn together. Each day upon the hills, they played their "Rural ditties" (32) to the amusement of satyrs, fauns, and old Damaetas. True education, the poem suggests, is autodidactic, and the young men learn by composing songs and singing them to one another. In this regard, while old Camus with his slow footing and hairy mantle is a curse upon them, university experience itself is a blessing, since it enables the boys to find themselves through their own private studies. Unlike the Irish Sea—a place of unraveling and disjunction, as Lycidas's body is dismembered and dispersed—Cambridge is a place of cohesion and intimacy, as the boys enjoy close companionship.

However, at Cambridge the Swain finds only the memory (not the person) of Lycidas, and so he continues his search for his friend, turning at last to England. But instead of praising the nation as he did in Elegy I, Milton presents a vision of national decay epitomized in the corrupt clergy. In Elegy I, Cambridge was everything London was not, but in *Lycidas*, it is England that is not England. Saint Peter's diatribe against the national church is replete with images of judgment: the "little reck'ning" the priests make (116, a pun on the reckoning they would soon receive); their inability to "hold / A Sheep-hook" (119–20, an instrument of discernment); and his reference in line 118 to a parable of the Last Judgment (the parable of the wedding banquet, Matt. 22:1–14) when indicating that the priests would be cast out at Christ's return, while the lowly and despised would take their place.[31] As the Swain propels us from one location to the next, we find that no place—not even England—is an adequate habitation for the exceptional Lycidas. King, Milton suggests, is too good for all the places of this world, and as the faithful remnant of a once holy English nation, his true home is among the blessed saints above.

Milton uses the figure of Michael the archangel to precipitate a shift in perspective from England to *ecclesia*, as we cease looking for Lycidas on Earth and find him in heaven. In biblical accounts of the end times,

Figure 3. John Speed, *The Kingdome of Great Britaine and Ireland* (1611).

Figure 3. (Continued)

Michael protects the faithful remnant in the days before the Last Judgment. Daniel prophesies that Michael would "stand up, the great Prince which standeth for the children [i.e. the remnant] of thy people" (Dan. 12:1) and Revelation states, "There was warre in heaven, [and] Michael and his Angels fought against the dragon" (Rev. 12:7).[32] Michael not only guards the remnant but also symbolizes God's divine action of reckoning between the faithful and the wicked. In *Lycidas*, Michael performs the same function, and Saint Peter invokes him when warning, "But that two-handed engine at the door / Stands ready to smite once, and smite no more" (130–31). One meaning of "engine" in Milton's England was a person who functions like an engine, and this is exactly the role in which we find Michael, who works on the one hand to protect the faithful, and on the other, to assail the wicked.[33] "Two-handed," moreover, refers to Christ's prophesy that at the Last Judgment, "then shall the King say unto them at his right hand, Come ye blessed of my Father, inherit the kingdome prepared for you [. . .] Then shall he say also unto them on the left hand, Depart from mee, ye cursed, into everlasting fire" (Matt. 25:34, 41). Michael is the embodiment of divine reckoning, and he fulfills the scriptural promise to separate the faithful from the wicked at the world's end.

But in the seventeenth century, Michael was also the guardian angel of the English nation, and the conflation of his two roles in *Lycidas*—the one patriotic and political, the other ecclesiastical and spiritual—registers a larger perspectival shift taking place in the poem, as we move from earthly concerns to spiritual ones and from impure nation to pure *ecclesia*.[34] The Swain's command to Michael, "Look homeward Angel now, and melt with ruth" (163), captures the essence of this shift, as Michael moves from guarding England to guarding the remnant, Lycidas. Given the Swain's recent search for Lycidas from the Hebrides to the Irish Sea, we are tempted at first to interpret "homeward" geographically, as looking toward England. But the true home of angels is in heaven, and it is there that we find Lycidas.[35] Glimpsing Lycidas among *ecclesia*, the Swain declares,

> So *Lycidas* sunk low, but mounted high,
> Through the dear might of him that walk'd the waves;
> Where other groves, and other streams along,
> With *Nectar* pure his oozy Lock's he laves,

And hears the unexpressive nuptiall Song,
In the blest Kingdoms meek of joy and love.
There entertain him all the Saints above,
In solemn troops, and sweet Societies
That sing, and singing in their glory move,
And wipe the tears for ever from his eyes.
Now *Lycidas* the Shepherds weep no more;
Hence forth thou art the Genius of the shore,
In thy large recompense, and shalt be good
To all that wander in that perilous flood.

(172–85)

Lycidas's apotheosis is modeled on Revelation, when Saint John sees a vision of the Last Judgment and then "a new heaven, and a new earth" (Rev. 21:1).[36] As in Elegy III, Milton transcends the difficulties of the present with a vision of the future, in which the faithful remnant enjoys the heavenly kingdom. As the saints wipe the tears from Lycidas's eyes, they fulfill the end-time prophecy that "God shall wipe away all teares from their eyes: and there shall bee no more death, neither sorrow, nor crying, neither shall there bee any more paine: for the former things are passed away" (Rev. 21:4). The search for Lycidas is finally over. Neither dismembered in the Irish Sea, nor remembered at Cambridge, nor corrupted in London, Lycidas is finally discovered among the universal community of the saints in heaven.

Yet *Lycidas* does not end there, and Milton's final turn toward the Swain, who sings to the oaks and the rills, is a return to temporality, the nation, and life in the present. The Swain explains that Lycidas has supplanted Michael as the "Genius of the shore," and he prophesies that others who "wander in that perilous flood" would find their way out through him. In a man of no nation, Milton locates the hope of the nation, and he suggests that King's singular virtue is a model for all the faithful in England who might follow in his track. Like *In Quintum Novembris* and Elegy III, *Lycidas* blesses England with time and opportunity to labor faithfully until Christ's return. The Swain's final observation, "To morrow to fresh Woods, and Pastures new" (193), writes that tomorrow into being and gives the nation hope. Because the day of their laboring has not yet drawn to a close, Milton's readers have an opportunity to establish true religion and become the pious English yet again.[37]

It is worth repeating that *Lycidas* is an English poem in a largely Latin collection, and that Milton (who was already an exceptional Latinist, and knew it) chose to write in the vernacular for a reason.[38] *Lycidas* is not as patriotic as *In Quintum Novembris* or Elegy III; it is, in fact, quite critical of the nation in a way the earlier poems were not. But the critiques of the nation found in *Lycidas* render its praise of the same all the more valuable, and that praise is embedded in the very language of *Lycidas*. "To morrow to fresh Woods, and Pastures new" is a string of mainly Anglo-Saxon words that echo of the English countryside, and among the neo-Latin poems of *Justa Edovardo King Naufrago*, Milton's praise of the English vernacular stands out. "To morrow to fresh Woods, and Pastures new" is an offer of hope in the form of time, as Milton's readers seize the opportunity before them and remake the nation after King's own example.

"From These May Grow / A Hunder'd-fold": The Waldensian Remnant in Sonnet 18 "On the Late Massacher in Piemont"

Two decades later, Milton would expand upon the ideas in *Lycidas* and map out new spaces in which a nation-remnant might exist. He would also theorize how he might give England more time when time has run out. Much had changed in the years between *Lycidas* and Milton's political sonnets. After witnessing just how slow the progress of reform could be, first under the Commonwealth and then under the Protectorate, Milton wrote a series of sonnets that linked England to the lukewarm Laodicea in Revelation, which is "neither cold nor hot" (Rev. 3:16) and is about to be expelled from *ecclesia*. The theme of Sonnets 15, 16, and 17 (to Fairfax, Cromwell, and Vane) is England's leadership of the Reformation, and as we shall see, Sonnets 18 and 19 are concerned with the same.[39] The tie that binds the latter two sonnets is the theme of the faithful remnant. Whereas *In Quintum Novembris* and Elegy III defined England in terms of geographic place, its *fluentisonis albentia rupibus arva* (25, wave-resounding cliffs and white fields) and *Angliaco solo* (4, English soil), respectively, Sonnets 18 and 19 follow the lead of *Lycidas* in locating the nation-remnant in unconventional spaces outside England's borders.

Building upon Elegy III, which construed England's identity in relation to its European partners in the Reformation, Sonnet 18 reads England's status as the remnant through comparison with another nation-remnant: the Waldensians. The Waldensians were a Protestant community who, following persecution from French lords, had been given two valleys in the Piedmont region of the Alps as a safe refuge. To Milton and other English Protestants, they were known as pre-Reformation Protestants, whose faith predated that of the Lollards and Hussites and perhaps derived from Saint Peter himself.[40] In Sonnet 18, Milton relates the interconnectedness of England and the Waldensians by describing the latter as they who "kept thy truth so pure of old / When all our Fathers worship't Stocks and Stones" (3–4). The faith of the Waldensians enabled England's conversion from Anglo-Saxon heathenism to Christianity, and in the present, England has an opportunity to repay that kindness.

On April 24, 1655, under orders from the Duke of Savoy and led by the Marquis of Pianezza, several thousand soldiers slaughtered the Waldensians who had taken up residence beyond the territory originally granted to them. England was implicated in the event, since Pianezza's force consisted in part of Irish Catholics who had fled from Cromwell and sought refuge on the continent.[41] England had a debt to pay not only in aiding its Protestant brothers but also in righting a wrong its own subjects helped commit.

Imagining the massacre as an end-time event, Milton's Sonnet 18 appropriates words and images from Revelation to present the Waldensians as the remnant:[42]

> Avenge O Lord thy slaughter'd Saints, whose bones
> Lie scatter'd on the Alpine mountains cold,
> Ev'n them who kept thy truth so pure of old
> When all our Fathers worship't Stocks and Stones,
> Forget not: in thy book record their groanes
> Who were thy Sheep and in their antient Fold
> Slayn by the bloody *Piemontese* that roll'd
> Mother with Infant down the Rocks. Their moans
> The Vales redoubl'd to the Hills, and they
> To Heav'n. Their martyr'd blood and ashes sow
> O're all th'*Italian* fields where still doth sway

The triple Tyrant: that from these may grow
A hunder'd-fold, who having learnt thy way
Early may fly the *Babylonian* wo.

The opening plea, "Avenge O Lord thy slaughter'd Saints," associates the Waldensians with the martyrs in heaven, whom Saint John hears crying, "How long, O Lord, holy and true, doest thou not judge and avenge our blood on them that dwell on the earth?" (Rev. 6:10). Similarly, the speaker's prayer to "avenge" invokes the Last Judgment as the means of the Waldensians' vindication. The plea that follows, "Forget not: in thy book record their groanes," refers to the Book of Life in scripture, out of which the dead would be "judged out of those things which were written in the books, according to their works" at the Last Judgment (Rev. 20:12). Synchronizing these two moments in scripture, Sonnet 18 draws the Last Judgment into the present in the minds of its readers, as the speaker orders justification for the Waldensians without further delay.

Sonnet 18 uses two biblical prophecies of the end times to describe the Waldensians as the remnant. Milton's account of bones scattered on the mountainside, as well as blood and ashes that give rise to a hundredfold, evoke Ezekiel's apocalyptic vision in the valley of the dry bones. The vision was interpreted by Protestants as a type of the General Resurrection, but in its ancient Jewish context, it was a political narrative of national unification. Previously in the book of Ezekiel, God had declared, "My sheepe wandered through all the mountaines, and upon every high hill: yea my flocke was scattered upon the face of the earth" (Ezek. 34:6). Here, as Ezekiel walks through the valley, skeletons take on flesh before his eyes, and God proclaims, "Behold, I will take the children of Israel from among the heathen wither they be gone, and will gather them on every side, and bring them into their owne land: And I will make them one nation in the land upon the mountaines of Israel, and one King shall be king to them all: and they shalbe no more two nations, neither shall they bee divided into two kingdomes any more at all [. . .] And David my servant *shall be* king over them, and they all shall have one shepheard" (Ezek. 37:21–22, 24). In the literal sense of scripture, the passage foretells the reunification of Israel and Judah (symbolized in the jointure of bone to bone and sinew to sinew), as the lost Ten Tribes are reunited with their brothers in the Jewish homeland. In the anagogical sense of scripture, however, the passage typifies the reunion of the faithful remnant with its kin community, *ecclesia*, at the end of the world. Just as the Assyrian Conquest scattered the Ten Tribes, so too the remnant would be scattered throughout the world until the appointed time of reunification. The messianism of the passage illustrates its eschatological significance. King David has, of course, been dead for centuries. The man Ezekiel sees is his antitype, the messiah, who rules over the saints in the New Heavens and New Earth for eternity.

Milton's appropriation of this narrative of national unification shapes the relationship between two sister nations, England and the Waldensians, in the poem. Milton relocates Ezekiel's vision in the valley of the dry bones to the valleys of the Piedmont, where the moans of the bones of the faithful cry for vengeance. Milton suggests that like Israel and Judah, the Waldensians and the English are one nation. Like the remnant of Israel, which was cut off from Judah for a time, the Waldensians are a remnant removed from their Protestant brethren until the time of reunification at the Last Judgment. The literal and anagogical senses of Ezekiel's vision converge in Milton's poem, as the reunion of the Waldensians with its sister nation, England, at the Last Judgment models the reunion of the faithful remnant with *ecclesia*.

Milton loves interweaving biblical narratives, and his reworking of Ezekiel's vision is accompanied by a second biblical prophecy of the faithful remnant. The poem's closing prayer, that "from these may grow / A hunder'd-fold, who having learnt thy way / Early may fly the *Babylonian* wo," echoes Revelation, when an angel declares, "Babylon the great is fallen, is fallen, and is become the habitation of devils" (Rev. 18:2), and then beckons to the faithful, "Come out of her, my people, that yee be not partakers of her sinnes, and that yee receive not of her plagues" (Rev. 18:4). In its first-century context, the passage offered hope to early Christians against the oppression of Rome, but in its anagogical sense, the passage describes the remnant's choice to extricate itself from wicked nations at the world's end. But in Milton's poem we are no longer talking about the Waldensians. This is a second remnant—a mysterious "hunder'd-fold"—who learn the way from their predecessors and accordingly flee from the Babylonian woe.

Milton's references to Christ's parable of the sower explain what this second remnant is. In the parable, a sower casts seeds upon the ground. Some fall by the wayside and are eaten by birds, some wither in the sun, some are choked by thorns, and a final few—a remnant—fall "into good ground," where they flourish and bring "foorth fruit, some an hundred folde, some sixtie folde, some thirty folde" (Matt. 13:4–8). Christ explains that the seeds that fell onto good ground are "he that heareth the word, and understandeth it" (Matt. 13:23). Those seeds, then, are they who hear the good news of Christ's coming and believe it. In Milton's sonnet, this is the news of the Easter Massacre. Like the gospel, some would hear the news of the Waldensian slaughter and turn a deaf ear, but others would use that news to cultivate their own faith and become a new remnant—the hundredfold.

This remnant of a remnant, which is born of the bones strewn across the Alps, which inherits the Waldensians' legacy of faithfulness, and which is heralded by Milton with prophetic force—this remnant is England. In the past, the Waldensians cleared the way for the English through their ancient faith, and in the present, the Waldensians show England the way to remain faithful through the witness of their blood and bones. Sonnet 18 is a call not only for divine action, as God avenges his slaughtered saints, but also for political action on the part of the Waldensians' sister nation. Using the Easter Massacre to stir his readers into activity, Milton indicates that England must pick up where the Waldensians left off. He calls upon his readers to defend the true faith, as the Waldensians did, and thereby become the hundredfold. And in a skillful paralleling of form and content, just as one remnant prepares the way for another, so too does Sonnet 18 set the stage for Sonnet 19, which offers yet another perspective on the remnant's union with *ecclesia*.

"They Also Serve": The English Remnant in Sonnet 19 "When I Consider How My Light is Spent"

Sonnet 18 ends in anticipation of the Last Judgment, and Sonnet 19 "When I Consider How My Light is Spent" inherits its concern for an imminent national reckoning. With its call for vengeance, Sonnet 18 invokes the Last Judgment and draws it near, but Sonnet 19, with its emphasis on waiting for the bridegroom, Christ, delays that event. Sonnet 19 first appeared in the 1673 collection *Poems, & c. upon Severall Occasions. by Mr. John Milton*, and while the poem has long been read biographically as a commentary on Milton's fading eyesight, nothing in the 1673 collection indicates that it should be read as such. In fact, the biographical tradition was established in the eighteenth century, when the editor Thomas Newton dubbed the poem "On his blindness"—a title it did not originally possess.[43] Centuries later, many critics continue to read the poem biographically as a moment of self-reflection at a pivotal point in Milton's life.[44] Though John Shawcross and William Riley Parker prove notable exceptions in arguing for the poem's fictitiousness, no one has considered the possibility that this famous and endearing sonnet is a political poem—not a personal one.[45] While Sonnet 18 wears its politics on its sleeve, the political concerns of Sonnet 19 are far more subtle, and the poem's intimate tone has for centuries caused scholars to overlook its contemporary relevance and religious topicality.

I suggest, then, that Sonnet 19 is a political poem, the second in a diptych exploring the idea of a national remnant, and the fifth in a sequence of five political sonnets that address the progress of religious reform in England.[46] As Milton coopts the intimate form of the sonnet to reflect public concerns, Sonnet 19 addresses the nation's fitness to become the remnant through an anonymous poetic speaker with whom any contemporary reader familiar with the rhetoric of reform might identify.[47] The poem might have been written any time after the Waldensian Massacre, but given the optimistic tone of Milton's *The Readie & Easie Way to Establish a Free Commonwealth* (which was written on the eve of Charles's return and holds out hope for a reformed English republic), more likely it dates to a period after the Restoration, since its themes of patient waiting and singular fortitude have a great deal in common with Milton's faithful remnant in *Paradise Lost*, as we shall discuss in chapter 5. Precisely because the poem resists easy anchoring to a specific historical event or figure, it is mistakenly interpreted as an apolitical work, but its relationship to antiprelatical treatises by Milton and others suggests that Sonnet 19 is a political text. The poem does not reflect Milton's personal anguish at his blindness but rather the collective anguish of a nation caught in the "work" that accompanies "the birth of reformation," as Milton described it in *The Reason of Church-Government*.[48]

The key to unlocking the political nature of Sonnet 19 is the parable of the talents. As Dayton Haskin observes, the parable was a biblical site of personal importance to Milton, but as I have shown elsewhere, it was also integral to a national rhetoric of reform during the prelacy controversy of the 1640s.[49] As we saw at the beginning of this chapter, Milton used the parable to describe England's labors in *Of Reformation* when he suggested that if it abolished episcopacy, the nation would receive "*Nationall Honours* and *Rewards*" at Christ's return, like the faithful servants in the parable. Tyrannous nations, by contrast, would be hurled into "the *darkest* and *deepest Gulfe* of HELL" like the wicked servant.

In *The Reason of Church-Government*, as well, Milton described the debate over church government as a "heavenly Traffick" of spiritual truths, in which he and other reformists "labour[ed]" (*CPW* 1:801) on behalf of true religion. Like the faithful servants in the parable, he and other reformists invested their "entrusted gifts" (*CPW* 1:801), but the bishops hid their talents and trade instead with "deceitfull wares" and "trash" (*CPW* 1:802), like the wicked servant. Through their attempts to blockade the dissemination of truth, the priests hindered exchanges by good servants like Milton, who sought to use publication to create a scripturally inspired dialogue on church government.

But Milton was not alone in politicizing the parable, and during the prelacy controversy it served as a rhetorical *locus communis* for reformists advocating change in England. For instance, in the works of Smectymnuus (an acronym for Stephen Marshall, Edmund Calamy, Thomas Young, Matthew Newcomen, and William Spurstowe), "talents" came to signify England's opportunities for godly reform.[50] Calamy preached, "It cannot be denied but that God hath done much for England, but England hath done much against God, [. . .] [for] every *new mercy* we receive from God is a *new talent*, (for mercies are talents, betrusted with us by God as stewards, for which we must give a severe and strict account at the day of Judgement)."[51] He went on to state that England, with its opportunities for reform, had been given "many hundred talents of mercies," and that its MPs could either "*improve* them" or "*mis-improve* them to the service of sin and Satan."[52]

Like Calamy, Marshall expressed his hope that "the Lord should now reforme this [church] government."[53] He instructed the people to use their talents of prayer on behalf of the nation: "now, there is one talent which I am sure every childe of God that is effectually called hath, though they be never so poore, and that is the talent of prayer [. . .] And this talent the Lord requires they should use and imploy for the good of his Church and people."[54] As Marshall saw it, the prayers of the English people were "like so many Talents put into Gods bank."[55] In Marshall's rhetoric, the danger of England becoming the unprofitable servant was balanced against the hope that the nation would become the faithful servant.

Milton's boyhood tutor, Thomas Young, who made a lasting impression on the young man, also nationalized the parable as a means of urging reform.[56] In a sermon to the Commons, he exhorted MPs to fortify their "Christian courage" and stated that "the ready way to have them [i.e., their courages] to encrease and *multiply*, is faithfully to *employ* them [. . .] This is evidently set forth to us in the parable of the Talents."[57] Young equated improving the nation's talents with improving the nation's religion—that is, replacing episcopal government with presbyterian government. He condemned those who, like the wicked servant, "labour not to *improve* the graces they have received," but he praised those who have "improved" the "good beginnings of a Reformation" begun under Thomas Cromwell.[58] "Improve that which they happily begunne," he challenged the MPs, for "this is the duty which God requires of you."[59] Like Calamy and Marshall, Young used the parable of the talents to illustrate the nation's opportunities for reform, to admonish against England becoming like the wicked servant, and to mobilize his audiences into action.[60]

While the parable of the talents uncovers the contemporary political topicality of Sonnet 19, the poem in fact employs three parables of the Last Judgment, as though one parable were insufficient to capture to complexity of the poetic speaker's predicament. As the poem shifts from one parable to the next, readers are encouraged to identify with different models of service and assess their own labors of reformation in light of an imminent national reckoning:

> When I consider how my light is spent,
> E're half my days, in this dark world and wide,
> And that one Talent which is death to hide,
> Lodg'd with me useless, though my Soul more bent
> To serve therewith my Maker, and present
> My true account, least he returning chide,
> Doth God exact day-labour, light deny'd,
> I fondly ask; But patience to prevent
> That murmur, soon replies, God doth not need

Either man's work or his own gifts, who best
Bear his mild yoak, they serve him best, his State
Is Kingly. Thousands at his bidding speed
And post o're Land and Ocean without rest:
They also serve who only stand and waite.

In the poem, the parables are framed by an Old Testament reference to the splintered kingdoms of Israel and Judah. As in his account of the Waldensians, in Sonnet 19 Milton appropriates the story of the divided kingdoms to suggest that England has reached its tipping point: it can either prove worthy of its calling as the remnant, or not. The phrase "E're half my days," which has long caused debate among scholars, echoes Habakkuk, a prophet of the remnant of Israel (the southern kingdom of Judah) who lamented the idolatry of his people and worried that they, too, would fall subject to a national reckoning like the northern kingdom.[61] "O LORD," Habakkuk cries, "revive thy worke in the midst of the yeeres, in the midst of the yeeres make knowen; in wrath remember mercy" (Hab. 3:2). The plight of Judah as a rebellious remnant is a fitting analogy for Milton's lukewarm and half-reformed England. In the prayer of the prophet, the poet finds words fitting for his own plea that now, when the godly work of reformation is half done and the nation is in "the midst of the yeeres," God would not forsake his people but return them to repentance.

Sonnet 19 acquires from Habakkuk the notion that God might provide mercy in the midst of his wrath. Similar to Elegy III and *Lycidas*, Milton channels the idea of England-as-remnant through the experience of a single person—an everyman—the poetic speaker. In Sonnet 19, however, the nation is at last fully unmoored from the geographic spaces to which it had previously been tethered and is now considered synecdochically through the mind and conscience of a single citizen.[62] And as the speaker imagines the Last Judgment coming upon him (and upon all England), he turns to three parables of judgment as an attempt to both describe his experience and mitigate the effects of wrath.[63] Significantly, all three parables use imagery of light and darkness to describe the divine action of reckoning. In a reworking of that imagery, Milton creates a poetic chiaroscuro that emphasizes the speaker's panic at his crisis of service, now that the Last Judgment has arrived and he is unable to labor further.

Sonnet 19 uses light to register time, and the point at which Milton's speaker enters each parable—always at the final moment of reckoning—is significant. The poem's opening reference to light being spent alludes to the parable of the wise and foolish virgins, in which young women await the coming of the bridegroom and some fall asleep and let their lamps go out. Christ explains that when they went out to buy more oil, "the bridegrome came, and they that were ready, went in with him to the marriage, and the doore was shut" (Matt. 25:10). To his dismay, the speaker of Sonnet 19 discovers that like the foolish virgins, he has not remained vigilant. His light has been spent, he has nothing with which to illuminate the way of Christ. Like the foolish virgins, he is about to be shut out of the marriage celebration.

But Milton reads this parable through another—the poem's opening line also alludes to the parable of the laborers in the vineyard.[64] In the parable, a lord hires men at different times of the day to work in his vineyard, but he pays each man the same amount. When those who worked long in the heat of the day complain, the lord responds, "Friend, I do thee no wrong: didst not thou agree with me for a penie? Take that thine is, and goe thy way, I will give unto this last, even as unto thee" (Matt. 20:13–14). Milton's poetic speaker, however, cannot accept this grace. Altering the biblical narrative, he imagines Christ as a far harsher taskmaster than the lord of the vineyard. He wonders, will God "exact day-labour" from him in the darkness? What more can he do, now that the light has faded?

Having been condemned (one way or another) by the first two parables, the speaker then turns to a third—the parable of the talents—in an attempt to resolve his crisis of service. Imagining himself at the moment of his lord's return, he fears that he is the wicked servant clutching "that one Talent which is death to hide" and that he, too, is about to be cast into outer darkness. The parable of the talents reveals what the speaker's service to God is. From the pulpit to the pamphlet, the parable had been used by men like the Smectymnuans to describe religious reform and to mobilize the faithful into action. Milton's use of the parable would have resonated with the reading public, who saw themselves as participants in the national conversation on the progress of the Reformation in England.[65] Recognizing the sonnet's political implications, readers may have seen in Sonnet 19 something akin to what they saw in *Of Reformation* and *The*

Reason of Church-Government: a description of England struggling to reform itself and a summons to participate in that godly work. The speaker's service to God in Sonnet 19, then, is the labor of religious reform on behalf of a lukewarm nation.

In the octave, the three parables work together to condemn the speaker, but at the volta, a fourth story of the Last Judgment is introduced, and it offers hope. This is the story of the faithful remnant as told by Patience, who informs the speaker that what he had thought was a vice—his immobility—is in fact the virtue of the faithful. She transforms the speaker's thinking and teaches him that by doing no more than standing and waiting for the Last Judgment, he has fulfilled the duty asked of him. Like Elegy III, Sonnet 19 constructs a panoramic vision of divine busyness, as *ecclesia* (those thousands who at Christ's bidding "speed / And post o'er Land and Ocean without rest") hovers above the speaker and threatens, at any moment, to disrupt his inward reveries.

But Patience explains that England has nothing to fear from this imminent national reckoning. In her admonition to "stand and waite," she frees the poetic speaker from the parable of the talents, which had condemned him, and draws him back to the parable of the wise and foolish virgins. As the parable of the virgins teaches, standing and waiting is not slothfulness but the virtue of the remnant (the parable concludes with the admonition, "Watch therefore, for ye know neither the day nor the houre, wherein the Sonne of man commeth" [Matt. 25:13]). Patience teaches the speaker of Sonnet 19 that this is, in fact, the very activity in which he is presently engaged, and that to prove faithful in the final days of testing is simply to do what the remnant does, which is to stand firm and await the coming of Christ.

The speaker's experience in Sonnet 19 teaches Milton's readers that the virtue of the faithful is their ability to remain in the faith. "Remain in me," Christ tells his followers in the gospels, "that I may remain in you" (John 15:4), and Sonnet 19 imparts the same lesson, which is that the highest form of service to God is to remain faithful when everyone else does not.[66] Milton's readers learn along with the poetic speaker that working out one's faith with fear and trembling is itself the labor of religious reform and, consequently, the service God requires. Sonnet 18 presented England with an opportunity to become the hundredfold—the remnant fleeing Babylon at the end of the world—and Sonnet 19 responds to that challenge by suggesting that England would indeed prove worthy of the calling it has received.

The nation's hope is now located in its readers, who respond to Milton's call to action and recognize that as the remnant, England still has a vital part to play before Christ's return. When the light has faded at last and all labors have ceased, England's role would be to do as the wise virgins did and stand and wait for the bridegroom and light the way of his coming. Sonnet 19 teaches that so long as faithful readers await Christ's coming with joy, the remnant would live on. The end of the world would mean the end of many things—but not, assuredly, the end of the nation.

2

POSTPONING THE LAST JUDGMENT

Biblical Sovereignty and
Political Messianism in Hobbes's Leviathan

The publication of Hobbes's *Leviathan* in 1651 prompted many fiery responses, most viciously from John Bramhall, bishop of Derry and later archbishop of Armagh. The debate between Hobbes and Bramhall had deep roots. It began in 1645 as a dispute at the Paris residence of William Cavendish, marquess of Newcastle, and from there, it expanded into a heated pamphlet war with many salvos fired and sustained by both sides.[1] In *Castigations of Mr. Hobbes*, Bramhall targets Hobbes's unconventional eschatology, in particular:

> And why should I not be confident in this cause? Grant me but that there is a God, that he is just, and true, and good, and powerfull, that there is an Heaven, and an hell, and a day of judgement, that is, rewards and punishments; That good and evil, virtue and vice, holinesse and sin, are any thing more than empty names [. . .] and I cannot fall in this cause. There is no doubt but the best doctrines may be abused.[2]

The passage shows that for Bramhall, at stake is not simply the nature of government but the fundamental doctrines of Christianity. Here and in

The Catching of Leviathan (which was often bound with *Castigations*), Bramhall focuses on the threat Hobbes poses to readers' belief in the last things, and he accuses Hobbes of calling these fundamental doctrines into question. By insisting that these doctrines are "more than empty names," Bramhall suggests that for Hobbes, that is all they are. Bramhall is a keen reader of Hobbes, albeit an unhappy one, and it is telling that he both hones in on eschatology's place in *Leviathan* and reacts violently to the kind of eschatology Hobbes offers him. By desacralizing judgment, Hobbes has undermined a spiritual economy of "rewards and punishments" that Bramhall sees as the moral foundation of society. In this regard, Hobbes has endangered not only the future but also the present.

Reading *Leviathan* in light of such contemporary responses, Nicholas Jackson, Jon Parkin, and A. P. Martinich reclaim Hobbes from his status (maintained for much of the twentieth century) as an early proponent of atheism and unearth Hobbes's investment in religious controversy and his intellectual debts to the reformers.[3] I would argue further that Hobbesian sovereignty is based on Christian eschatology and that Hobbes's sovereign is modeled on Christ at the Last Judgment, as *Leviathan*'s title page indicates.[4] This eschatological basis has national implications, and Hobbes presents *Leviathan* to his English readers as an instruction manual for repairing the complex machinery of the national government in the aftermath of the civil wars.[5] In the Old Testament, the leviathan is an incomparable "dragon in the waters" (Ps. 74:13), and in the Jewish *Chaoskampf* tradition, the monster represents unchecked human power at the end of days.[6] In the twentieth century, Carl Schmitt admired Hobbes's leviathan (as only Schmitt could) as an "all powerful, resistance-destroying, and technically perfect mechanism of command."[7] What better symbol, then, for England, the "sceptred isle," towering over its European neighbors, safe and secure in its ocean home?[8] Capitalizing on the messianic expectations of his countrymen, Hobbes works to transform widespread eschatological hope in Christ into the political hope for a national *deus mortalis*. Rather than await Christ's return, Hobbes suggests, the English people might make their own messiah instead.[9]

The Last Judgment is useful to Hobbes as a tool for rebuilding the nation in a time of turmoil, but it also threatens to undermine the same with its promise of a greater ruler to come and a one-world, theocratic government. Like Milton, Hobbes sees the Last Judgment as an opportunity to reshape the nation, but unlike Milton, who awaits his "Eternall and shortly-expected King" with joy, Hobbes dreads Christ's return. Hobbes plays a dangerous game. On the one hand, eschatology allows him to show England the godlike status it might attain as the leviathan, but on the other, he must work to delay the outcome of that eschatological expectation—the Last Judgment—since it would entail the end of English sovereignty. In an era when many Englishmen believed Christ would soon "gather all nations" and reckon between them (Matt. 25:32), Hobbes realized that the Last Judgment was a powerful tool for rebuilding England, but one that needed to be contained, regulated, and—at times—delayed.

Leviathan's Title Page and the Visual Tradition of the Last Judgment

Hobbes's appropriation of the Last Judgment is apparent in *Leviathan*'s famous title page, which reveals his indebtedness to Christian eschatology (see figure 4). The illustration was created by the French artist Abraham Bosse, likely with Hobbes's instructions and oversight.[10] What might an early English reader have thought of the title page? Who would he or she have seen in this gigantic man looming over a city, a sword in one hand and a bishop's crosier in the other? The image was a familiar one, but in the context of religious iconography—not political philosophy. The figure's large body evokes the ancient concept of *makros anthrōpos* (the great man), which had been employed in visual representations of Christ at the Last Judgment since the Middle Ages and was commonly used in tympana on the facades of medieval cathedrals, both in the British Isles and on the continent.[11]

The European Reformation gave rise to new and exciting visualizations of Christ's return, and *Leviathan*'s title page evinces how Hobbes, too, in directing Bosse's hand, reinvented eschatological iconography for his own purposes.[12] Not coincidentally, the Last Judgment tympana on Paris cathedrals—where Hobbes had been living since 1640 for fear of reprisal against his absolutist treatise *The Elements of Law*—bear a striking resemblance to *Leviathan*'s title page.[13] On the west portal of the Last Judgment at Notre-Dame Cathedral in Paris, for instance, a superhuman Christ towers over angels, saints, and sinners, his hands raised in a posture

Figure 4. Abraham Bosse, title page to Thomas Hobbes, *Leviathan* (1651).

of power like that of Hobbes's sovereign (see figure 5).[14] In the sculpture, the celestial arch above the oversized Christ evokes the expansive frame of *Leviathan*'s sovereign, who mirrors Christ's position by crowding the visual space and brushing up against the heavens.[15] The Last Judgment tympanum on the Abbey Church of Saint Denis, also in Paris, features another such arch, beneath which a massive Christ stretches out his arms in memory of the cross but also in a display of his authority at the world's end (see figure 6).[16] In these and other tympana of the Last Judgment, the smaller figures are subordinate to Christ, but in Hobbes's reworking of the image, they form the body of Hobbes's sovereign—as if to say, our messiah is who we make him. This major alteration to the traditional iconography exemplifies Hobbes's larger method throughout *Leviathan* of politicizing Christian messianism and suggesting that his countrymen hold in their own hands the tools of their redemption.[17]

In revolutionary England, the image of a supersized Christ at the Last Judgment would have resonated with readers. Many of them had seen the same and similar sculptures on cathedrals across France and England, but all of them were familiar with the great man image from a more ubiquitous source: English Bibles. Since William Tyndale's de Keyser New Testament of 1534, the image of a domineering Christ staring down from on high had appeared in illustrations to Revelation, many of which were adapted from woodcut engravings by Lucas Cranach for Luther's September Testament of 1522, which were in turn inspired by Albrecht Dürer's *Apocalypse* series.[18] In the earliest editions of English Bibles, Revelation was the only book to receive full-page illustrations, which quickly became part of the visual heritage of the English Reformation and continued to appear (in differing variations and sizes) in editions of the Great Bible, the Bishops' Bible, and the King James Bible.[19] What seems (at first glance) a supersized Christ at the Last Judgment resurfaces again in *Leviathan*'s title page, as Hobbes capitalizes on his readers' familiarity with the iconic image—both from church architecture and from English Bibles—to show the nation the godlike power it might possess as the leviathan.

The title page to *Leviathan* establishes a method Hobbes continues to deploy throughout the treatise, in which he constructs an idea of Christ's unmatched power at the Last Judgment only to supplant Christ with the sovereign. Hobbes's strategy is to equip the sovereign with Christ's own authority while simultaneously emphasizing that the Last Judgment is a future event and therefore a present nonreality.

Figure 5. Tympanum of the Last Judgment, Notre-Dame Cathedral, Paris (ca. 1220).

© French Moments.

Figure 6. Tympanum of the Last Judgment, Abbey Church of Saint Denis, Paris (ca. 1135–44).

© James B. Kiracofe.

Figure 7. Tympanum of the Last Judgment,
Notre-Dame Cathedral, Laon (ca. 1155–1210).

© Alec Harthill.

Figure 8. Tympanum of the Last Judgment, Basilique
Saint-Seurin, Bordeaux (ca. 1267).

© Markus Schlicht.

Figure 9. *The Last Judgment*, the Bishops' Bible (1568), sig. Uiiir. RB 32904, the Huntington Library, San Marino, California.

The relationship between sovereign and Christ in *Leviathan* is thus both typological and teleological. Suggesting that his *deus mortalis* is the type (*figura*) of Christ (*veritas*) who is to come, Hobbes declares, "this is the generation of that great LEVIATHAN, or rather (to speak more reverently) of that *Mortall God* to which we owe under the *Immortal God*, our peace and defence."[20] The sovereign reigns until the appointed end of the world, when Christ would return and "rule all nations," as foretold in scriptural prophecy (Rev. 12:5).

This has major implications for Hobbes's readers, who in *Leviathan*'s title page are subsumed into the *deus mortalis*—this great man who resembles Christ yet is not Christ—as Hobbes metaphorizes the contract between citizens and sovereign.[21] The smaller figures are no longer passive recipients of judgment but become implicated in the activity that has replaced it, which is the rule of the sovereign. For an early modern Protestant, this may have been disturbing, to say the least. To see oneself in the smaller figures is to recognize one's complicity in the act of establishing human sovereignty and, by extension, displacing Christ. The title page to *Leviathan* offers readers the dangerous idea that God is not in control of human affairs, and in his absence, people make the world what they will.

Hobbes's politicization of Last Judgment iconography exposes the eschatological foundation of his concept of sovereignty. Hobbes feels compelled to find a scriptural basis for his political system, but as he does so, he shows himself perfectly willing to alter scriptural narrative when such alteration works in his favor. Throughout *Leviathan*, Hobbes's model of sovereignty rests upon a notion of Christ's sovereignty at the Last Judgment. But as we shall see, Hobbes is quick to keep divine sovereignty safely fenced off in the future and to emphasize instead the unchecked agency of the human sovereign in the present. In the Old Testament, Hobbes found several powerful narratives of judgment that—with a little tweaking—could accomplish just what he wanted.[22]

Personating God: Abraham, Moses, and the Origin of Sovereignty

The Old Testament provided Hobbes with a principle central to his philosophy, which is that the sovereign is he who judges. Like Milton, Hobbes was a profoundly Hebraic thinker.[23] His Hebraism is evident in his materialism, his rejection of scholasticism and Aristotelian philosophy, and his search for *Hebraica veritas* in the Old Testament.[24] Reading the Old Testament typologically, Hobbes saw moments of judgment in Jewish history as anticipations of Christ's sovereignty at the Last Judgment. The English word "judgment" and its variations ("to judge," "judged," and "judge") appear 558 times in the King James Version of the Old Testament. Forty instances (7 percent) occur when judging is a human activity carried out by a ruler exercising power over his subjects; 239 instances (43 percent) describe the judgments of God, God as judge, or God meeting the nations in judgment. Clearly, the Old Testament envisions judgment as primarily a divine phenomenon. However, in transferring sovereignty from the realm of the divine to that of the human, Hobbes transforms judging into the rule by which the human sovereign exercises his absolute power.

Basing his political system on the ancient Jewish idea of judgment, and drawing upon a rich western tradition of juridical kingship, Hobbes describes the sovereign's ability to rule as an act of judging.[25] In his readings of the Old Testament, Hobbes found that sovereign power is often described as an act of judgment, such as when God "raysed up Judges, which delivered [the Israelites] out of the hand of those that spoyled them" (Judg. 2:16); God's command to Solomon to "execute my Judgments" (1 Kings 6:12); the axiom that "the king by judgement stablisheth the land" (Prov. 29:4); and the prophecy that "a King shal reigne in righteousnes, and princes shal rule in judgement" (Isa. 32:1). When we turn to Hobbes's *Leviathan*, we find the same idea expressed: "To judge," Hobbes affirms, is "to be king in this world" (3.42.107). While scholars note that the sovereign's power is ultimately the ability to preserve life or take it, they do not recognize this as an eschatological phenomenon—the divine act of judging.[26] These acts look back to the judgments of God in the Old Testament, but they also look forward to Christ's reckoning between the faithful and the wicked at the Last Judgment.

In order to transfer judgment from God to the sovereign, Hobbes develops his theory of personation.[27] Personation derives from the Latin *persona* (character) and the Greek *prosōpon* (face), and it offers a logic of political representation. The *OED* defines the verb "personate" as the act of "assum[ing] the person or character of (another person)," and in *Leviathan*, Hobbes states that people can not only personate one another, but also personate God. "The true God may be personated," Hobbes writes, "as he was, first by *Moses*" (1.16.12). Hobbes is cautious. He knows he is treading on dangerous ground, since this same argument had been used by the Catholic Church for over a thousand years to validate the pope as the vicar of God. Hobbes does not state directly (but rather implies) that current sovereigns personate God, inasmuch as they bring judgment to the people, just as Abraham and Moses did.

Moses and Abraham enable Hobbes to bring divine judgment into the *saeculum* of human history and make judging the trademark of sovereignty. They practiced a "divine politics" of God, Hobbes claims, and their function as judges was to deliver "the laws of the kingdom of God" (1.12.12). Hobbes insists that the judgments of Moses and Abraham, as personators of God, anticipated the judgments of sovereigns in seventeenth-century Europe. Reading his own political theory into the Bible, he asserts the "Sovereign Rights of Abraham" and that Abraham was "sole Judge, and Interpreter of what God spake" (3.40.1–4, side gloss). In personating God as judges, Hobbes insists, they established themselves as rulers, and he writes, "though the name of *King* be not yet given to God, nor of *Kingdom* to Abraham and his seed, yet the thing is the same" (3.35.4). In Hobbes's reworking of scripture, Abraham becomes a sovereign whose absolute power, as a personator of God, justifies the absolute power of sovereigns in Hobbes's own day.

In Hobbes's political theory, Moses also personated God and prefigured Christ's sovereignty at the Last Judgment. Hobbes privileges Moses by stating, "Moses was (under God) Sovereign of the Jews" (3.40.7, side gloss), which echoes Christ's title as King of the Jews. Hobbes writes that the Israelites were contracted to Moses as their sovereign and "obliged themselves to obey whatsoever he should deliver unto them" (3.40.6). Using Moses to demonstrate the absolute authority of the sovereign, Hobbes identifies Moses as a "sovereign prophet" (3.36.13) and verges on blasphemy by equating him with Christ:

> For as Moses and the high priests were God's representative in the Old Testament, and our Saviour himself as man, during his abode on earth, so the Holy Ghost, that is to say the apostles and their successors in the office of preaching and teaching, that had received the holy Spirit, have represented him ever since. But a person (as I have shown before, ch. [16]) is he that is

represented, as often as he is represented. And therefore God, who has been represented (that is, personated) thrice, may properly enough be said to be three persons. (3.42.3)

By privileging the sovereign to the extent that Moses becomes Christ's equal, Hobbes desacralizes judgment and transfers it to a human ruler while outlining for his readers a course of political action. As the examples of Moses and Abraham show, sovereigns engage in an activity specific to the divine person—the authority and ability to judge. Consequently, if England's citizens wish to see judgment return to the land, they must restore the nation's sovereignty by renouncing their own democratic claims to power through the Commonwealth and instead transferring those rights to a strong ruler.[28] The English people must work judgment for themselves, in other words, rather than simply awaiting judgment at Christ's return. All sovereigns, good and bad, bring God's judgments into the historical present, and Hobbes's greatest fear is that without a master to govern them, the English people will become "scattered upon the hilles, as sheepe that have not a shepheard" (1 Kings 22:17), as scripture puts it.

Saul and the End of the Kingdom of God

In addition to illustrating how sovereignty is established, *Leviathan* postulates how sovereignty can fail—and specifically, how the effects of that failure played out in the English Revolution. Hobbes's theories of sovereignty and personation are politically topical and speak to the current state of affairs in England. When arguing for the indivisibility of the sovereign's rights, for instance, Hobbes states that if it had not been incorrectly believed in "*England*, that these powers were divided between the King, and the Lords, and the House of Commons, the people had never been divided and fallen into this civil war" (2.18.16). Throughout *Leviathan*, Hobbes presents Israel—which is also guilty of backsliding, dethroning its sovereign, and paying the consequences—as a forerunner of England. Both nations imperil their citizens by bringing them closer to the natural state of man, which is "solitary, poor, nasty, brutish, and short," and wherein citizens are exposed to "continual fear and danger of violent death" (1.13.9). Whether Israel or England, a nation without its sovereign is a nation divided, and as scripture warns, such a kingdom cannot stand (Mark 3:24).

Nowhere is this clearer than in the story of Israel's first king, Saul, which Hobbes uses in *Leviathan* to desacralize judgment, limit the power of Christ, and increase the power of the sovereign. In allocating judgment to the sovereign through personation, as we saw with Abraham and Moses, Hobbes humanizes a divine phenomenon thought to belong exclusively to God. But Hobbes recognizes that in order for the sovereign's rule to be absolute, the sovereign must be the only one who judges. This conclusion draws Hobbes toward one of his most controversial claims, which is that God does not govern human affairs, and the kingdom of God does not currently exist.

One of the most important discoveries of the Reformation was that the kingdom of God began at Christ's epiphany, when "John the Baptist initiate[d] the Kingdom of Christ [and] usher[ed] in a new era," as Luther wrote.[29] The reformers preached that from that moment onward, death was conquered, Satan was bound, and Christ was king upon the Earth.[30] Hobbes, however, refutes this claim, since it conflicts with his principle that ruling is judging and the sovereign is the only one who rules. He asserts that the kingdom of God began at "the very creation" (3.35.3), when God reigned over all men, but it has been lost since Saul and would not be regained until the Last Judgment, at which time "God shall reign (at the coming again of Christ) in Jerusalem" (3.38.23). The mistake of Christ's contemporaries, Hobbes points out, was to herald him as a king in their own time, when in fact, "our Saviour came into this world that he might be a king, and a judge *in the world to come*" (3.41.3, emphasis mine). When confronted with Christ's majestic sovereignty, John the Baptist humbly says, "Hee must increase, but I must decrease" (John 3:30); when confronted with the same, Hobbes's response is rather the opposite: to increase human sovereignty by decreasing Christ.

Downplaying the sovereignty of Israel's judges, which Milton and other antimonarchists in the 1650s used to justify English republicanism, Hobbes favors Saul as the first sovereign invested with the divine power to do as he wished.[31] Hobbes proudly depicts Saul as a usurper of divine rule, rather than God's "Anointed" (1 Sam. 26:9), as scripture calls him. A sovereign, Hobbes recognizes, cannot personate God if God needs no personation. In the story of how Saul becomes Israel's first king, Hobbes finds justification for the total rule of the sovereign and a way of detaching the kingdom of God from human history.[32] As Hobbes tells it, the crowning of Saul signaled the end of God's rule in this world and the beginning of human sovereignty leading up to the present day. 1 Samuel records that Israel grew frustrated with the corrupt sons of the prophet Samuel, who ruled as judges over them. The elders approached Samuel and demanded that they be given "a King to judge us" (1 Sam. 8:5). When Samuel told them of the misfortune a monarch would bring upon Israel, they responded: "Nay; but we wil have a King over us: That we also may be like all the nations, and that our King may judge us, and goe out before us, and fight our battels" (1 Sam. 8:19–20). The elders forgot that God was already their sovereign, and in an act of sin, they asked Samuel for a human one.

The *a priori* assumption in the biblical passage is that God has been reigning over the Israelites all along. God explains to Samuel, "They have not rejected thee, but they have rejected mee, that I should not reigne over them" (1 Sam. 8:7). He commissions Samuel to fulfill their request, and Israel has its first king in the short-tempered and phobic Saul. When adapting the passage for his own political system in *Leviathan*, Hobbes focuses on the end of theocratic government, which he interprets as proof that the sovereign's power is absolute. As Martinich observes, for Hobbes "there has already been a divine kingdom in the past; none exists now; and a second, final kingdom is reserved for the indefinite future."[33] God grants the Israelites' request and gives them Saul, and sovereignty is now the prerogative of human rulers alone. Significantly, Hobbes ignores the next chapter in 1 Samuel, which suggests an alternative reading: Saul was divinely appointed to "save my people out of the hand of the Philistines," as God says (1 Sam. 9:16).[34] Such an appointment would make Saul into another personator on level with Abraham and Moses. But if Hobbes's claim about the end of the kingdom of God is to work, and if the human sovereign is to be truly sovereign, it is essential that Saul be different from Abraham and Moses. More than a personification of God's power, as they were, Saul is the first human sovereign invested with the divine authority to do as he alone—not God—pleases.

When insisting that divine sovereignty was lost with Saul, Hobbes materializes the kingdom of God and locates it within the *saeculum* of human experience.[35] As J. G. A. Pocock points out, Hobbes's determinist materialism entails "a radical temporalization of salvation," such that judgment, heaven, and hell all occur within time, since Hobbes denies the existence of any reality outside of time, including the Augustinian Eternal Today and the Boethian *nunc stans*.[36] The kingdom of God becomes a political kingdom (not a spiritual one) that God held over the ancient Israelites before Saul, and that Christ would hold again at the Last Judgment. In chapter 35 of *Leviathan*, Hobbes declares,

> The kingdom of God is a civil kingdom, which consisted first in the obligation of the people of Israel to those laws which Moses should bring unto them from Mount Sinai (and which afterwards the high priest for the time being should deliver to them from before the *cherubims* in the *sanctum sanctorum*), and which kingdom having been cast off in the election of Saul, the prophets foretold should be restored by Christ, and the restoration whereof we daily pray for when we say in the Lord's Prayer *Thy kingdom come*, and the right whereof we acknowledge when we add *For thine is the kingdom, the power, and the glory, for ever and ever, Amen.* (3.35.13)

Hobbes's declaration that "the kingdom of God is a civil kingdom" is a bold statement, and it demonstrates his method of reworking scriptural narrative to extend the sovereign's reach. Claiming that the kingdom of God is a civil kingdom is as much as claiming that it is an earthly one. Because that kingdom has been lost, Hobbes suggests, every sovereign since Saul is supreme in matters political and ecclesiastical. Hobbes's argument about Saul amplifies human agency at the expense of divine omnipotence and (as we shall see) therefore irritated his critics to no end because of its materialist implications. Elsewhere, Hobbes states that "*motion* [is] attributed to God, and consequently *place*" (3.34.5)—that is, that God has a physical body. As Hobbes would have it, God's material absence on Earth is the greatest evidence that he does not currently reign. An early English reader might have asked: if divine government was lost with Saul, and if God is no longer in charge, who governs human affairs now? Hobbes's answer was simple: the English people do.

Moreover, Hobbes's account of Saul appropriates a national rhetoric of revolution and turns it back against the revolutionaries. In *Eikonoklastes*, Milton characterized Charles I as a Saul figure who tyrannized his people and showboated a false piety. Attacking Charles for thinking himself "zeal[ous]" in matters of faith, Milton claims, "so thought *Saul* [. . .] for which he lost his Kingdom" (3:491). Although Charles "labours to have it thought that *his fearing God more then Man* was the ground of his sufferings," Milton writes, so too "boasted *Saul* to have *perform'd the Commandment of God*" (3:434), when in fact Saul did nothing of the sort. By contrast, in *Leviathan*, Saul is a strong sovereign, though a usurper. Led by Saul, Hobbes writes, the Israelites "cast off God's yoke" (3.33.20), thereby opening the door for the total absolutism of sovereigns in the present. Hobbes and Milton thus both identify Saul as a usurper but differ in the conclusions they derive from that fact. For Milton, Saul is proof that monarchy is abhorrent to God and the English Revolution justified, while for Hobbes, Saul's actions unshackled humanity from the chains of divine sovereignty. Had Saul not usurped God's throne, England would never have had the opportunity in the mid-seventeenth century to exercise its sovereignty and become the leviathan Hobbes hoped it would be.

For both Hobbes and Milton, interpreting Saul as a usurper had profound implications for English nationalism. The different views they held of Saul illustrate the elasticity of scriptural narrative during the English Revolution, as a royalist used the story to support monarchy, while a republican used it to support the Commonwealth. Milton's analogy between Charles I and Saul, for instance, criticizes kings as villains and praises liberty-loving citizens as heroes. "The ears of a free Nation," Milton writes, find the commands of a tyrannical Charles or a Saul simply "odious" (3.435). Hobbes, by contrast, finds fault not with Saul but with his rebellious subjects—the Israelites, who "rejected God" (3.35.10) in transgressing God's law and demanding a king. As Hobbes sees it, the Israelites' decision enabled the absolute sovereignty of human rulers, but it also began a national decline that rendered such absolutism necessary, since God's perfect government was no more. Noting that this mistake had been repeated of late in England's civil wars, Hobbes pillories the English for dividing and thereby destroying their sovereignty.

Significantly, this is the same act that Milton (by contrast) sees as the godly popularization of sovereign power, and for which he praises the English above all peoples of the world. Whereas Milton sees the English Revolution as an opportunity for the English people to rebuild the nation into a godly republic, Hobbes sees only nation diseased with the cancerous notion that sovereign power is divisible and citizens have a right to rebel.[37] While both men harness eschatological expectation to reinvent the nation, Milton hopes that the Commonwealth might prove precursor to the democratic rule of the saints in *ecclesia*. Hobbes hopes, however, for a strong sovereign who might draw Christ's judgments into the historical present, thereby bringing salvation to the nation.

"In the Meantime": Postponing Christ and Rebuilding the Nation

Throughout *Leviathan*, the Last Judgment serves as the *telos* of sovereignty, but it is a *telos* that is repeatedly slighted, put off, or otherwise passed over with a hastiness untypical of Hobbes's dogmatic prose style. "The kingdom of Christ is not of this world," he often reminds his readers, and Christ will not reign "till the day of judgment" (3.42.6). As a materialist, Hobbes like Milton imagines eternity as endless duration of time (rather than atemporality) and the Last Judgment as a historical event occurring within the *saeculum* of human experience.[38] But while Hobbes acknowledges that "the day of judgment is the day of the restoration of the kingdom of God" (3.43.17), he is not happy about it. For all the times Hobbes speaks of the Second Coming or the Last Judgment (forty-six in the 1651 edition), he says remarkably little about it but often uses it as a referent for describing the authority of sovereigns in the present.

The Last Judgment is useful to Hobbes precisely because it is the last or ultimate judgment—that is, because it is safely locked away in the future. It is a future event that does not infringe on the present but which can be used to manipulate the present. As Hobbes explains in part 1 ("Of Man"), "The *present* only has a being in nature; things *past* have a being in the memory only; but things *to come* have no being at all, the *future* being but a fiction of the mind" (1.3.7). As a "fiction of the mind," then, the Last Judgment is not a reality, and we might think of it as Jacques Derrida thought of nuclear war: as a "non-event" that has not occurred in history—and perhaps never will—and exists only in the imagination.[39] The Last Judgment is an appropriate *telos* for Hobbes's project in *Leviathan* because, as a "non-event," it forever remains an ideal—and a powerful one at that. That ideal at the end of history, like the model of Abraham and Moses at the beginning of history, has the power of legitimating Hobbes's philosophy and the absolute authority of the sovereign. Whether the ideal of sovereignty is ever realized, Hobbes suggests, is beside the point. Hobbes's sense of history, we might say, folds in on itself, as genesis and terminus work from opposing ends of time to validate the present.

Hobbes refers to the Last Judgment in order to politicize the messianic expectations of his countrymen and rebuild England into a new political machine: the leviathan. When discussing Saul, for instance, Hobbes is adamant that the kingdom of God came to an end. The implication is that England, like all other nations since Saul's Israel, has the right to establish its own sovereignty. Hobbes writes,

> The kingdom of God is a civil kingdom [. . .] and which kingdom having been cast off in the election of Saul, the prophets foretold should be restored by Christ, and the restoration whereof we daily pray for when we say in the Lord's Prayer *Thy kingdom come*, and the right whereof we acknowledge when we add *For thine is the kingdom, the power, and glory, for ever and ever, Amen*, and the proclaiming whereof was the preaching of the apostles, and to which men are prepared by the teachers of the Gospel—to embrace which Gospel (that is to say, to promise obedience to God's government) is to be in the *Kingdom of Grace*, because God hath *gratis* given to such the power to be the subjects (that is, children) of God hereafter, when Christ shall come in majesty to judge the world, and actually to govern his own people, which is called *the Kingdom of Glory*. (3.35.13)

When stating that the kingdom of God would be restored with Christ, Hobbes does not welcome in the new sovereign, as Milton does, but rather insists that Christ's reign has not yet come. Capitalizing on the power of ritual to shape the imagination, Hobbes takes a daily activity— the recitation of the Lord's Prayer—and uses it to teach his readers that Christ is not yet sovereign. Christ's kingdom has not yet come, and for this reason the faithful pray, "*Thy kingdom come*." Instead, the English rule themselves through a strong sovereign until Christ's return. In this way, the Lord's Prayer reminds readers on a daily basis that the kingdom has *not* arrived.

Throughout *Leviathan*, Hobbes uses temporal adverbs and the subjunctive mood to postpone judgment and cordon it off into the future. The forty-six times Hobbes mentions the Last Judgment are saturated with qualifying words and phrases: "when," "till," "until," "in the meantime," and the like. In the passage above, he writes of "*when* Christ shall come in majesty to judge the world, and *actually* to govern his own people, which is called *the Kingdom of Glory*" (my emphasis). As the *OED* notes, "actually" signifies doing something "in fact, [or] in reality," as opposed to "potentially, [or] theoretically" doing something.[40] The distinction that Christ will someday govern but does not *actually* govern now delays the Last Judgment while allowing human sovereigns to exercise, in the present, all of Christ's own authority at that imagined future event.

Hobbes wants to harness Christ's authority at the Last Judgment, but he does not want himself or anyone else to be under that authority. Rather, his focus is on the time that remains before Christ's return. He writes,

> But spiritual commonwealth there is none in this world. For it is the same thing with the kingdom of Christ, which he himself saith is not of this world, but shall be in the next world, at the resurrection, when they that have lived justly and believed that he was the Christ shall (though they died *natural* bodies) rise *spiritual* bodies; and then it is that our Saviour shall judge the world, and conquer his adversaries, and make a spiritual commonwealth. In the meantime, seeing there are no men on earth whose bodies are spiritual, there can be no spiritual commonwealth amongst men that are yet in the flesh. (3.42.128)

Hobbes acknowledges that the kingdom of God would begin again at the Last Judgment, when "our Saviour shall judge the world." However, he is quick to assert that that moment has not yet come. Humanity still dwells "in the meantime" between eschatological anticipation and the fulfillment thereof. Christ's sovereignty does not, in fact, concern Hobbes. His concern is only for the "meantime" between Saul and the Last Judgment, in which the *deus mortalis* is sovereign and England has an opportunity to fashion itself into the epitome of Christ's own sovereignty—the leviathan.

In this regard, Hobbes endeavors to create a community of readers who envision, as he does, the restoration of English sovereignty. That restoration depends first and foremost upon the use of reason, which Hobbes says is the talent God has entrusted to England:[41]

> We are not to renounce our senses and experience, nor (that which is the undoubted word of God) our natural reason. For they are the talents which

he hath put into our hands to negotiate till the coming again of our blessed Saviour; and therefore not to be folded up in the napkin of an implicit faith, but employed in the purchase of justice, peace, and true religion. (3.32.2)

As we saw in chapter 1, the parable of the talents was central to the rhetoric of national reformation in the 1640s, and Milton employed it when describing the work that accompanies "the birth of reformation" (1:795) in England. By using it here, Hobbes too capitalizes on the parable's cultural cachet—although his end game is quite different from Milton's. Hobbes suggests that England has been given many talents, which are indeed (as the reformists preached) an opportunity to pave the way for the kingdom of God. But unlike the reformists, who saw those talents as the opportunity for religious reform, Hobbes identifies them as a political tool—human reason—which might be used to rebuild England.

Rather than waiting for Christ to save them, the English people could take advantage of the fact that they still live "in the meantime" before his return. Employing the talents God gave them, they could manufacture their messiah and bring judgment into the present by becoming the leviathan and the semblance of Christ's unmatched power. The English people are their own masters for the time being, Hobbes seems to say, and if they cannot fix the nation they have broken, then they squander the talents God has given them.

"He Deposeth Christ": The Critics Respond

As we saw at the beginning of this chapter, Bramhall and other opponents of *Leviathan* focused on the threat Hobbes posed to the last things. As Parkin points out, Hobbes was "too useful to ignore, but too dangerous to leave unchallenged."[42] Hobbes's enemies assaulted his theology and labeled him an atheist, and their incisive attacks began a project of defamation that continued well into the twentieth century.[43] As they saw it, the problem was not that Hobbes was eschewing eschatology (that, at least, could be easily dismissed as antichristian), but that Hobbes had desacralized it. Hobbes had stripped judgment of its divine mystique so that it became an uncomfortably human phenomenon.

Critics of *Leviathan* objected in particular to Hobbes's politicized messianism, his delay of Christ's sovereignty, and his reallocation of Christ's power to the sovereign. In a period when the hopes of so many Englishmen rested on Christ's imminent sovereignty, Hobbes had robbed them of the comforting thought that the nation was under the aegis of God's protection. No more could they rely on Christ's sovereignty in the present (which Hobbes says does not exist) nor await its instauration at the Last Judgment (which Hobbes says might never occur). Rather, they must seize the power within their grasp since Saul's usurpation and work their own salvation.

Hobbes's critics correctly discerned that *Leviathan* empowered English sovereigns by reducing the power of Christ.[44] The divine Richard Baxter, for instance, railed against books that "slander or reproach [the] Magistracy, Ministry, or Ordinances of Christ."[45] He suggested they be burned, and singling out Hobbes, he added, "Specially *Hobbs* his Leviathan."[46] Baxter's use of the word "Magistracy" is telling, for it suggests that he too interpreted Christ's sovereignty as an act of judging. Baxter recognized that Hobbes has diminished Christ's role while increasing the authority of the human ruler.

Like Baxter, Sir Robert Filmer recognized the threat Hobbes posed to the magistracy of Christ in the present, and he honed in on Hobbes's treatment of the kingdom of God. Objecting to Hobbes's politicized reading of the Old Testament, Filmer claims, "The name of *King* is not given to God, nor of *Kingdome* to *Abraham*, yet the thing if we will believe Master *Hobs* is all one."[47] Filmer argues that God's status as the Almighty and Abraham's status as a prophet are quite different types of political power than that of the sovereign, but that Hobbes mistakenly reads them all as the same thing. Hobbes, Filmer complains, is twisting the words of scripture. On Hobbes's interpretation of Saul's accession, Filmer declares, "I see not that the Kingdome of God was cast off by the election of *Saul*, since *Saul* was chosen by God himselfe, and Governed according to Gods Lawes."[48] Filmer is adamant that the kingdom of God was not lost, and he sees what Hobbes is on about in claiming the contrary. Hobbes has voiced the dangerous idea that humanity is not protected by providence, and in response, Filmer is quick to reclaim Saul as evidence of God's concern for the wellbeing of the faithful.

Undoubtedly, *Leviathan*'s most hostile critic was Bishop Bramhall. Insisting that Hobbes was not "a fit adversary," Bramhall likened his opponent to a phantasm from Revelation, a "piller of smoake [. . .] threaten[ing] to take possession of the whole Region of the air, darkening the skie, and seeming to pierce the heavens."[49] Nor did Bramhall miss Hobbes's crafty maneuver of empowering human sovereigns by postponing the Last Judgment and the kingdom of God. Hobbes "deposeth Christ from his true kingly office," Bramhall exclaims, "making his *kingdom not to commence or begin before the day of judgement*."[50] The kingdom of God exists now, Bramhall claims, nor was Saul a sovereign in the political sense of the word. If Hobbes is correct and Saul was indeed sovereign, Bramhall notes tongue in cheek, then by implication "Samuel [who argued against Saul's appointment] was a false Prophet to contest with Saul a Soveraign Prophet."[51] In their attempt to rescue Christ, whom Hobbes had replaced with a sovereign, Bramhall and Filmer worked to expose Hobbes's spurious readings of scripture, as well as to tip the scales in God's favor by emphasizing divine jurisdiction. If Hobbes was determined to show his readers that they could create the messiah for whom they waited, then Bramhall, Baxter, and Filmer were just as determined to subdue such sinful ambitions and restore Christ to his rightful throne in the hearts of the people.

Ironically, by opposing Hobbes and emphasizing the current sovereignty of Christ, Hobbes's critics also drew judgment into the present. Like Hobbes, they too made use of the "meantime" between Saul's accession and the end of the world. Bramhall, for instance, filled the time before Christ's return with bishops rather than sovereigns. Asserting that the bishop is God's lieutenant on Earth, who alone personates the divine, Bramhall borrows Hobbes's own rhetorical maneuver and posits that bishops—not sovereigns—bring God's judgments to the people. Translating the Mosaic law as "the Bishop shall be Judge" (Num. 35:24), Bramhall quietly alters the meaning of the Hebrew *eidah*, which the Great Bible, the Bishops' Bible, the Geneva Bible, and the King James Bible all render correctly as "congregation"—not bishop.[52] Despite his complaints that Hobbes is a poor exegete, Bramhall too was not above playing with scripture to endorse his own political views.

Between them, Bramhall and Hobbes outlined two routes to national reconstruction that lay before the English people in the final days of the world. One depended upon restoring episcopalianism and the national church, and the other upon restoring England's sovereignty by transforming it into the leviathan. Despite the hostilities between them, and much like Milton before them, both Hobbes and Bramhall held an optimistic view of human agency at the end of days. Both Hobbes and Bramhall were unsure how or when the nation would be rebuilt, but both were equally confident that at the moment of Christ's return, the English people would be actively employed as faithful laborers in the process of their own regeneration.

3

Turning Swords into Plowshares

Diggers, Ranters, and Radical Eschatologies of Class Revolution

In the early days of the young Commonwealth, the Ranter Abiezer Coppe published two treatises announcing that the Last Judgment had arrived in England. The title page to the first treatise, *A Fiery Flying Roll,* plays on eschatological immanence and delay (see figure 10). "Now the Lord is come," it proclaims, and yet Coppe's treatise is "the last Warning Piece at the dreadfull day of Judgement."[1] In the space between revelation and reckoning, the treatise suggests, there is still time to repent. The title page to *A Second Fiery Flying Roule* pronounces the Last Judgment as an economic leveling, and it warns England's wealthy citizens of the class revolution about to take place. "Howle, rich men," the title page admonishes, for "the rust of your silver is rising up in judgment against you, burning your flesh like fire."[2] Now that the Day of the Lord has come, the rich will pay (literally) for their crimes against the people of God.

The type of radical expectation of the world's end espoused by the Ranters and Diggers is often studied as a mode of cultural critique during the English Revolution.[3] This captures only half its sense, however, for

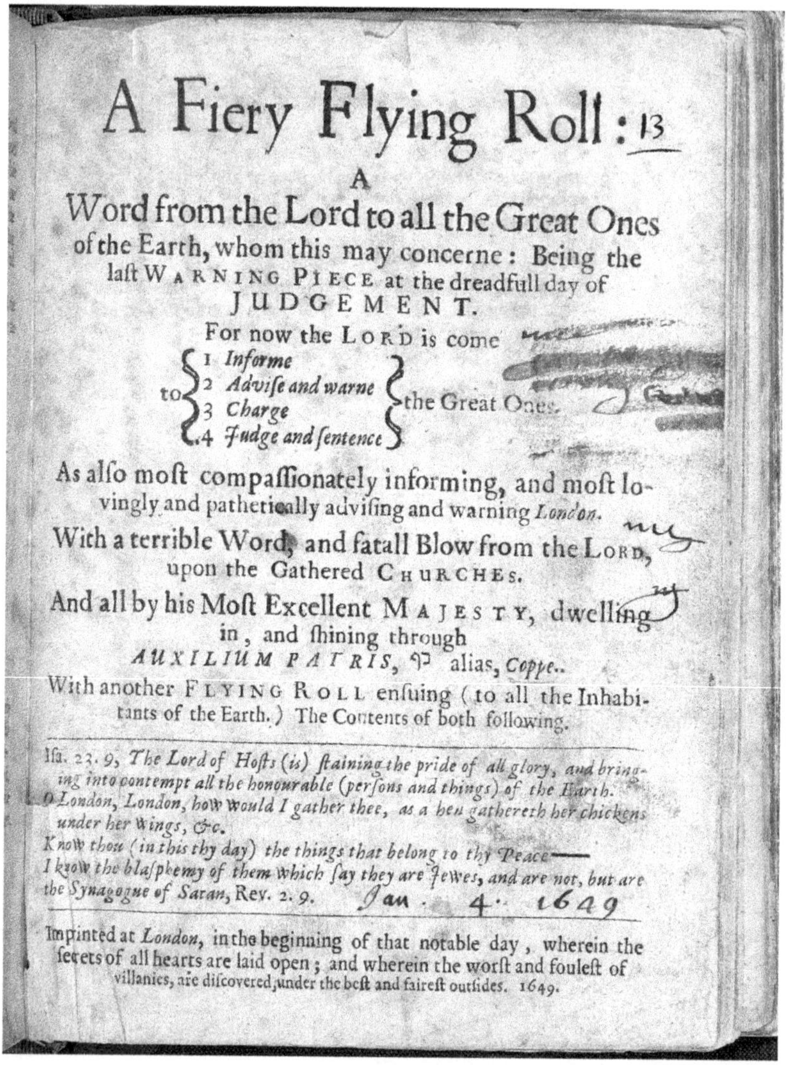

A Fiery Flying Roll: 13

A

Word from the Lord to all the Great Ones of the Earth, whom this may concerne: Being the last WARNING PIECE at the dreadfull day of JUDGEMENT.

For now the LORD is come

to 1 *Informe* 2 *Advise and warne* 3 *Charge* 4 *Judge and sentence* the Great Ones.

As also most compassionately informing, and most lovingly and pathetically advising and warning *London.*

With a terrible Word, and fatall Blow from the LORD, upon the Gathered CHURCHES.

And all by his Most Excellent MAJESTY, dwelling in, and shining through *AUXILIUM PATRIS,* אבי alias, *Coppe.*

With another FLYING ROLL ensuing (to all the Inhabitants of the Earth.) The Contents of both following.

Isa. 23. 9, *The Lord of Hosts (is) staining the pride of all glory, and bringing into contempt all the honourable (persons and things) of the Earth.*

O London, London, how would I gather thee, as a hen gathereth her chickens under her wings, &c.

Know thou (in this thy day) the things that belong to thy Peace——

I know the blasphemy of them which say they are Jewes, and are not, but are the Synagogue of Satan, Rev. 2. 9. Jan. 4. 1649

Imprinted at *London,* in the beginning of that notable day, wherein the secrets of all hearts are laid open; and wherein the worst and foulest of villanies, are discovered, under the best and fairest outsides. 1649.

Figure 10. Title page to Abiezer Coppe, *A Fiery Flying Roll* (1649/50).

© The British Library Board, E.587 (13).

anticipation of the Last Judgment encouraged the faithful not only to critique their current reality but also to consider alternatives to it. Eschatology does not merely disrupt the present order and dispense with it; it also generates new social possibilities and explores the conditions under which those possibilities might play out. In chapters 1 and 2, we saw how Milton and Hobbes used the Last Judgment to rebuild the nation, and in chapters 3 and 4, we shall see how Gerrard Winstanley, Abiezer Coppe, and Henry Vaughan used it to dismantle the nation and create new communities fit for the arrival of *ecclesia*.

For Winstanley and Coppe, the Last Judgment was a bridge to the *aevum aureum* they believed would follow the end of episcopacy, monarchy, and classed society. Shortly after the civil wars, John Lilburne wrote that though "this much wasted Nation" had suffered greatly, yet "the people may at length be comforted" with economic prosperity, and from the Levellers, the Diggers and Ranters learned that the plight of the poor would improve once the king had been dethroned.[4] But the Rump's seeming disregard for the poor after the king's imprisonment frustrated religious radicals and catalyzed sweeping programs of social change.[5] When their promised bounty failed to appear, the Diggers and Ranters deployed something else they had inherited from the Levellers: a radical eschatology of class revolution that threatened to topple the social status quo.[6]

But like nationalism, counternationalism in the period was plagued by contradiction, and in the works of Winstanley and Coppe, a fundamental paradox dominates their opposition to the nation. Despite the fact that they define their followers as faithful remnants opposed to England, both writers are reluctant to abandon the nation entirely, even when faced with persecution. At times, their rhetoric of national reckoning is also an expression of hope for England, as they try to swell the ranks of the faithful by borrowing members from the nation or converting it altogether. And therein lies a second paradox. Though Winstanley and Coppe both invoke a class revolution that would liberate the poor from an oppressive economic system, they are nonetheless aware that religion and economics share an overlapping network of signification in their society, no less in the Bible itself.[7] Though they inveigh against the fetishization of money in England, Winstanley and Coppe struggle to reconcile their utopian visions of a moneyless society with the fact that the Bible often compares spiritual righteousness with financial success. It is the servant who doubles his talents, after all, who gains his master's favor, and in the New Testament, the Last Judgment is likened to a "reckon[ing]" (Matt. 25:19), an "account" (Matt. 12:36, Ro. 14:12, 1 Pet. 4:5), the paying of "penn[ies]" and "wages" (Matt. 20:1–15, Ro. 6:23), a rendering of "talents" (Matt. 18:23–34, 25:14–30), and the collection of "debt" (Matt. 18:27–34, Luke 16:1–8). To put it another way, while Winstanley and Coppe would gladly have the writing on the wall and the word of judgment upon an idolatrous nation, they could do without the financial "*MENE, MENE, TEKEL UPHARSIN*" that accompanies it, as well as the heavenly invoice, "thou art weighed in the balances, and art found wanting" (Dan. 5:25, 27).

Consequently, if capitalism (and the classed society it engenders) is the problem and the Last Judgment is the solution, then for both writers, judgment must be reinvented according to new conceptual models. To overcome the paradox, reckoning can no longer be understood in terms of money and earthly riches, for such worldly things are passing away; rather, it must be made to reflect the eternal riches of the millennial kingdom. For the Diggers, those eternal riches are the natural world, and in Winstanley's ecological eschatology, the dirt of England becomes a device for reckoning between the faithful and the wicked. For the Ranters, those riches are the glorified bodies promised to the faithful at the world's end (1 Cor. 15:42), and in Coppe's embodied eschatology, corporeal motions distinguish the enlightened from the unenlightened. Both writers transform reckoning into a tactile experience and phenomenalize the Last Judgment as a decision in the mind.

Digging in the dirt for one's salvation, cuddling prostitutes, and bowing to beggars are seemingly foolish things, but in these acts, the Diggers and the Ranters discover eternity. The Bible tells that in the end times, God "shall judge among the nations, and shall rebuke many people: and they shall beate their swords into plow-shares, and their speares into pruning hookes" (Isa. 2:4). By announcing the Last Judgment's arrival, Winstanley and Coppe strive to fulfill this prophecy in revolutionary England. Christ's reign has begun, they declare, and the nation must make way for communities more appropriate for citizenship in *ecclesia*: the Diggers as new Adams, and the Ranters as a mass organism of one flesh.[8]

Dirt and Dust for "a Bleeding Dying Nation"

When Gerrard Winstanley and his followers planted seeds in the wind-blown dirt of St. George's Hill on Sunday, April 1, 1649, they were creating a new society that rejected the idea of a class-based nation and the capitalist system upon which it was based.[9] "The Father," Winstanley proclaimed, "is now raising up a people to himself out of the dust" who would replace the corrupt English.[10] As scholars have shown, Winstanley's endeavor was an experiment in social class, economics, and religious freedom.[11] These different concerns converge in Winstanley's attempts to reveal the Last Judgment to England and lead the faithful into an *aevum aureum* of peace and plenty.

The new community Winstanley envisioned—these new Adams rising "out of the dust"—was predicated on the belief that the Last Judgment had arrived and that April 1st was the first day of Christ's millennial reign on Earth. National reckoning was already taking place, and as Winstanley's faithful remnant removed itself from an idolatrous nation preoccupied with money, they proved their citizenship in *ecclesia* by digging and holding all things in common. For Winstanley's followers, digging was holy work and even "a sacralization of opportunities afforded by the present to the reforming will" of their project, as Joanna Picciotto puts it.[12] The Diggers began their work on Sunday for a reason. The Christian Sabbath is a day of resurrection, and on Sunday the 1st, they announced the beginning of the millennium and *ecclesia*, which happened to be congregating for the first time in Surrey.

Amid the economic recession of the late 1640s, the Digger project began out of a discontentedness with the Commonwealth and the belief that Cromwell had betrayed the English people.[13] Winstanley had supported Parliament during the civil wars, and he expected the Commonwealth to recompense him and everyone else by revitalizing the national economy.[14] "You called upon us to come and help a bleeding dying Nation," he declares in *An Appeal to the House of Commons*, "and we did come with purse and person, and under-went great hardship, and you stil promised us freedom in the end, if in case you and we prevailed over the Norman successor [i.e. Charles I], and we have prevailed" (2:68). Where then, Winstanley asks, is their promised reward?

When that reward failed to appear, Winstanley's response was to forsake England and its capitalist system and grow his own end-time community, the Diggers. We might call Winstanley's approach an ecoeschatology, wherein he discovers the eternal salvation of the faithful in England's black soil. Mindful of scriptural truths that "we are dust" (Ps. 103:14), humanity came from "the dust of the ground" (Gen. 2:7), and the righteous man is "like a tree planted by the rivers of water" (Ps. 1:3), Winstanley imbues dirt with soteriological significance. It is not dirt the Diggers till on St. George's Hill, he says, but themselves. In the crop of the world, the new Adams are the first fruits of God's labor of *renovatio mundi*. Salvation, Winstanley teaches, does not come from above but from below—from the dirt beneath one's feet, which is the very stuff of the self and the matter of eternity.

For Winstanley, dust is a nexus of typological associations between a biblical past and an eschatological future, both of which meet in the present.[15] His new Adams define themselves as resurrected saints, and scriptural passages on the end times supply Winstanley with the ideological framework for the Digger project. In *The Mysterie of God*, Winstanley writes that on the Day of Judgment, God "raises up the bodies of believers, and unbelievers out of the dust again, wherein he hath reserved them all the time of the battel, between the anointing and the Serpent, as a man would keep his jewels in a box for an appointed time" (1:283). Like the bodies that arose from their graves at Christ's resurrection (Matt. 27:52), the new Adams arise out of England's soil to proclaim a new age. They declare that capitalism is a thing of the past, and in the bright future now unfolding, all goods are held in common.

The poor, in particular, who suffered under the old economic system, are privileged with becoming new Adams. Winstanley asserts that the Last Judgment is a great social leveling currently taking place in England. In *The New Law of Righteousness*, he claims, "The Father is now raising up a people to himself out of the dust, that is, out of the lowest and despised sort of people, that are counted the dust of the earth, man-kind, that are trod under foot" (1:508). Winstanley echoes Christ's admonishment to the Pharisees: "Thinke not to say within your selves, Wee have Abraham to *our* father: For I say unto you, that God is able of these stones to raise up children unto Abraham" (Matt. 3:9).

Winstanley's revision of scripture is a damning commentary on England. In the gospels, Christ criticized the Pharisees for thinking that Jewish identity was based on outward signs (for example, circumcision and the dietary laws of *kashrut*), which he condemned as idolatrous. Instead, Christ claimed, a true Jew is one "inwardly," as Saint Paul would later put it (Ro. 2:29). Applying the passage to England, Winstanley assumes a Christ-like role and reprimands a hypocritical nation that defines itself, as he sees it, in terms of its wealth. A new people, he warns, is on the rise. Covered with the dust of the fields, and making their way by the sweat of their brows, the Diggers would supplant England's Pharisees as the true people of God. Dirt is thus an engine of reckoning for Winstanley, since it quite literally marks the Diggers as God's people and separates them from the wealthy people in England.

Yet for all his railing, Winstanley was reluctant to abandon England entirely. At times, he envisions dirt paradoxically as the salvation of both the Diggers and the nation. In his correspondence, Winstanley writes that "the Nation cannot be in peace [. . .] so long as the poor oppressed are in want, and the land is entangled and held from them by bondage" (2:126). He warns General Fairfax that "England cannot bee a free Commonwealth, unless all the poore commoners have a free use and benefitt of the land; for if this freedome bee not granted, wee that are the poore commoners are in a worse case then we were in the King's dayes" (2:415). Consequently, if England is to be saved, it must move both forward and backwards in time. To become the epicenter of Christ's millennial reign, it must reclaim its Edenic identity and embrace the earth, as Adam did.[16] In *The New Law of Righteousness*, for instance, Winstanley indicates that England has a part to play in the return of the faithful to an Adamic state. The idea is not to extirpate England, but rather to grow this new Eden out of the nation's dying husk:

> Therefore, O thou first Adam, take notice, that the Lord hath set before thee life and death, now chuse whether thou wilt, for the time is near at hand that buying and selling of land shall cease, and every son of the land shal live of[f] it.
>
> Divide England into three parts, scarce one part is manured: So that here is land enough to maintain all her children, and many die for want, or live under a heavy burden of povertie all their daies: And this miserie the poor people have brought upon themselves, by lifting up particular interest, by their labours. (1:523)

This is a matter of salvation and damnation, and the reader has a choice to participate in widespread cultivation—or not. If a person would be saved, Winstanley indicates, he or she must turn to England's earth, recognize its misuses, and work to improve the land.

In Winstanley's ecoeschatology, dirt calls to dust, and the former is the means by which men and women, the latter, are redeemed from death into life. His texts perform judgment upon readers by asking them to participate in the work of land cultivation (which is also the work of self-cultivation) and thereby become new Adams—or resist this higher calling and be damned to the hell of class, capitalism, and other devices of Satan. In *An Appeale to All Englishmen*, Winstanley entreats his readers to "come, take Plow & Spade, build & plant, & make the wast Land Fruitfull" (2:243). The singsong sequence of monosyllabic words mirrors the beautiful simplicity of Winstanley's message of salvation to the faithful in England: dig and be saved.

"Jacob Hath Bin Very Low, but He is Rising"

As Winstanley imagines a national reckoning occurring in England, the Last Judgment becomes internalized as a choice within the minds of his readers. Although his phenomenalized eschatology would ultimately prove untenable, it sheds light on how he appropriates scriptural narratives to shape his readers' understanding of the economic crisis in England.[17] As he would have it, readers must choose between membership in the new Adams or the old Adams, between a long awaited exodus or continued life in captivity, and between Esau (whom God hated) and Jacob, who, God promised, would supplant his elder brother. At the beginning of the millennium, what was being unveiled was nothing less than eternity in the earth, which the Diggers had begun to dig up with joy.

Winstanley insists that the obstacle to England's enjoyment of the millennial reign is agrarian capitalism, which divides the nation's people into classes.[18] God may not discriminate between persons, he suggests, but the Commonwealth does, and it is wrong to do so. God is Reason, Winstanley claims, and the "great day of Judgment" is when reason "sit[s] upon the Throne in every man and woman" (1:529).[19] The Last Judgment, in other words, is when men come to their senses (as they are starting to do), dispense with social classes and capitalist economics, and labor together toward a common goal.[20] Winstanley entreats Parliament to "let the common people have their Commons and waste lands set free to them, from all Norman enslaving Lords of Mannors" (2:69). Reinventing the biblical Fall of Man (Gen. 3), Winstanley asserts that while the Earth was originally a "common Storehouse of Livelihood to all Mankinde," the Adamic curse was "buying and selling of Land" (2:32)—or the subjection of the soil to capitalism. He believes that if everyone in England has his own plot of ground to cultivate, then the nation would enter the promised millennial reign indeed.

As Winstanley draws the Last Judgment into the present in his readers' minds, scriptural narratives of judgment help him to phenomenalize eschatology into a choice. The first narrative is the Fall of Man from Genesis. In Winstanley's typology, the old Adams represent a people who struggle against the Earth (and consequently themselves), since the cursed ground brings forth "thornes also and thistles" (Gen. 3:18) for the English, just as it did for the first Adam after the Fall. But as all died in Adam, so all would be made alive in Christ, who is "the last Adam," as Saint Paul calls him (1 Cor. 15:45). The new Adams, then, have reclaimed the ground that was cursed and, by sharing it among themselves, have liberated it from the capitalist forces that kept it in a fallen state. The Diggers' digging is the antitype to the Fall of Man. Their resurrection as new Adams is one and the same as the resurrection of Christ, and by their teachings the spiritually dead citizens of the nation find new life as Diggers. The war between soil and self is no more, for the work of digging reveals to the faithful their eternal selves in the black earth of England.

Winstanley was a creative theologian, to be sure, and the new typological associations he created pressured readers to reevaluate their current political affiliations. In *The True Levellers Standard Advanced*, he rails against the old Adams, the English, who hold to the old idea of the nation, with its classes and capitalism:

O you A-dams of the Curse, or else live in great straits and beggery: O you A-dams of the Earth, you have rich Clothing, full Bellies, have your Honors and Ease, and you puffe at this; But know thou stout-hearted Pharaoh, that the day of Judgement is begun, and it will reach to thee ere long; Jacob hath bin very low, but he is rising, and will rise, do the worst thou canst; and the poor people whom thou oppresses, shall be the Saviours of the land; For the blessing is rising up in them, and thou shalt be ashamed. (2:17)

Donning the persona of an Old Testament prophet, Winstanley synthesizes three biblical narratives. The first is the Fall of Man, which, as we have seen, encourages readers to look upon England's land with the eyes of a new Adam. An old Adam sees only property, financial gain, and the alienation of labor, but a new Adam sees natural resources for building the kingdom of God.

The second narrative central to Winstanley's model of the Last Judgment is the Israelite exodus from Egypt. Its typological associations teach readers they are part of a new community—a faithful remnant—emerging from a corrupt nation.[21] In Exodus, Pharaoh resists the departure of the remnant, for his "heart is hardened: [and] he refuseth to let the people goe" (Exod. 7:14)—but the people of God go anyway. Winstanley, however, reads the exodus of his new Adams as an eschatological event and the entrance of God's people into the millennial kingdom. Consequently, reckoning comes at Winstanley's readers from two directions, as both Old and New Testaments force them to choose whether they would be new Adams or old Adams, Israelites or Egyptians, the Diggers or the English.

The third narrative, of Jacob and Esau, synthesizes Winstanley's desire for a new community with his promise that the Diggers would be rewarded for their labors. Just as God loved Jacob and hated Esau, so too are the Diggers God's beloved and the old Adams the objects of his wrath. And just as Jacob, the younger brother, stole the birthright that was Esau's, so too, Winstanley states, are the new Adams being entrusted with the material goods that the old Adams squandered. But these goods are not coins and bank notes but something far more valuable: the very treasures of the Earth. Isaac blesses Jacob with "the fatnesse of the earth, and plenty of corne and wine," and the "nations bow downe" before him (Gen. 27:28–29), and though he is hunted by Esau for the blessing he received, Jacob rises over him as a man of great wealth. The poor of England are Jacob's heirs, Winstanley states. Their rise to power is a redistribution of the nation's wealth, as the land's true riches—the fruit of the fields and the milk of the cows—is reallocated into the Diggers' hands.

"England [. . .] Know for All This Thou Shalt Come to Judgement"

Despite the vim and vigor of Winstanley's ecoeschatology, at some point in 1649, he abandoned his idea of a Last Judgment of the mind and relocated the Last Judgment to an event in history. Judgment, in other words, ceased to be immanent and became imminent, and the nation—which he had claimed was obsolete, now that the millennial reign had come—again took center stage in his newly historicized eschatology. The shift in Winstanley's thinking was almost certainly due to persecution. When reckoning was a matter of personal discrimination, heaven and hell became nothing more than metaphorical states of mind. In a sense, Winstanley had brought the Last Judgment too far into the present. As a psychological phenomenon, it lost its fearful associations with hellfire, brimstone, and damnation.

Winstanley then worked to postpone the Last Judgment into the future, where the threats of God's omens upon a wicked nation might be imagined but not yet realized. And therein lies the paradox at the heart of Winstanley's counternationalism: despite his defense of the Diggers and his claims of the nation's obsolescence with the arrival of *ecclesia*, Winstanley nonetheless held out hope that his adversaries would come to their senses and join the ranks of the faithful. His threats of national reckoning serve both to shield the Diggers from persecution and to warn England that time is running out and judgment "come[s] quickly" (Rev. 3:11). Winstanley's threats of reckoning upon England hint, in fact, at his continued concern for the English people, despite their misplaced hatred for himself and his followers.

From the beginning of their digging project, Winstanley and his new Adams were vilified as a hazard to the nation. A frequent refrain was that the Diggers, with their principle of "all things in common," endangered the existing structure of England's economy by disrupting the relationship between land and landowners. For example, one anonymous critic warned that "much trouble befall[s] the Nation" by "such as were called Diggers."[22] "To me," he writes, the Diggers "incroach not only upon Commons, but upon the very foundation of every mans just propriety."[23] If the Diggers were uprooted from England, he claims, "the Nation will undoubtedly be setled in so happy a condition."[24] Similarly, the horticulturist Walter Blith warned that the Diggers disrespected property boundaries and that, as vagrants, they endangered the land-based system upon which English capitalism was based. "Though the poor are or ought to have advantage upon the Commons," Blith writes, "yet I question whether they [i.e. the Diggers] as a society gathered together from all parts of the Nation could claim a right to any particular Common."[25] The transience of the new Adams, which Winstanley saw as evidence of their higher calling, was to nonmembers a threat to England's historic identity and economic future.

For the pamphleteer Marchamont Nedham, the Diggers endangered the nation's God-given opportunities for growth and expansion under the Commonwealth. His harsh criticisms recall Milton's early attempts to pin down the nation in time and space, which we saw in chapter 1. The Diggers' plea for men to return *ad tuguria* (to huts), Nedham claims, reduces them and everyone who follows them into savages. He warns that if the Diggers' work continues unimpeded, the English would soon "renounce Towns and Cities, live at *Rovers*, and enjoy all in common."[26] Temporally, the Diggers constitute a threat to what Nedham sees as England's phoenix-like rebirth, as it arises from the darkness of monarchy into a bright republican future. By castigating them as "old *Parthians* [. . .] and other wild *Barbarians*," Nedham counters the Diggers' bold claims that they alone—as the faithful remnant preparing the way for *ecclesia*—were the custodians of the future.[27] Instead, Nedham casts them as barbarians from humanity's base beginnings—specters of a primal past darker even than that of monarchy, in which men lived savage lives. Spatially, Nedham counters the Diggers' claims of a special relationship with the land by uprooting them from England. No better than *"Scythian Nomades,"* Nedham asserts, the Diggers have no place in a nation that, under the Commonwealth, is undergoing rapid territorial expansion, as its sovereignty extends across the British Isles, its adjacent seas, and the world.[28]

Criticisms such as Nedham's were not the worst of what the Diggers endured, and their communities were repeatedly exposed to physical attacks from landed gentry and army soldiers. The summer of 1649 was a bad time to be digging, and Winstanley's followers were waylaid, beaten, run down by horses, and harassed by villagers.[29] Angered and dismayed, Winstanley realized that the threat of divine judgment and national reckoning might mitigate the situation. He turned again, as the radicals often did, to the printing press to remedy the situation.[30] In the second Digger manifesto, *A Declaration from the Poor Oppressed People of England*, he warns the gentry against interfering with his project. "Such coveteous, proud, unrighteous, selfish flesh," he declares, would be left "without excuse in the day of Judgment" (2:35). Winstanley's treatises from this period target the army in particular—that vicious body that had turned its back on the poor—and he warns Fairfax that both he and his soldiers would be "left without excuse in the day of Judgement [. . .] [because they] have been spoken to sufficiently" (2:47).[31] The Last Judgment, Winstanley suddenly asserts, is an imminent historical event, at which God's enemies would be called to account for their actions.

Embedded within Winstanley's threats of national reckoning is the hope that England can change its ways and join the faithful remnant—rather than hinder it. In *A Declaration of the Bloudie and Unchristian Acting of William Star and John Taylor of Walton*, Winstanley responds to a specific assault upon the Cobham community, when William Star and John Taylor rode the Diggers down with their horses and ruined their crops. "We have peace and purposes to go on," Winstanley writes, "and we are lively witnesses, and shall be at the day of Judgement, against these and all others that have and may so furiously oppose us" (2:61). He then turns his attention to the nation and admonishes, "Well, England take thy course, but know for all this thou shalt come to Judgement" (2:62). When faced with the brutal reality of persecution, ideology gives way to necessity. Winstanley removes the Last Judgment from the historical present and displaces it into the near future. This allows him to threaten reckoning upon his enemies and prompt them to reconsider their actions against the Diggers.

But Winstanley's menacing words of national reckoning are also a challenge for England to prove itself the godly nation it claims to be. In Revelation, Saint John warns the church of Sardis to "be watchfull, and strengthen the things which remaine, that are ready to die" (Rev. 3:2), and in his printed defenses of the Diggers, Winstanley offers the same warning to England—a warning that is, essentially, both a threat and an encouragement. Like Coppe, who proclaims both that "now the Lord is come" and that his treatise is "the last WARNING PIECE at the dreadfull day of JUDGEMENT," Winstanley uses temporal delay to his advantage. He hopes that his pamphlets might find purchase with those in England who have ears to hear and eyes to see in the final days before Christ's return.

In the end, Winstanley's ecoeschatology collapsed under persecution and ultimately proved untenable. By ushering the Last Judgment into the minds of his readers, he had familiarized it and removed the fear of the Last Judgment as *Dies Irae*—the fear of being judged and punished by almighty God. Frustrated and out of options, later that year Winstanley turned to a scriptural passage that provided him with comfort. "My Talent," he wrote, "was, to procure Englands peace inward and outward, and yet all along I have found such as in words have professed the same cause, to be enemies to me" (2:80). As it did for Milton and Hobbes, the parable of the talents allowed Winstanley to evaluate his labors through the lens of an imminent national reckoning. But it was also an ironic admission of his own entrenchment in the capitalistic system he had renounced, as the man who once preached "things in common" found solace in a biblical story that presents salvation as financial gain. This connection between finance and faith would disturb another radical, as well, who also rewrote scriptural narrative to mitigate the economic disparity in England.

"The Day of the Lord [is] at Hand": Coppe and the Community of One Flesh

Rather than teaching the faithful to capitalize on the riches they had received, as Winstanley did, Abiezer Coppe convinced them that the road to salvation lay in giving their riches away. Both social agendas entailed a radical reinvention of reckoning as a tactile experience: Winstanley's ecoeschatology used dirt to reckon between laborers and nonlaborers, and Coppe's embodied eschatology used bodily touch to separate the enlightened poor from the unenlightened rich. Winstanley carved out a new, faithful remnant in his new Adams, and in the same way, Coppe turned away from the nation and proclaimed a new community of one "FLESH" (*A Fiery Flying Roll* sig. B3v). Eternity, Coppe teaches them, is to be seized and caressed in the flesh of London's homeless and destitute, and so the Anointed (as Coppe calls his followers) bow to beggars, cuddle prostitutes, and shout obscenities. By privileging the poor as part of themselves, the faithful put into practice the true equality and sainthood of all believers.[32]

Coppe's celebration of the body as a conduit for judgment traces back to his childhood fascination with what Nigel Smith calls the radicals' belief in "the divine signifying power of language."[33] As a child, Coppe was horrified at the thought of sinning with his mouth. To eliminate that possibility, he wrote "yea" and "nay" on two pieces of paper, which he tied to his wrists and used to communicate without speaking.[34] His body thus became the remedy for its own malady, and the part most likely to offend—his mouth—was mitigated by another part—his wrists. Coppe's act was a performance of judgment, since it allowed him to discriminate his "yeas" and "nays" through a corporeal medium. His body became an apparatus for steering him toward righteousness, and during the English Revolution, Coppe would again come to see bodies as agents of reckoning.

Like Winstanley, Coppe phenomenalizes the Last Judgment as a decision within the mind. In *Some Sweet Sips, of Some Spirituall Wine*, he declares that England has moved beyond eschatological expectation and into eschatological realization. He challenges his readers to "arise out of Flesh into Spirit, out of Form into Power, out of Type into Truth, out of Signes into the thing signified."[35] A world greater than they know "Sparkles throughout these Papers" (sig. A3v), Coppe writes, and readers who have eyes to see will see it. The Christian, Coppe asserts, no longer exists *in statu viatoris* but has arrived, today, at eternity.

Transforming the last things into present things, Coppe structures his community of flesh around the Last Judgment, which he claims is already dawning in the minds of the Anointed. Modeling his authorship on Saint John in Revelation, Coppe defines his faithful remnant in opposition to the nation, just as John criticized the seven churches when instructing the faithful to prepare for the coming of *ecclesia* (Rev. 2:1–3:22). "Doomes Day [has] come already upon some flesh" (sig. A5v), Coppe declares, and "the day of the Lord [is] at hand" (sig. A8v). In *A Fiery Flying Roll*, Coppe attacks England's classed society and the capitalist system upon which it is based. Coppe frequently reads London in synecdoche for England, and his threats of national reckoning often localize in urban conflicts between the poor and the rich.[36] Coppe tells of how he walks through "the streets of the great Citie, and in Southwark," where he proclaims that the day of the Lord has come to the "Cavalliers" and the "Gentry" (sig. C4r).

To Cavaliers and cavilers alike, he preaches that the Last Judgment has arrived, and he asserts that there is no place for poverty, vagrancy, or class within the millennial kingdom.[37]

Envisioning Christ as a "mighty Leveller" (sig. Bv) whose arrival would mean the end of classed society, Coppe privileges bodies as the new riches of the millennial kingdom. "The prime Levelling," Coppe proclaims, "is laying low the Mountaines, and levelling the Hills in man" (sig. B2v). Coppe's readers are encouraged to see the rich and poor alike as the fleshly appendages of one holy body, the community of flesh. The impediment to doing so, he states, is capitalism, which blinds the rich from seeing the poor as the flesh of their flesh. But God has come to strip away that wealth, and *In A Second Fiery Fly Roule*, Christ reprimands England's upper classes:

> 2. Thou hast many baggs of money, and behold now I come as a thief in the night, with my sword drawn in my hand, and like a thief as I am,—I say deliver your purse, deliver sirrah! deliver or I'l cut thy throat!
>
> 3. Deliver MY money to such as poor despised Maul of Dedington in Oxonshire, whom some devills incarnate (insolently and proudly, in way of disdaine) cry up for a fool, some for a knave, and mad-man, some for an idle fellow, and base rogue [. . .]
>
> 4. I say (once more) deliver, deliver, my money which thou hast to him, and to poor creeples, lazars, yea to rogues, thieves, whores, and cut-purses, who are flesh of thy flesh, and every whit as good as thy self in mine eye. (sig. A2v)

In a display of rhetorical acrobatics, Coppe takes the image of Christ as a thief in the night (1 Thess. 5:2, 2 Pet. 3:10), flips it on its head, and uses it to describe England's economic crisis. Coppe's Christ goes after the "baggs of money" of London's rich and affluent. The image inverts cultural norms, and Christ—the thief—is a hero for going after the money-bags of England's wealthy citizens. Like Robin Hood, Christ delivers the money to the poor, so that people like Maul of Dedington will no longer suffer. Submission to the Last Judgment as a social leveling is mandatory, and he or she who refuses can look forward to Christ's promise, "I'l cut thy throat!"

Condemning England's idolatrous fetishization of money, Coppe also inverts the parable of the talents. In his retelling of the parable, the man who gives away all his money—rather than he who capitalizes on it and earns more—is reckoned faithful in his master's eye. Instead of valuing money, Coppe teaches, the true servant of God values the bodies of the poor. Coppe relates how, riding through the countryside, he comes across a beggar and calls out because "the day of the Lord [. . .] burned as an oven" within him (*A Second Fiery Flying Roule*, sig. A3v), an echo of the fourth chapter of Malachi. Seeing the man's need, Coppe offers him a shilling in exchange for six pence. But the vagrant has no pennies, so Coppe keeps his money and moves along:

> Whereupon with much reluctancy, with much love, and with amazement (of the right stamp) I turned my horse head from him, riding away. But a while after I was turned back (being advised by my Demilance) to wish him cal for six pence, which I would leave at the next Town at ones house, which I thought he might know (*Saphira* like) keeping back part.
>
> But (as God judged me) I, as she, was struck down dead. And behold the plague of God fell into my pocket; and the rest of my silver rose up in judgement against me, and consumed my flesh as with fire: so that I, and my money perisht with me.
>
> I being cast into that lake of fire and brimstone.
>
> And all the money I had about me to a penny [. . .] did so rise up in judgement against me, and burnt my flesh like fire: and the 5. of James thundered such an alarm in mine ears, that I was fain to cast all I had into the hands of him, whose visage was more marr'd then any mans that ever I saw. (sigs. A4r–A4v)

Coppe's initial plan is to make change for the shilling at a friend's house and there to leave six pence for the vagrant to call upon later. While the idea at first seems generous, his scriptural reference evokes the story of Ananias and Sapphira, who sold their land and gave some of the proceeds to Christ's apostles (Acts 5:1–10). Claiming that they gave the whole sum, they withheld a portion for themselves, and for that sin God struck them dead. Thus, "*Saphira* like," Coppe too is intent on withholding some of his money from the vagrant and giving him only six pence, when he might have given the whole shilling.

But then the Last Judgment consumes Coppe, and his thinking is transformed. "The rest of my silver rose up in judgement against me," he writes, and "consumed my flesh as with fire." He is reminded of the fifth chapter of James, which warns the rich men of the world that "the Judge standeth before the doore," ready to convict them (James 5:9). Coppe suddenly turns back. He gives the beggar not only the shilling, but indeed everything he has. He then removes his hat and "bow[s] to him seven times," to the man's astonishment (sig. A4v). In doing so, Coppe institutes a new value system that holds the bodies of the poor in higher esteem than the silver in his pocket. How might the parable of the talents have been different, he may have wondered, if one of the servants responded to his master, "I gave what you gave me to the poor?" Coppe's encounter with the vagrant affords him an opportunity to rewrite the parable and do just that. Now that the Last Judgment has come, the only godly way to invest one's silver is to give it to the poor, to whom belongs the kingdom of God (Luke 6:20) and who are themselves the priceless treasures of that kingdom.

"Paradox, Hetrodox, Riddle, or Ridiculous"

As the encounter with the vagrant suggests, Coppe was fascinated with the performative nature of judgment, and he used his own cryptic language as an extension of his body and an instrument of reckoning. Coppe was a skilled linguist, having studied Latin, Greek, and Hebrew as a student at All Souls, Oxford, and the innovative uses to which he puts the English language register his careful engagement with the genres, styles, and literary forms of scripture.[38] Speaking with divine authority, Coppe's language teaches readers about true value in the millennial kingdom and separates enlightened readers from unenlightened ones.[39] In this regard, we might compare him to the Fifth Monarchist Anna Trapnel, who claimed that only those who spoke the righteous "language of Canaan" could understand her, while those who spoke the evil "language of Ashod" would be confused.[40]

The holy language of both radicals borrows its method from scripture, in which figurative language conveys truths to the faithful while safeguarding them from the wicked.[41] Saint Paul, for instance, declared that "the preaching of the Crosse is to them that perish, foolishnesse: but unto us which are saved, it is the power of God" (1 Cor. 1:18). Another important passage appears in the Gospel of Matthew, when Christ tells the crowds,

> Who hath eares to heare, let him heare.
>
> And the disciples came, and sayd unto him, Why speakest thou unto them in parables?
>
> He answered, and said unto them, Because it is given unto you to know the mysteries of the kingdome of heaven, but to them it is not given.
>
> For whosoever hath, to him shall be given, and he shall have more abundance: but whosoever hath not, from him shall be taken away even that hee hath.
>
> Therefore speake I to them in parables: because they seeing, see not; and hearing, they heare not, neither doe they understand. (Matt. 13:9–13)

As Christ explains, figurative language is an instrument for discriminating between believers and unbelievers. While the faithful see wisdom in Christ's words, the wicked see only foolishness. "Why speakest thou unto them in parables?" the disciples ask Jesus, and no doubt, many Englishmen in revolutionary England wondered the same of Coppe and Trapnel.

In *Some Sweet Sips*, Coppe presents his figurative language as a portal through which readers can access the Last Judgment and the community of flesh. He asserts that his words are "neither Paradox, Hetrodox, Riddle, or ridiculous to good Scholars, who know the *Lord in deed*" (sig. C7v). Punning on "in deed," Coppe hints that only when readers perform bizarre acts such as those the Ranters perform will they know the Lord both "in deed" (through their actions) and "indeed" (in fact). In a similarly playful manner, Coppe describes his language as a "stumbling stone to some," while to others, it is a route *"Inside"* to the Last Judgment and the community of flesh (sigs. B2r-B2v). Again, Coppe puns, this time on the Greek word *skandalon* (a stumbling stone) and its English derivative—"scandalous."[42] Readers who are scandalized by his language, Coppe suggests, will trip over his words and never discover the precious truths they hold. Educated only in the language of Ashod, as Trapnel would say, they can neither understand the Anointed nor appreciate the Ranters' newfound freedom in Christ.

Coppe's bizarre language, then, functions like his bizarre bodily movements, inasmuch as it marks off the community of flesh from outsiders.

Just as the bodies of the faithful engage in strange motions, so too do their mouths speak strange things. In this way, the Ranters used their bodies to protest England's obsession with wealth. In *A Fiery Flying Roll*, Coppe orders that on this day, the Day of Judgment, the great ones of England must salute the poor, embrace their lousy bodies, and engage in intimate human touch:

> 4. bow before those poore, nasty, lousie, ragged wretches, say to them, your humble servants, Sirs, (without a complement) we let you go free, and serve you, & c.
>
> Do this (or as I live saith the Lord) thine eyes (at least) shall be boared out, and thou carried captive into a strange Land.
>
> [. . .]
>
> Hide not thy self from thine own flesh, from a creeple, a rogue, a begger, he's thine owne flesh. From a Whoremonger, a thief, & c. he's flesh of thy flesh, and his theft, and whoredome is flesh of thy flesh also, thine owne flesh. (sig. B4r)

Coppe's phrase, "flesh of thy flesh," evokes Adam's declaration that Eve is "flesh of my flesh" (Gen. 2:23) and speaks to the physical connectedness of this community of one flesh. But the phrase also recalls and revises the Mosaic *lex talionis*, a judicial system of reckoning which dictated that "life *shall goe* for life, eye for eye, tooth for tooth, hand for hand, foot for foot" (Deut. 19:21). Channeling both scriptural passages, Coppe suggests that on this day of reckoning, the faithful will be found justified in God's sight by endorsing an altogether new value system, which recognizes bodies as the riches of the New Heavens and New Earth.

In effect, Coppe is offering his readers a new model of commerce based on the holy exchange of flesh. This should replace the nation's obsolete commerce based on the exchange of money. The Anointed have learned a new type of accounting, in which they value one another's bodies as equal to their own. For Coppe, the only commerce fit for life in the millennial kingdom is the commerce of flesh. This commerce consists of seemingly strange (but in fact holy) transactions: exchanging embraces with the poor, repaying a prostitute's touch with a touch of one's own, and recompensing sensual pleasure with more of the same. Strange though this may seem to those on the outside, who "seeing, see not; and hearing they heare not," as Christ said, to those who are on the "*Inside*," it is a route into the community of flesh. Those on the inside, who are part of that fleshly community, have ceased associating value with money and now associate value with people, who bear the image of God, rather than the image of the sovereign.

Coppe's Recantations and England's Redemption

While Coppe's new economy of flesh may have liberated his mind, it made no such provisions for his body. Shortly after publishing his treatises, he was arrested, imprisoned, and interrogated at Warwick, Coventry, and Newgate. He later wrote that his "sore, tedious, and long continued imprisonment" took a tremendous physical toll on him (*Copp's Return*, sig. A3r). When he was brought to trial on October 1, 1650, he refused to take off his hat, and he mumbled to himself while flinging "apples, pears, and nutshells about the room," which caused many of those present to consider him insane.[43] While at Newgate, Coppe was forced to write two recantations of his heterodoxical views, titled *A Remonstrance of the Sincere and Zealous Protestation of Abiezer Coppe* and *Copp's Return to the Wayes of Truth*. Seemingly, like Winstanley, persecution had forced Coppe to abandon his radical eschatology of social leveling and endorse a more orthodox view of the end times.

But how sincere was Coppe's conversion? The final section in *Copp's Return*, titled "The Answer of A. C. to Mr Duries Proposals," is the only passage in either text to repudiate his claims of a present and phenomenal Last Judgment. However, this chapter is clearly a late addition and not consistent with the content of *Copp's Return* and *A Remonstrance*. Moreover, when professing orthodoxy, Coppe suddenly abandons his distinctive prose style and simply mimics the language of the King James Bible. Instead of offering his own view of the Last Judgment, for instance, Coppe just echoes Saint John: "I believe, that the dead, both small and great, shall stand before God the Judge of all" (*Copp's Return* sig. E3v; Rev. 20:12). The catechistical nature of this confession suggests that Coppe was merely appeasing his persecutors and using the King James Bible to put up a show of orthodoxy, rather than stating what he actually believed.

On the contrary, *A Remonstrance* and *Copp's Return* indicate that Coppe never forsook his embodied eschatology and his idea of an immanent Last Judgment. Unlike Winstanley, whose labor-based Last Judgment collapses under pressure, Coppe's body-based Last Judgment survives under a cloak of seeming orthodoxy. Denying that he is recanting, Coppe explains that his purpose is rather "the clearing up of those mistakes, and the wiping away those aspersions, which (through malice, weakness, ignorance, and mistake) have been cast upon me."[44] If his words have been misunderstood as blasphemous, it is because they have been read by the unenlightened, who do not have the eyes to see. In this way, Coppe's followers live on in a way the Diggers could not, in no small part because of the Ranters' lack of centralized organization and geographical fixedness. Unlike the Diggers, who were easily identifiable by their communes and the dirt on their hands, the Ranters were uncoordinated and widely dispersed. As Ariel Hessayon points out, Ranter communities were likely polygenetic rather than monogenetic, and this accounts for the sporadic evidence of their gatherings.[45] Flesh, as Coppe gleefully observes, is everywhere, making the Anointed no easy targets for persecution.

In *Copp's Return* (which shows little evidence of an actual return on his part), Coppe reiterates his earlier declaration that the Last Judgment has arrived in the minds of the faithful. To truly recant, Coppe would need to abandon his embodied eschatology—but he does nothing of the sort. Instead, he offers yet another account of how the Last Judgment ambushed him one day when he was out on a walk. The story reinforces (rather than denies) his earlier claims that the Last Judgment has arrived:

> But at length the terrible, *notable day of the Lord, stole upon me unawares, like a thiefe in the night.*
>
> *Even that DAY burst in upon me, which burneth like an oven, and NO FLESH, (no not the FLESH of FOWLES which sore aloft) can stand before it,* Malach. cap. 3. *and* chap. 4.
>
> *So that I can very well take up* Habbacuks *expresse,*
>
> Hab. 3. when I saw him———
>
> *My bowels trembled, my lipps quivered, rottenness entered into my bones,* &c. (sig. A4v)

Coppe's experience is similar to his encounter with the vagrant in *A Second Fiery Flying Roule,* when the Last Judgment burned like an oven within him. Here in *Copp's Return,* however, Coppe models his authorship on the Old Testament prophet Malachi, and his depiction of the

Last Judgment incorporates a harsh critique of the nation lifted from that biblical book.[46] "Where is the God of judgement?" (Mal. 2:17) is Malachi's frequent refrain, and in revolutionary England, Coppe poses the same question to his readers. And his response is also Malachi's: God is right here, and national reckoning is near. "Beholde, the day commeth, that shall burne as an oven," Malachi proclaims, "and all the proud, yea and all that doe wickedly, shalbe stubble" (Mal. 4:1). Malachi was written during the Babylonian captivity of the Jews, and in *Copp's Return*, the Ranter positions his renewed emphasis on the immanence of the Last Judgment against a backdrop of impending national exile. Like Judah before it, Coppe indicates, England would soon pay for its idolatry with the loss of its sovereignty.

While the book of Malachi supplies Coppe with his language of national reckoning, couched in the midst of that language is a reference to another biblical book—one that offered hope to the Jews in a similar time of political crisis. Significantly, this is the same reference to the third chapter of Habakkuk that Milton used in Sonnet 19 "When I Consider How My Light is Spent." Now as before, the reference suggests that even on the Day of Judgment, the nation might yet find redemption. Wrapped up in a vision of ultimate reckoning, Habakkuk prays, "O LORD, revive thy worke in the midst of the yeeres, in the midst of the yeeres make knowen; in wrath remember mercy" (Hab. 3:2). Like Milton, Coppe "*take[s] up* Habbacuks *expresse*," which is the hope that the nation might find mercy in the midst of wrath. By becoming the faithful remnant, England might yet find favor in its master's eye. Coppe's recantations are an opportunity to lash out, one last time, against the nation that oppresses him. But they are also an invitation for England to join him within the millennial kingdom, if only the nation's citizens will learn to embrace the divine human body.

Coppe and Winstanley respond to persecution differently, and the routes they take elucidate a larger difference between their sects while speaking to the wide range of antinomian beliefs during the English Revolution. Reasoning is reckoning for Winstanley, and the Last Judgment is the day when all men are governed by reason and, consequently, labor together in common. When persecuted, Winstanley tries to reason with those who will see no reason, and when he fails, he abandons his project. Coppe, however, is guided not by reason but emotional impulse and the promptings of the Holy Spirit.[47] The Last Judgment is an oven burning within him, and the only way to pacify that burning is to open the door and let the fire out. Winstanley reaches a point when continuing his work seems unreasonable, but Coppe reaches no such point, nor is unreasonableness a reasonable deterrent to his labor. Like the nature of radical religion itself, which only grows bolder in the face of persecution, Coppe perseveres, indefatigably and unreasonably, to seek new expressions for the divine truths burning within him.

4

THE FIRE AND THE SCYTHE

Hermeticism, Husbandry, and Welsh Politics in the Works of Thomas and Henry Vaughan

On February 22, 1649/50, the Rump passed the Act for the Propagation of the Gospel in Wales, which removed Welsh priests from their churches and replaced them with reformists. The act was an assault on the entire Welsh nation, as the anonymous Welsh author of *Gemitus Ecclesiae* saw it. With their evangelical fervor, the English mistook the "condition of *Wales* as most sad, and deplorable, overspread with Ignorance and Profannesse [. . .] as though *Wales* were still a *Land of Darknesse*, the poore Inhabitants thereof out of *Christendome*, sitting in the *Region and shadow of Death.*"[1] The act, the writer claims, was the result of a fundamental misconception about Welsh religion: Welsh episcopalians are Protestants, not papists, yet the English tried to evangelize them all the same. The writer admits that this misunderstanding was partly due to Welsh puritans, who helped bring "this *Trojan* horse"—the act—"into their Countrey."[2] Likely, he has in mind men like Morgan Llwyd and Vavasor Powell, who were preaching in London about the vestiges of popery in the Church of Wales. Though these are men "of our owne Nation," the writer states, they have betrayed their country by endorsing the new religious settlement.[3]

The act and the responses it engendered give us an idea of eschatology's place in nationalist discourses of revolutionary Wales, as the English attempted to evangelize the Welsh into *ecclesia* and the Welsh resisted such manipulation. John Kerrigan and other scholars have shown the complex nature of Welsh identity during the period, such that Welsh writers employed a "double orientation" of political association, in which they identified themselves paradoxically through difference and sameness with England.[4] But such paradoxes in Welsh nationalism ran vertically as well as horizontally, and the expectation of *ecclesia* both aided and frustrated Welsh attempts to codify a political identity. Welsh writers were caught in a double bind, as it were, as they labored to welcome in a universal community while rebuilding a particular community that was, in many ways, at odds with it. As they navigated the dual axes of political association, the needs of the universal community often outweighed the needs of the particular community. This is why Welshmen like Llwyd and Powell could "betray" their countrymen, because for them (as for Welsh episcopalians) saving souls took precedent over saving the nation.

The writings of Thomas and Henry Vaughan, in particular, illustrate the paradoxical nature of Welsh counternationalism during the English Revolution. Thomas, an alchemist, imagines himself as a modern Moses, and he hopes to lead the faithful from both England and Wales into the magical environs of the Last Judgment. By contrast, Henry commits himself to "walk[ing] in our forefathers way," and he transforms the devotional mode of his mentor, the English poet and parson George Herbert, into a Welsh weapon against their foreign oppressors.[5] Yet while both brothers use the expectation of *ecclesia* to renegotiate the relationship between England and Wales, their models of national reckoning ultimately prove incompatible with their belief in the ancient doctrine of *apokatastasis* (universal salvation).[6] One must be quite crafty to privilege both the universal and the particular at once, as we saw in chapter 1, but whereas Milton succeeds in his endeavor, the Vaughans fail in theirs. Preaching that reckoning would be a refinement by fire, Thomas's praise of England is undermined by his idea of cosmic transformation. Meanwhile, Henry invokes reckoning upon England by coopting Herbertian scenes of husbandry, but he proves unable to execute his revenge, and the reaping imagery that invigorates *Silex Scintillans* ultimately falls flat.

Fire and the scythe, consequently, capture the end-time politics of the Vaughan brothers. In their hands, eschatology was a force powerful enough to tear down the world as they knew it. But fire and the scythe are tools of destruction *and* rejuvenation. As such, they also illustrate how the end of one world is the beginning of another, as new knowledge and new societies are built upon the wreckage of things past.

"My Dear Mother, the Most Famous University of Oxford"

As a royal soldier under Colonel Herbert Price of Brecon Priory, Thomas possessed firsthand knowledge of the civil wars and their effect upon his homeland.[7] As a pastor after the war, he also was quite familiar with the Act for the Propagation of the Gospel in Wales, which expelled him from his rectorship at St. Bridget's in Llansantffraed on charges that he was "a comon drunkard, a common swearer, no preacher, a whoremast^r, & in armes personally against ye Parliament."[8] The English Revolution took a personal toll on him with the loss of his younger brother, William, who likely died of wounds incurred during the wars. Henry wrote elegies in William's memory, and when Henry More joked that perhaps William "killed himselfe by unmercifull studying of *Aristotle,*" Thomas fired back that his brother had died *"by a far more glorious imployment."*[9] Thomas had many reasons to hate the English, but for all this, he moved to England after his sequestration and lived out the rest of his life there. Seeking, perhaps, to make himself anew, Thomas was drawn to centers of intellectual exchange, and his deep appreciation for English learning enabled his reconciliation with the people he once fought against.

In his works, Thomas privileges England as an incubator for *ecclesia*. The church universal would come into being through an increase in knowledge that only the English could provide, and that had already begun at Oxford. Thomas was a leading member of the most extensive network of scientific information in revolutionary England, the Hartlib circle. The leaders of the circle were all Oxford trained, and their head,

Samuel Hartlib, resided there. Convinced that they were living in the bib-lical *eschaton*, the period preceding the Last Judgment, members of the circle saw it as their moral duty to become "partakers" with God in the divine plan to "make all things new," as the ecumenicist John Dury put it.[10] Their aim was nothing less than the total renovation of the world, beginning in England, by means of the rapid accumulation and dissemina-tion of knowledge about natural phenomena.[11]

The Hartlib circle labored to prepare the way for the Second Coming by initiating a scientific revolution first imagined by Francis Bacon. In *Novum Organum*, Bacon had theorized that the end of the world would be preceded by a period known as the *instauratio magna* (the Great Instauration).[12] Knowledge that was lost with the Fall of Man would be regained in the final days before the Last Judgment. Bacon drew this sup-position from the book of Daniel, which prophesies that at "the time of the ende," many people "shall runne to and fro, and knowledge shall bee increased" (Dan. 12:4). Hartlib and his compatriots saw themselves ful-filling this Old Testament prophecy, and Hartlib wrote, "Mee thinkes the tyme drawes neere that this Great *desideratum* [i.e., the Great Instaura-tion] drawes neere."[13] Thomas Vaughan included the verse from Daniel on the title page of *Anthroposophia Theomagica*, indicating that his own discoveries were part of a divine plan to uncover hidden knowledge in the last days of the world.[14]

Thomas's hermeticism is governed by a sense that he is living "in these last days," as he puts it.[15] The centrality of eschatology to his theory of magic is suggested in a copy of his *The Fame and Confession of the Fra-ternity of R[osi]: C[rucians]* at the Huntington Library, which contains a telling comment by a contemporary reader (see figure 11).[16] Thomas ends the preface by declaring that Adamic knowledge has been found, after which the reader writes (my translation below),

Amen. Γένοιτο. *Ita fiat.*
Ἀληθεῦς ὕτως ποιήσαι Κύριος.
Ἀμὴν ναὶ ἔρχου κύριε Ἰησοῦ.

[Amen. Let it happen. Thus let it be.
In this way the Lord is made manifest.
Amen, yes, come Lord Jesus.][17]

admiring contemplation of Na
ture, to his honour and praiſe, an
to the love, help, comfort an
ſtrengthening of our Neighbors
and to the reſtoring of all th
diſeaſed. *Amen. Γένοιτο. Ita fiat.*
Ἀληθῶς ὕτως ποιήσαι Κύριος.
Ἀμὴν ναὶ ἔρχȣ Κύριε Ἰησȣ.

Figure 11. Reader inscription in Thomas Vaughan, *The Fame and Confession of the
Fraternity of R: C:* (1652), sig. A8v.

The reader's language borrows from Revelation, which concludes with the words, "Amen. Even so, Come Lord Jesus" (Rev. 22:20). Like St. John, the reader pleads for Christ's imminent return, and like Thomas, he understands that hermeticism is an eschatological endeavor. The recovery of Adamic knowledge would prepare the way for Christ, and by means of hermetic experimentation, God would be made manifest to the world.

In Thomas's alchemical eschatology, England above all nations has been endowed with the ability to regain Adamic knowledge. Oxford, in particular, holds a privileged place as the training ground for members of the Hartlib circle. The Vaughans attended university there, and Thomas's treatise *Lumen de Lumine* is dedicated to their "dear Mother, the Most Famous University of Oxford" (239).[18] Addressing the university, Thomas writes,

> For my own part, I can present thee with nothing that is voluminous; but here is a mustard-seed which may grow to be the greatest amongst herbs. The draught itself hath nothing of Nature but what is under the veil [. . .] give me leave to make it my opportunity, that I may return the acknowledgment where I received the benefit. I intend not my address for the Banks of Isis; thou hast no portion there, unless thy stones require my inscription. It is thy dispersed body I have known, and that only I remember. Take it then, wheresoever thou art, in thy sad removes and visitations. It is neither Sadducee nor Pharisee but the text of an Israelite and Thy Legitimate Child EUGENIUS PHILALETHES. (239)

Thomas creates a typology between Egypt and Oxford that interweaves the hermetic and scriptural traditions. According to the hermetic tradition, occult philosophy originated in Egypt, and Thomas indicates that England—specifically, Oxford—has succeeded it as the custodian of Adamic secrets. He finds a place for himself within this new typology. Setting himself up as a Mosaic leader, Thomas suggests that he, too, has a divine mandate to bring the elect nation out of the slavery of ignorance and into the freedom of knowledge. Renaissance hermeticists claimed Moses as one of their greatest leaders, since he drew water from a rock, and Thomas refers to him fondly as "a natural magician" (163). Here, Thomas presents himself as a second Moses who is bringing similar miracles to England *via* Oxford.

Throughout *Anthroposophia Theomagica*, Thomas attempts to rally his English readers into an awareness of their newfound gifts. "We should therefore pray continually that God would open our eyes," he writes, "whereby we might see to employ that talent which He hath bestowed upon us but lies buried now in the ground and doth not fructify at all" (49). England is in danger of repeating the wicked servant's mistake, and Thomas's reference to the parable of the talents is doubly appropriate because hermeticism was often understood as an unearthing of buried truths. Like Milton, Thomas nationalizes the parable, such that the threat of national reckoning is upon all readers who refuse to recognize England's special gifts in the unveiling of hidden knowledge.

Thomas returns to the exodus narrative when dividing England between its enlightened hermeticists and its unenlightened school divines. In that division, Oxford becomes a battleground for the fate of the nation. "Now will the Peripatetics," he writes, "brand me with their *contra principia* and the school divines with a *tradatur Satanæ*" (50), as though he were an unschooled amateur and a dangerous heretic. Condemning scholasticism, Thomas encourages "all the true sons of my famous Oxford Mother to look beyond Aristotle and not to confine their intellect to the narrow and cloudy horizon of his text" (59). Instead of the "vomit of Aristotle, which his followers—with so much diligence—lick up and swallow," Thomas offers instead "a positive express of principles as I find them in Nature. I may say of them as Moses said of the FIAT: 'These are the generations of the heavens and the earth'" (9). Likening the school divines to the ignorant Egyptians in the Bible, Thomas assumes a Mosaic role as the liberator of God's chosen people and an intermediary between the human and the divine.

Moses appealed to Thomas not only because he was a powerful magician but because he, too, was a man of two nations. A Hebrew by birth, Moses was raised as an Egyptian, and he underwent a radical realignment of national identity when God charged him to "bring forth my people the children of Israel out of Egypt" (Exod. 3:10). Thomas writes for an English audience, but he is all too aware that he is not an Englishman. He publishes his treatises under the penname Eugenius Philalethes ("the well-born lover of truth"), which obscures the foreignness of his Welsh surname but retains the Vaughans' proud family heritage. "English is a language the author was not born to" (60), Thomas admits at the end of

Anthroposophia Theomagica, and he apologizes for any plainness in his speech. Like Moses, Thomas is an outsider preaching to a people who likely regard him with suspicion. His Oxford background allows him to pass as an Englishman, to a certain degree, and his repeated emphasis on his *alma mater* makes him familiar to his readers. Like Moses leading the Israelites, he would guide England by means of fire and bring the nation out of captivity and into a new era of enlightenment.

"Salvation Itself is Nothing Else but Transmutation": The Last Judgment as Alchemical Process

The greatest secret Thomas hoped to reveal to England was that the Last Judgment would be an alchemical process of refinement by spiritual fire. Thomas adapted this idea from the many passages in scripture that imagine divine judgment as a fire. "Behold, I have refined thee," God declares in the book of Isaiah; "I have chosen thee in the fornace of affliction" (Isa. 48:10). Of the Day of the Lord, Malachi asks, "Who may abide the day of his comming? and who shall stand when he appeareth? for he *is* like a refiners fire" (Mal. 3:2). Zechariah writes that in the last days, God would bring Israel's remnant "through the fire, and wil refine them as silver is refined, & will try them as gold is tried" (Zech. 13:9). From these and like passages, Thomas learned that reckoning was refinement and the Last Judgment would be the transmutation of earthly nations into *ecclesia*.

As an alchemical experience, the Last Judgment would be a divine process of breaking down humans, dissolving them into their *prima materia*, and rebuilding them into a higher state.[19] In *Anthroposophia Theomagica*, Thomas writes that God has even now begun "refin[ing] His creatures" (22). Similar to the monist materialism of Hobbes and Milton, Thomas imagines the physical and spiritual as "two extremes" (199) along the same spectrum of matter generated by *prima materia*, which emanates from God and out of which the world was formed.[20] The Fall of Man caused the human to become mired in sin and death, but the Last Judgment would strip away that dross and reconcile people with their true selves—their tincture—beneath.

As a hermeticist, Thomas sees sin as the product of an imbalance between humanity's pure and impure elements. The prelapsarian man,

Adam, was dominated by spiritual matter, but fallen people are subject to the whims of their baser materials. Good vies with evil, and the celestial nature of the *imago Dei* within them vies with the lowly dust from which they were formed. Thomas indicates that as a second Moses, he would lead the faithful into God's fires and thereby initiate the Last Judgment's refinement process. He explains that his intention in writing is to "reduce" the human to "his first simplicity and separate his mixtures of good and evil" (10). The human can then arise a "pure intellectual essence" (38) and prove fit company for God.

In Thomas's alchemical eschatology, "salvation itself is nothing else but transmutation" (302), and the Last Judgment is the furnace in which that change occurs. Like an object exposed to an alchemist's fire, the human is exposed to God's reckoning:

> I am now to speak of man as he is subject to a supernatural judgment; and—to be short—my judgment is this: I conceive there are—besides the empyreal heaven—two inferior mansions or receptacles of spirits. The one is that which our Saviour calls τὸ σκότος, τὸ ἐξώτερον [the outer darkness], and this is it whence there is no redemption—Ὅθεν ὄυποτε ἐξίαοι [from whence no one comes out]; *unde animae nunquam egrediuntur*, as the divine Plato hath it. The other, I suppose, is somewhat answerable to the Elysian fields, some delicate, pleasant region, the suburbs of heaven [. . .] But let it be where it will, my opinion is that this middlemost mansion is appointed for such souls whose whole man hath not perfectly repented in this world. But notwithstanding they are *De salvandorum numero* [of the number that must be saved], and are reserved in this place to a further repentance in the spirit for those offences they committed in the flesh. I do not here maintain that *ignis fatuus* of purgatory. (56–57)

At the Last Judgment, people would be filtered into different receptacles, and like common metals subjected to the alchemist's fire, their baser parts would be burned away. A person would enter the furnace of God's judgment as a base and mixed creature, but after reckoning, he or she would emerge as pure, spiritual gold. All things were made from the fires of God's forge (16), Thomas states, and so it is fitting that spiritual fire is the means by which all things would be reconciled to God. This is the meaning of Revelation's prophecy that each saint would receive a white stone with his or her true name on it (Rev. 2:17). "This, Reader," Thomas asserts, "is the Christian Philosopher's Stone" (113), a stone given to the faithful to mark their purity after the refinement of reckoning.

However, Thomas's belief in universal salvation negated his concept of reckoning. The Vaughan brothers' universalism drew upon the Origenic heterodoxy of *apokatastasis*, or *restitutio in pristinum statum*, which entailed a "restoration" and a "return to [an] original position."[21] Origen taught that at the end of the world, all creation would return to its original and pristine state, so that God might become "all in all" (1 Cor. 15:28).[22] Hermeticism similarly teaches that all creation is part of God, and that nothing that exists can cease to exist, since then a part of God would cease to exist. The *Corpus Hermeticum* states,

> For death is destruction; but of the things that are in the world, nothing is destroyed [. . .] [and consequently] the instauration of earthly bodies is their consistency, and the dissolution of that consistency restores them to indissoluble, that is, immortal bodies. Even so there comes about a deprivation of sense-perception, but not a destruction of bodies.[23]

According to hermeticism, death is not *apōleia* (destruction) but merely transmutation. Matter does not vanish from creation but is transformed into new forms.[24] Adapting this principle for his idea of an alchemical Last Judgment, Thomas includes both the faithful and the wicked in the process of refinement. Just as all people must endure a reckoning, so must all be invited into *ecclesia*, once they have been purged of their baser parts, and England would lead the way. They in turn would be led by a second Moses, who would guide the faithful into the promised land, and they as well, like the ancient Israelites, would follow a spectacle of fire that symbolizes their own refinement and regeneration.

"O Thou Man of Wales!": The Henry More Debate

Thomas's vision of the Last Judgment relies upon a paradox, since his claims of greatness for himself and England are only true to the extent that English readers can identify with him and include him in a nation to which he was not born. For Thomas to truly bring about the reconciliation of England and Wales, in other words, he needed to deliver on his claim to be a man of two nations. But this Thomas proved unable to do. His biggest critic would find a way to expose the fissures in his argument by poking holes in that which Thomas held most dear—his pride in his *alma mater*, the University of Oxford, and his claims to be at the center of an English community of great learning. No longer a well-educated man of two nations, as Moses was, Thomas would be humiliated before his readers and reduced to a Welsh wolf in English clothing.

Shortly after Thomas announced himself as a Moses-like national leader, the Cambridge Platonist Henry More responded with *Observations upon Anthroposophia Theomagica, and Anima Magica Abscondita*, published anonymously under the name Alazonomastix Philalethes.[25] More was ignorant of his opponent's identity (since Thomas had used a pen name), but he mocked Thomas as his "brother" in the family of Phila-lethes, or "truth-loving."[26] "You magnifie your self," More writes, and debunking Thomas's pride in his Oxford education, More accuses, "you are a very unnaturall son to our mother *Oxenford*, and to her sister University," Cambridge, which More himself attended.[27] More then coopts Thomas's own self-aggrandizing style and casts himself as a national savior as well. More claims that hermeticism is a "disease [that] is grown even Epidemicall in our Nation," and he says that he intends to provide the antidote.[28]

Alchemical fire is central to Thomas's vision of worldwide transmutation, and More turns it against him by fashioning it into a point of ridicule. Magicians, More jokes, promise fireworks and cannons but deliver only "fire-crackers and squibs," and he claims that Moses has been "much abused" through Thomas's association with him.[29] For Thomas, fire symbolizes the new creation that would emerge from the Last Judgment, but in More's hands, it becomes the embarrassing badge of a doomsday prophet. "Here *Philalethes* like the Angell of the bottomlesse Pit," More mocks, "comes jingling with the Keyes of Magick in his hands," but Thomas's hocus pocus reveals only empty palms.[30] "What can this voice of fire be?" More teases, and he claims that Thomas's fiery voice is his greatest trick as an alchemist.[31] Spewing out "Gypsie gibberish," Thomas's voice is a kind of alchemy, since it "attract[s] metall out of mens purses" and transforms it into Thomas's financial gain.[32]

Throughout *Observations*, More's strategy is to "other" Thomas as an unlearned foreigner. Thomas is not an Englishman but a gypsy, More asserts, and he is not a philosopher but a sad poet, since he writes "poeti-call pomp in prose."[33] "This affectation of humor and Rhetorick," More writes, "is the most conspicuous thing in your book. And shines as ori-ently, as false gold."[34] More claims that Thomas is given to "much canting language," and that for all his talk of refinement, Thomas lacks "the skill to winnow away all the chaffe of humorous words, and uncouth freaks and fetches of phansie, and affected phrases" that clutter his speech.[35] This rhetorical ornamentation, More indicates, is part of Thomas's magic trick, as readers buy his treatises, and the alchemist transforms their gold into his own.

The debate between More and Vaughan continued in two treatises that escalated this war of cultural othering and increased attention to the end times. Thomas learned that his opponent was Henry More, and in response, he published *The Man-Mouse Taken in a Trap, and Tortur'd to Death for Gnawing the Margins of Eugenius Philale-thes.* Demonizing both Cambridge and his opponent, Thomas writes, "*Cambridge*! *Cambridge*! what a *monstrous mother* art thou! I never thought the *same womb* could *labour* with *Moores* and *Christians*."[36] More is the true charlatan, he argues, since Thomas offers only Chris-tian truths to his readers, but More peddles the worthless wares of his "*Sodomit* Patron *Aristotel*."[37] "This is *Cambridge* Philosophie," Thomas exclaims; "it is not *worth*—."[38] And bolstering his Oxford connection, Thomas declares, "Sirrah I will *teach you*, and now that you have taken your *degree* of *Master* in *Cambridge*, you shall have the *honor* to be a *Pupill* to *Oxford*."[39] In Thomas's hermetic treatises, Oxford lent a degree of credibility, and here in *The Man-Mouse*, Cam-bridge serves the reverse function in ostracizing More as an unlearned Moor.

To further castigate the Cambridge scholar, Thomas interprets More's disbelief as symptomatic of a national apostasy in the final days before the Last Judgment. Addressing More, Thomas writes,

> It is no wonder indeed thou doest condemn my work, when thou doest slight and scorn the works of God. Truly, if thy severall *horrible Blas-phemies* meet not with a *Christian reproof* and *correction*, I shall say of *England*, as *Abraham* said of *Gerar*, *Surely the fear of God is not in this place.*[40]

Reading England into the Genesis narrative, Thomas suggests that the nation is unable to recognize a true prophet when it sees one. Like Abraham, Thomas sees himself as one holy man in the land of the godless. Yet in the biblical story, the people of Gerar were given an opportunity to repent before judgment came upon them. Abimelech, their king, undid the wrong he committed, and he praised Abraham as a true servant of God (Gen. 20). By referencing this passage, Thomas indicates that like Gerar, England is being given a moment of grace before its national reckoning. In the final days before the Last Judgment, the nation has an opportunity to repent, change its ways, and seek out wisdom from holy prophets like Thomas.

More responded to *The Man-Mouse* with *The Second Lash of Alazonomastix Laid on in Mercie upon that Stubborn Youth Eugenius Philalethes*, which argued that Thomas's alchemical eschatology was the result of his superstitious upbringing in rural Wales. More was embarrassed at having been publicly outed in a frivolous debate. "Consider what disservice," he later complained, "to the rest of my Writings, which are so grave and serious, and how they [i.e. the exchanges with Thomas] may cause the Reader, through incogitancy, to think of me in good earnest no where having once found me so much in jest."[41] In *The Second Lash*, then, More returned the favor. "Is not your name *Tom?*" he chides; "They tell me it is *Tom Vaughan* of *Jesus Colledge* in *Oxford*."[42] Comparing Thomas to the Tom-fool character in stage plays like Shakespeare's *King Lear*, More paints his opponent as an actor playing the fool. Mocking Thomas for his fiery temper and his fiery occupation, More writes, "He has too much naturall heat."[43] Thomas, it seems, is not only a fool but effeminate, since his fiery actions are motivated by an imbalance in the passions.

The Second Lash surpasses *Observations* in blackening Thomas's reputation, and it presents the alchemist as a country yokel who dreams of life in the big city. More insists that like Shakespeare's Tom o' Bedlam, Thomas is unskilled in language and in learning. The only people who would say things as ridiculous as Thomas has said, More exclaims, are "such as are no Englishmen, as you say somewhere you are not, and so do not understand the language."[44] To deny Thomas the English language is to deny him a credible scholarly voice. More claims that whether mangling English or misquoting classical authors, Thomas the Welshman speaks English most "barbarously."[45]

The natural world is key to More's strategy of othering Thomas into a rustic, and More associates the alchemist with the plants and trees of his Welsh homeland. Wondering why Thomas is so foul mouthed, More asks, "has thou devoured an Orenge like an apple, pulp and pill and all, and so made thy mouth bitter, O thou man of Wales! But it is to wash *hur* mouth from bawdry."[46] In early modern Europe, oranges were grown in southern climates and imported to northern cities as treats. More's joke, then, is that as a rustic, Thomas has never encountered an orange before and has foolishly eaten the entire thing, rind and all, which has turned his mouth sour. More even parrots Thomas's Welsh accent and broken English when saying, "it is to wash *hur* [i.e. your] mouth from bawdry," and suggests that the Welshman wears his ignorance of English manners and city life on his sleeve.

Wales's rurality also comes into play when More repudiates Thomas's hermetic vision of the Last Judgment. As we have seen, Thomas believed in the universal refinement of creation and held to the doctrine of *apokatastasis*, wherein all the world would return to its prelapsarian state at the Last Judgment. In *The Second Lash*, More accuses Thomas of letting "Chymistrie" guide his understanding of the New Heavens and New Earth, rather than the scriptures.[47] "He's for an Eden with flowry walks, and pleasant trees," More writes; "I am for a *Paradise*, Ἔνθ' ἀρετὴ σοφία τε καὶ εὐνομία συνάγονται, [or] *Where Virtue, Wisdome, and good Order meet.*"[48] More quotes Chaldean oracle 107, which declares natural phenomena to be mere *athurmata* (playthings) and warns readers against seeking spiritual truths in the earth. The reference is poignant. More accuses Thomas of broadened his ark of salvation to include flowers, trees, stones, and all creation. Saint Paul admonished against those who "worshipped and served the creature more then the Creatour" (Ro. 1:25), and in a similar manner, More condemns Thomas for idolizing nature like a superstitious country bumpkin.

Despite his zeal for national leadership, Thomas proved outmatched when facing a formidable foe like More, who had the upper hand in both rhetoric and intellect. Repeatedly, More harangued Thomas for being a Welshman and posturing as a scholar. The truths Thomas hoped to share with England were poisoned by More's accusations of heresy, materialism, and shoddy scholarship. For all this, at the end of his life, Thomas still saw himself as a workman who had no need to be ashamed. Thomas wrote in his diary, "I have not bushnelled my light nor buried my talent in the ground" (118), and he believed that despite the attacks leveled against him, he had done his part in publishing truths that were essential to humanity's regeneration at the end of the world. His failure to become a national leader would be mirrored, in a sense, in the life of his brother, who would become the finest poet in the Herbertian tradition but who—like Thomas—would prove unable to reconcile his love for a nation with his hope in *ecclesia*.

Silurist

Like Thomas, Henry interpreted the English Revolution as a sign of the world's end and the nearness of *ecclesia*. But unlike Thomas, who sought reconciliation with England, Henry worked to antagonize the Commonwealth and frustrate its efforts to manipulate Welsh religion. Since their patriarch, Dafydd Gam, died defending King Henry V at the battle of Agincourt, the Vaughan family had been a bulwark of royalism. Historical evidence indicates that Thomas (and possibly Henry) fought in the civil wars on the side of the king.[49] Henry's poem, "An Elegie on the death of Mr. R. W.," celebrates the king's cause at the Battle of Rowton Heath. Boasting a lineage few families in Wales could match, Henry and Thomas Vaughan were related to three powerful families with royalist sentiments: the Vaughans of Tretower, the Herberts, and the Somersets.[50] Their relatives included the Catholic recusant Thomas Somerset, who defended traditional religion in the time of Queen Elizabeth; the antiquarian John Aubrey, who complained about "puritanicall zealotts" swarming the land; and the poet George Herbert, who was born in Powys in Mid Wales.[51] Thomas and Henry Vaughan both expressed pride in their royalist heritage, but they nonetheless chose markedly different paths following the civil wars.

For both brothers, a sense of place and belonging was central to their postbellum politics. Oxford was dear to Thomas, and the activities of the Hartlib circle assured him that England would lead the way in worldwide renovation. In a similar way, Henry derived his sense of self from the forests, flowers, and fields of Breconshire, which inspired him to see God's reckoning as an act of divine husbandry and the Last Judgment as a pruning away of bad growth. But while Thomas moved to England after the wars, Henry remained in Breconshire, and the plethora of mountains, trees, and flowers in his poetry reflects his love for the rurality and innocence of Wales.[52]

For Thomas, fire symbolized the transmutation of the faithful into *ecclesia*, but Henry was inspired by a common harvesting tool that also symbolized reckoning: the scythe. Henry was drawn to scriptural stories that depict reckoning as a reaping. In *Silex Scintillans*, references to three recurring parables of judgment—the parables of the tares, the sower, and the seed growing secretly—constantly remind his readers that the Last Judgment is near. In Revelation, an angel commands, "thrust in thy sickle and reape [. . .] for the harvest of the earth is ripe" (Rev. 14:15), and as Henry saw the Breconshire countryside overrun with Englishmen after the wars, he no doubt agreed that the time for reckoning had come.[53]

Wales's influence on Henry's sense of self is evident in the epithet, "Silurist," which he appended to his name on the title page of *Silex Scintillans* and other works. "Silurist" refers to the Silures, a tribe of Britons who engaged the Romans in guerrilla warfare and were described by Tacitus as *gens non atrocitate, non clementia mutabatur* (a people changed neither by cruelty nor compassion).[54] Henry's epithet is a declaration of political defiance. By associating himself with his ancient ancestors, he suggests a parallel between Roman incursions into Wales and the Commonwealth's attacks on Welsh religion, most especially the Act for the Propagation of the Gospel in Wales. In his poetry, Henry lays claim to a British identity that precedes that of these Anglo-Saxon upstarts, as well as to an authentic episcopalian faith dating back centuries (what he calls the "antient way" of his forefathers ["The Proffer," ln. 43]) that precedes the newfangled evangelical frenzy under the Commonwealth.[55]

Today, Henry's tombstone in the churchyard of St. Bridget's, Llansantffraed, brandishes "SILURIS" beneath his name. It is engraved with the Vaughan coat of arms: three boys' heads with a snake entwined about their necks. The stone is a fitting tribute to Henry, since it cements the Vaughan family's legacy and Henry's own political defiance directly into the Welsh landscape Henry loved. The stone is also appropriate given the rigid and uncompromising nature of Henry's resistance to the Commonwealth. His brother may have found a new life in England, but such a move was unthinkable for the Silurist, who mounted a one-man campaign against his English oppressors and used their own poetry to do it.

"I'le Not Stuff My Story / With Your Commonwealth and Glory": *Silex Scintillans* and the Episcopal Faithful

Henry's response to the Act for the Propagation of the Gospel and other forms of English oppression was the second and more politically combative edition of *Silex Scintillans*, published in 1655. Henry's great achievement in *Silex Scintillans* is the politicization of Herbert's devotional mode, and he codes his threats toward England in images of husbandry borrowed from Herbert's great devotional work, *The Temple*.[56] In this way, Herbert supplied his Welsh relative with the tools the latter needed to oppose the Commonwealth.[57] As Henry appropriates *The Temple*'s imagery for his own revolutionary context, he labors tirelessly to adapt Herbert's English verse for the Welsh political agenda. As Achsah Guibbory observes, "Contradictory religious impulses lie at the center of Herbert's poetry," and by celebrating both the elaborate liturgical rituals of the episcopalians and the inward faith of the puritans, *The Temple* makes itself accessible to both ceremonialists and anticeremonialists.[58] Appropriating his mentor's praise of liturgy and ritual, Henry struggles, as we shall see, to reconcile these treasures of the episcopal community with his mentor's praise of the puritans who were now oppressing Welsh episcopalians.

Throughout *Silex Scintillans*, Henry codes his invectives against England through the Herbertian language of religious devotion.[59] In place of the outlawed Book of Common Prayer, *Silex Scintillans* offers itself as a vehicle for liturgical worship and traditional meditation.[60] Written in English, it was published in London and intended for Welsh and English episcopalians, who could appreciate the edition's ritualistic elements and sympathize with the plight of Welsh Protestants.[61]

Under Henry's tutelage, the reader's spiritual progress in *Silex Scintillans* is also progress toward a correct political perspective. Henry's use of iambic meter, rhyming couplets, monosyllabic words, ballad-like stanzas, and what Gerrard Manley Hopkins called the "consonant-chime" of

Welsh lyric are all designed to make *Silex Scintillans* easily accessible.[62] Henry's use of a familiar and intimate genre, the Herbertian devotional lyric, encourages readers to identify with the poetic speaker, thereby internalizing Henry's messages of opposition to the Commonwealth. Henry creates, in effect, a transnational reading community of episcopal faithful—a holy remnant from the Church of England and the Church of Wales, which had both been disbanded—who worship together through the liturgical act of reading his poetry.[63]

Henry acknowledges his debt to Herbert in the preface to *Silex Scintillans*, which reveals his method of politicizing Herbert's devotional mode. Henry praises his predecessor as "the blessed man, Mr. *George Herbert*, whose holy *life* and *verse* gained many pious *Converts*, (of whom I am the least)" (391). Professing that *Silex Scintillans* is a "kinde of *Hagiography*, or holy writing," Henry hopes that he might "be able to write (with *Hierotheus* and holy *Herbert*) A *true Hymn*" (392). Elsewhere, Henry rails against those who "want the *Genius* of *verse*, [and therefore] fall to *translating*," wherein foreign works are "*naturalized* and made *English*" (389). Keen to distance himself from such poetasters, Henry is in fact performing his own act of translation in transferring Herbert from an English context to a Welsh one. The author's preface is likewise misleading when it denies a political motive. "I meddle not with the seditious and Schismatical" (389), Henry states. But Henry's poetry is fiercely political, and time and again, his opposition to the Commonwealth assumes the form of a national reaping.

To uncover Henry's method of Welshifying Herbert, we might begin by considering "The Proffer," which recycles images of husbandry from *The Temple*. In "Employment (I)," Herbert's poetic speaker experiences a crisis of service, and much like Milton's speaker in Sonnet 19, he is concerned with proving fruitful before the Last Judgment arrives. At once a personal and a vocational poem, "Employment (I)" is one of several poems in *The Temple* that explore the speaker's search for purpose in life against the backdrop of his clerical calling.[64] In the poem, expectation of the Last Judgment causes the speaker to exchange his personal identity for a collective one, as he reflects on the coming of *ecclesia*:

> If as a flowre doth spread and die,
> Thou wouldst extend me to some good,

Before I were by frosts extremitie
    Nipt in the bud;

  The sweetnesse and the praise were thine;
  But the extension and the room,
Which in thy garland I should fill, were mine
    At thy great doom.

  For as thou dost impart thy grace,
  The greater shall our glorie be.
The measure of our joyes is in this place,
    The stuffe with thee.[65]

As the sudden change from singular to plural pronouns indicates, consideration of the "great doom" helps the speaker remember that his true abode is not on Earth but in heaven. Herbert's redefinition of "stuffe" captures the perspectival shift taking place. In seventeenth-century England, "stuff" referred to mundane things, but Herbert uses it here to signify heavenly rewards that come to the faithful through God's kindness.[66] Content to be a reed and not a flower, the speaker takes solace in the fact that his meager sound would soon be amplified within the heavenly orchestra of *ecclesia*.

Henry's "The Proffer" Welshifies this Herbertian crisis and reads it in the context of Henry's own offer of employment. "The Proffer" suggests that at some point before 1655, Henry was approached by a representative of the Commonwealth, who likely offered advancement in exchange for Henry's cooperation with the new administration.[67] During the wars, parliament's ability to take advantage of local resources had helped secure its victory, and afterward, the English government continued to employ native recruits in local administration.[68] Henry's cousin, Charles Walbeoffe, was one such recruit, and he accepted the Commonwealth's proffer and became a magistrate. But as the vitriolic tone of "The Proffer" makes clear, Henry refused a similar deal. Henry begins by inverting the image of insect productivity in Herbert's "Employment (I)." Henry's bugs are the wrong type—flies, not bees—and their extraction of nectar results in the plants' death:

  Be still black Parasites,
    Flutter no more;

Were it still winter, as it was before,
    You'd make no flights;
But now the dew and Sun have warm'd my bowres,
    You flie and flock to suck the flowers.

  But you would honey make:
    These buds will wither,
And what you now extract, in harder weather
    Will serve to take;
Wise husbands will (you say) there wants prevent,
    Who do not so, too late repent.

                 (1–12)

The black parasites suggest the black-clad officials issuing out of London, who were then descending like a plague upon Wales. Under the reign of Charles I, these parliamentary parasites had been contained. Now, they bask in the warmth of their recent victory, and they swarm forth *en masse* upon the Breconshire countryside. Their interaction with the foliage is a kind of rape, and the flowers are powerless to stop the flies' penetration of their delicate insides. These English flies try to force honey out of Welsh flowers, but the buds wither instead, which suggests that the outcome of complicity is death—or that men like Henry would rather die than submit.

Henry's poem also uses reckoning as an engine of war against his enemies. Imagining himself among the martyrs in heaven, Henry wonders how the parliamentarians hope to tempt him with worldly baubles. "Having born the burthen all the day," he asks, "[Shall I] now cast at night my Crown away?" (29–30). Knowledge of the Last Judgment emboldens him, and he declares,

  No, No; I am not he,
    Go seek elsewhere.
I skill not your fine tinsel, and false hair,
    Your Sorcery
And smooth seducements: I'le not stuff my story
    With your Commonwealth and glory.

  There are, that will sow tares
    And scatter death
Amongst the quick, selling their souls and breath
    For any wares;

> But when thy Master comes, they'l finde and see
> There's a reward for them and thee.
>
> (31–42)

Reading his own situation through the parable of the tares, Henry envisions reckoning upon England as a reaping. In the parable, an enemy plants tares (weeds) in a field, and when the workers discover them growing among the good crop, they come in distress to their master. "Let both grow together until the harvest," he tells them, "and in the time of harvest, I will say to the reapers, Gather ye together first the tares, and binde them in bundles to burne them: but gather the wheat into my barne" (Matt. 13:30). Like the scythes of the reapers, the judgments of God would soon cut down the wicked and separate them from episcopal faithful. The speaker's resolution hinges on the word "stuff," which recycles the Herbertian idea that the true reward of the faithful is *ecclesia*.

Henry's "The Proffer" represents the Commonwealth through an image quite familiar to his Welsh readers: London bigwigs with tinseled garments weaving their way through Breconshire. Contrasting with the verdant countryside, their black clothes make them conspicuously foreign—like weeds in a field of wheat, as Henry suggests. As readers process this image and sympathize with the poetic speaker, they too come to anticipate with joy the moment of reckoning, when these black weeds would be cut down and the land return to unblemished green.

"Dear, Secret *Greenness!*": Underground Religion and Pastor Charles

Welsh episcopalians responded to the disestablishment of the Church of Wales and the Act for the Propagation of the Gospel by taking their faith underground. In a surprising twist of fate, those who once comprised the religious establishment were driven to meet in basements, barns, and wooded glens, just as the sectaries had done before them.[69] Jeremy Taylor, who had been driven from his rectory at Uppingham, wrote with pride that despite their persecution under the Commonwealth, the episcopalians still bravely met to "worship upon mountains and caves, in fields and Churches, in peace and warre, in solitude and society, in persecution and in Sun-shine."[70] In this sense, he claimed, they were like the early Christians, who avoided the "temples of the heathen [and] the fury of a persecution" and instead "hid themselves in caves, and wandred about in disguises, and preached in private."[71]

Henry's poetry celebrates underground religion as an act of defiance to the Commonwealth. South Wales was full of royalist sentiment, and after the war, the people paid dearly for their loyalty to Charles.[72] On January 4, 1644/5, the Book of Common Prayer was outlawed. Many divines were ousted from their churches, including Matthew Herbert, the brothers' schoolmaster, who was deprived of his rectory at Llangattock, and the family friend Thomas Powell, who was sequestered from his rectory at Cantref.[73] Henry's own brother, Thomas, was deprived of his rectorship at St. Bridget's. Henry likely attended the illegal congregation pastored by Herbert, which met in Llangattock and even collected tithes from parishioners.[74] Welsh episcopalians practiced their faith in secret while Welsh evangelicals with English sympathies taught new doctrines from ancient pulpits.

Amid this atmosphere of clandestine meetings, Henry's "The Seed Growing Secretly" traffics in issues of secret faith and hidden praxis. As with "The Proffer," Henry constructs his critique of the Commonwealth on a Herbertian foundation. "The Seed Growing Secretly" engages Herbert's "The Flower," which likens spiritual fickleness to a flower that grows and then fades. Herbert writes,

> Who would have thought my shrivel'd heart
> Could have recover'd greennesse? It was gone
>   Quite under ground; as flowers depart
> To see their mother-root, when they have blown;
>   Where they together
>   All the hard weather,
>   Dead to the world, keep house unknown.
>
> These are they wonders, Lord of power,
> Killing and quickning, bringing down to hell
>   And up to heaven in an houre;
> Making a chiming of a passing-bell.
>   We say amisse,
>   This or that is:
>   Thy word is all, if we could spell.
>   (8–21)

In his frustration, the speaker blames his fickle nature on God and the whimsies of divine judgment. The speaker is dandled between heaven and hell, and God's reckoning is as arbitrary as growing flowers one day and lopping off their heads the next. Herbert is unable to justify this divine action, so rather than pursue the theodicy any further, he accepts mutability as part of our mortal nature. The speaker concludes that "we are but flowers that glide" (44), planted by God in his heavenly garden—an unsatisfying resolution, if not a downright disingenuous one.

As he appropriates and politicizes Herbert's crisis, Henry filters it through two parables of judgment—the parable of the seed growing secretly and the parable of the mustard seed. In the first parable, Christ likens the kingdom of God to a seed sown in the ground by a farmer. The farmer sleeps at night, and if "the seed should spring, and grow up, he knoweth not how" (Mark 4:27). When the plant sprouts and "the fruite is brought foorth, immediately he putteth in the sickle, because the harvest is come" (Mark 4:29). Christ's point is that just as the seed grows in secret, so do the faithful grow undetected until the Last Judgment, when the scythe of reckoning would cut down their enemies. The parable of the mustard seed, as well, associates hidden faith with righteousness. The kingdom of God is like a mustard seed, Christ explains, which "when it is sowen in the earth, is lesse then all the seedes that be in the earth. But when it is sowen, it groweth up, and becommeth greater then all herbes" (Mark 4:31–32). The parable teaches that those things that are small and easily overlooked are most worthy in God's sight.

Adapting these parables to describe the current political situation, "The Seed Growing Secretly" celebrates the underground religion of the episcopal remnant, who produce spiritual fruit in anticipation of the harvest. In Herbert's "The Flower," dormant growth was a metaphor for spiritual entropy, but used here in a revolutionary context, it describes cultivating a secret faith in the absence of a national church:

Dear, secret *Greenness!* nurst below
Tempests and windes, and winter-nights,
Vex not, that but one sees thee grow,
That *One* made all these lesser lights.

If those bright joys he singly sheds
On thee, were all met in one Crown,
Both Sun and Stars would hide their heads;
And Moons, though full, would get them down.

Let glory be their bait, whose mindes
Are all too high for a low Cell:
Though Hawks can prey through storms and winds,
The poor Bee in her hive must dwel.

(25–36)

The changeableness that bothered Herbert becomes a virtue in Henry's poem and describes the religion of the faithful, which grows secretly beneath the storms brewing overhead. The sun and the stars hiding their heads alludes to the seventh seal in Revelation, at which "the thirde part of the Sunne was smitten, & the third part of the Moone, and the third part of the starres, so as the third part of them was darkened" (Rev. 8:12). Despite cataclysmic events as the world hurtles toward its end, Henry indicates, the seed of faith grows unperturbed below.

Moreover, "The Seed Growing Secretly" alludes to the title page of *Eikon Basilike*, in which Charles also practices a secret faith (see figure 12). After he surrendered to the Scots on May 5, 1646, Charles was imprisoned at Newcastle, Holdenby House, Hertfordshire, Hampden Court, the Isle of Wight, and finally at his London residences.[75] Then and after his death, royalists used imagery of Charles languishing in a prison cell to rally support for the king. One broadside personified Wisdom as Charles and lamented, "O *Heavens*! and dares an earthly power confine / My Soveraignes Head? and are my senses mine? / And is he wise? must heavenly Wisdome dwell, / Prefined to the Limits of a Cell?"[76] Another royalist text declared, "Such black Attendants Colonied Thy Cell, / But for thy Presence, *Car'sbrooke* had been Hell. / Thus basely to be Dungeon'd, would enrage / Great *Bajazet* beyond an *Iron Cage*."[77]

Of course, *Eikon Basilike* was revered as a sacred book, and royalists recorded births, marriages, and deaths in it.[78] In its title page, Charles's prayer book is open to a page that reads *In verbo tuo spes mea* (my hope is in your Word), while he gazes up to heaven with the words *Cæli Specto* (I look to the heavens) and meditates on the "crowne of glory" promised to the faithful at the Last Judgment (1 Pet. 5:4). In *Olor Iscanus*, Henry

Figure 12. Title page to John Gauden, *Eikon Basilike* (1649).

had used cell imagery to evoke *Eikon Basilike*'s title page. "*Content* [i.e. contentment]," Henry wrote, "most times doth dwell / In *Countrey-shades*, or to some *Cell* / Confines it selfe, and can alone / Make simple *straw*, a Royall *Throne*" ("*Casimirus, Lib.* 4. *Ode* 15," ll. 31–34).

In "The Seed Growing Secretly," Henry goes a step further and recreates Charles as the dutiful pastor of an episcopal remnant. His suffering as their pastor-king anticipated their own. While men like Cromwell would disdain to be in a cell such as Charles inhabited, the king accepted his fate, mindful of the true glory he would soon win at the Last Judgment. Resurrected in Henry's poem, Charles is present at their underground gatherings. He serves as a rallying point for episcopalians across England and Wales who struggle to fortify their faith amid persecution. Like Christ the good shepherd, who promised to raise up his followers on the last day (John 6:40), the resurrected Charles shepherds his people through the paths of righteousness in the final days of the world.

The poem concludes by returning to Henry's favorite parable, the parable of the tares, and reminding the faithful that they are the product of divine husbandry. In Herbert's "The Flower," men are subject to the whims of God's reckoning, but in "The Seed Growing Secretly," reckoning is the welcome end of holy suffering. "Then bless thy secret growth," Henry writes, "nor catch / At noise, but thrive unseen and dumb; / Keep clean, bear fruit, earn life and watch, / Till the white winged Reapers come!" (45–48). In the parable of the tares, the reapers are the angels at the Last Judgment (Matt. 13:39), and in his poem, Henry likens the episcopal faithful to the flowers of the Welsh countryside, just as he likened Englishmen to weeds before. Dislocated yet unmoved, trodden under foot yet still growing, leaderless yet led by Charles, the episcopal faithful look forward to the national reaping that awaits.

The Scythe Suspended

As the "The Proffer" and "The Seed Growing Secretly" suggest, the scythe is the discursive center of *Silex Scintillans*. By means of the scythe, Henry's poems speak to one another, to Herbert's poems, to political events, and to scripture—all in an attempt to remind the faithful that judgment is coming. *Silex Scintillans* mirrors the *Temple* by turning, at its end, toward judgment.[79] Herbert's penultimate poem, "The Church Militant," merges heroic and prophetic modes to chart the westward migration of Christianity from Judea to England to America.[80] To describe this migration, Herbert draws upon scriptural metaphors of husbandry, including Christ's declaration, "I am the true vine, and my Father is the husbandman" (John 15:1) and "I am the vine, ye are the branches" (John 15:5). The Church, Herbert writes, is "Trimme as the light, sweet as the laden boughs / Of Noah's shadie vine" (14–15). In Herbert's husbandry, the faithful wind their way toward the Son like a plant straining toward the sun, and whenever their growth is impeded, they branch out in glorious new directions.

Long before Henry Vaughan, Herbert's praise of the pilgrims in "The Church Militant" had raised eyebrows.[81] In 1633, *The Temple*'s publication by Cambridge University Press was delayed by the Vice Chancellor, who took issue with Herbert's prophetic claim that the true faith was migrating to America.[82] Presenting the American settlers as Christianity's faithful remnant, Herbert claims religion would abandon its "ancient place" (256) for a home in New World, until the arrival of the Last Judgment:

> Then shall Religion to *America* flee:
> They have their times of Gospel, ev'n as we.
> My God, thou dost prepare for them a way
>
> [. . .]
>
> But as the Sunne still goes both west and east;
> So also did the Church by going west
> Still eastward go; because it drew more neare
> To time and place, where judgement shall appeare.
> (247–49, 274–77)

Herbert's account of an itinerant Christianity is a reminder to his readers that "God attributes to place / No sanctitie," as Michael the archangel puts it in *Paradise Lost*.[83] Likening the Americans to early Christians, who sold their houses to nourish the whole community (Acts 4:34), the poem finds beauty in Christianity's dynamism, geographic dislocation, and elasticity of expression, as the faith weaves its way westward in search of Christ like a vine twisting around a pole.

The final poem in *Silex Scintillans*, "L'Envoy," similarly envisions the Last Judgment as the remedy to human suffering. Henry found his mentor's praise of the pilgrims distressing, and so he transforms Herbert's New World into the New Heavens and New Earth and Herbert's faithful remnant, the Americans, into his own, the episcopal faithful. In the poem, the remnant are "drest in shining white" (4), like those who "came out of great tribulation, and have washed their robes, and made them white in the blood of the Lambe" (Rev. 7:14). In Herbert's poem, the Son illuminates Christianity's westward path, and in Henry's "L'Envoy," a new sun dawns on the New Heavens and New Earth, as the Son meets his bride, *ecclesia*.

In "L'Envoy," Henry attempts to use the Last Judgment to portend reckoning upon the Commonwealth, as he had done before. But that endeavor is a surprising poetic failure. The imagery of "L'Envoy" is squeezed between Henry's nationalistic need for vengeance, one the one hand, and his mentor's vision of peace and his own convictions as a universalist, on the other.[84] His attempt to reconcile these dueling impulses reveals the inherent incompatibility of national reckoning and universal salvation. The poetic speaker prays that Christ will

> Frustrate those cancerous, close arts
> Which cause solution in all parts,
> And strike them dumb, who for meer words
> Wound thy beloved, more then swords.
> Dear Lord, do this! and then let grace
> Descend, and hallow all the place.
>
> [. . .]
>
> Therefore write in their hearts thy law,
> And let these long, sharp judgements aw
> Their very thoughts, that by their clear
> And holy lives, mercy may here
> Sit regent yet, and blessings flow
> As fast, as persecutions now.
>
> (39–44, 53–58)

Henry's attempt to imitate Herbert and envision a peaceful Last Judgment takes the edge off his scythe and dulls his threats of retribution against the Commonwealth. Throughout *Silex Scintillans*, reaping imagery is an effective rhetorical maneuver precisely because of the violence involved in cutting, severing, and piercing. But in "L'Envoy," the scythe is an alarmingly underdeveloped image. It appears as the "long, sharp judgements" of God, but it does not cut down the wicked, as it did before. Rather, it very unremarkably "awe[s]" their thoughts. As a message of Christian charity, this is perhaps acceptable, but as a poetic conceit—of a scythe *awing* people into goodness—it is disappointing, to say the least.

As he imagines the Last Judgment in "L'Envoy," Henry sacrifices poetic artfulness to stake a theological claim. The scythe's immobility, as it hangs suspended in the poem, is the product of Henry's mental uncertainty, as he himself hangs in the balance between vengeance and forgiveness. Unlike in his earlier poems, the scythe in "L'Envoy" does no reaping. Try though he might to channel his ancestors and bring the scythe crashing down upon the necks of his enemies, Henry is unable to complete the action he desperately wants to see performed.

As a result, the vibrant husbandry imagery that so invigorates the world of *Silex Scintillans* breaks down at its end. As a poet, Henry is at his best when he operates within the Silurian tradition of resistance and, like his ancestors, plots stunning assaults upon his opponents. In "L'Envoy," the scythe is a familiar image, but it does neither what we expect it to do nor what it is supposed to do. Grace wins at the end of *Silex Scintillans*, but poetry falters. The scythe of God's judgments, which had been so dreadful before, becomes nothing more than a clumsy contrivance, crude in its design and mechanical in its application.

The Trial of Charles I and the Redemption of Fallen Community in Milton's *Paradise Lost*

On Saturday, January 20, 1648/9, the prisoner Charles Stuart was brought to Westminster Hall to hear the charges laid against him by the Commons of England.[1] Flaunting his disdain for the court, Charles kept his hat on and smiled when accused of being "guilty of all the bloud that hath been shed in these warres."[2] The charges having been read, Charles refused to plead but instead questioned the court's jurisdiction, demanding, "I would know by what power I am called hither[?]"[3] Deriding the High Court as no better than a band of highwaymen, Charles reminded his spectators that the proceedings were part of a much greater trial taking place, which was the trial of England before God.[4] Mocking the lord president of the court, John Bradshaw, and his company as "pretended Judges," Charles warned, "Remember I am your King, your lawful King, and what sins you bring upon your heads, and the Judgment of God upon this Land, think well upon it."[5] The prosecution was not amused, and over the next two days, the court tried to suppress the unruly antics of this "royal actor" upon a national stage, as Andrew Marvell would later call him.[6] An irritated Bradshaw commanded Charles time and again, "You are not to have liberty to use this language," and "You may not be permitted to fall into these discourses," and he demanded that the king take his charges seriously.[7]

On Tuesday, January 23, Bradshaw's patience was at an end. He ordered Charles, "You are to give your positive and finall Answer in plain English, whether you be guilty or not guilty of these Treasons laid to your charge."[8] Charles, looking austerely upon his judges, complained that he had not been sufficiently heard. "[As] for the Charge," he added, "I value it not a rush," since it issued from "a new Court I never heard of before."[9] From the first day in court until the last, the trial of Charles I was a debate over the authority of subjects to judge their king, and both sides were keen to expose the other as usurping a juridical prerogative belonging solely to God.[10]

Charles's trial was the trial of the century, and it attracted a great deal of national and international attention.[11] The Restoration saw a revival of interest in the king's trial, and in the "image wars" of period, as Kevin Sharpe calls them, the king's representation was hotly contested in print.[12] Although David Loewenstein points out that Milton "exploits and revises the traditional symbols and language of monarchy and its power" in *Paradise Lost*, and Alison Chapman observes that the epic is "saturated" with the language of the courts, the poem's engagement with the controversy over Charles's trial has gone unremarked.[13] But that event looms large over the representation of judgment in *Paradise Lost*, and Milton uses trial-like scenes in the epic to participate in the national debate over Charles's sentence and to theorize how responses to God's reckoning might ruin or redeem an entire community. In *The Tenure of Kings and Magistrates* and *Eikonoklastes*, Milton argued that the sentence laid upon the king by the High Court was a divine decree, and in *Paradise Lost*, judgment is a litmus test for obedience, since it allows characters to practice Protestant virtues of humility and confession—or deny them and practice attitudes of pride and defiance.[14] From Eve's submission to reckoning to Satan's crafty evasions of the same, Milton's epic shapes the meaning and memory of Charles's trial in Restoration England while showing readers something they had not seen in history: how godly individuals seek out judgment, instead of avoiding it.

Figure 13. *Trial of King Charles I,* in John Nalson, *A True Copy of the Journal of the High Court of Justice* (1684), sig. T2v.

Similar to the twin paths of godliness outlined in *Samson Agonistes* and *Paradise Regain'd*, the figures of the Son, Abdiel, and Eve in *Paradise Lost* offer alternating models of how faithful individuals can seek out God's judgments in a time of apostasy.[15] In the politically oppressive atmosphere of Caroline England, when the faithful had fallen on "evil dayes [. . .] with dangers compast round"(*Paradise Lost* 7.25, 27), Milton returned to his method of seeking England's salvation in the remnant, whom the Bible prophesied would be "caught up together" with *ecclesia* at the world's end (1 Thess. 4:17).[16] *Paradise Lost* picks up where Sonnet 19 left off and champions individual persons as faithful remnants. Milton's epic is filled with types of the Last Judgment, and each fictional encounter with reckoning is both a criticism of the king's behavior and an opportunity for Milton's readers, that "fit audience [. . .] though few" (*Paradise Lost* 7.31), to show themselves of a different temperament.[17]

Consequently, in a tale of the world's beginning, Milton teaches a fundamental lesson about life in the final days before the world's end. Scripture promises that "Zion shall be redeemed with judgement" (Isa. 1:27), and Milton's epic suggests that England might yet be saved through a faithful remnant of readers who keep their lamps lit for the Last Judgment and *ecclesia*.[18] Awaiting the nation's redemption and their own union with the saints of history, Milton's readers learn that they can look upon the world's end without fear, for with the end comes judgment, and with judgment, grace.[19]

"We Have Been Mutually Punished": National Reckoning in *Eikon Basilike*

As he had done before the High Court, so in *Eikon Basilike* Charles claimed there was only one trial fit to judge a king: the Last Judgment. Written by Charles, John Gauden, and others, *Eikon Basilike* capitalized on the newly popular genre of spiritual autobiography as a way of telling the king's story.[20] By the time of the king's execution on January 30, 1649, copies were already in circulation at the staggering price of 15*s*.[21] On March 15, William Dugard printed his expanded edition, which included a new chapter, "His Majesty's Reasons against the Pretended Jurisdiction of the High Court of Justice, Which He Intended to Deliver in Writing on

Monday, January 22, 1648," allegedly written by Charles and handed to Bishop Juxon just before the king's execution.[22] In the chapter, Charles protests "not only against the illegality of this pretended court, but also that no earthly power can justly call me, who am your king, in question as a delinquent" (188). Balking at the death sentence he received, Charles declares, "I am most confident that this day's proceeding cannot be warranted by God's law" (189). Upholding the same position he held at his trial, Charles asserts that the High Court of Justice was illegal according to the laws of England and the laws of God.

Throughout *Eikon Basilike*, Charles displays himself as willing, even eager, to accept judgment from God. Claiming he has "no judge but God above me" (66), Charles appeals to divine judgment in order to assert a Christ-like humility and simultaneously discredit the High Court. "Those judgments God hath pleased to send upon me," he writes, "are so much more the welcome as a means, I hope, which His mercy hath sanctified so as to make me repent" (8). Charles prays,

> Teach me to learn righteousness by Thy judgments and to see my frailty in Thy justice. While I was persuaded by shedding one man's blood to prevent aftertroubles, Thou hast for that, among other sins, brought upon me and upon my kingdoms great, long, and heavy troubles.
>
> Make me to prefer justice, which is Thy will, before all contrary clamors, which are but the discoveries of man's injurious will. (10)

The reference to "one man's blood" alludes to the execution of Thomas Wentworth, Earl of Strafford, but also hints at Charles's own imminent execution. Reading his own death through Christ's death, when it was decided that "one man should die for the people, and that the whole nation perish not" (John 11:50), Charles reinforces his image as a national martyr who like Christ would die for his people.

In deflecting blame from himself, Charles's strategy was to nationalize judgment and disperse reckoning across his subjects, thereby transforming England into a sinful and fallen community.[23] The High Court was keen to pin all responsibility for the wars on Charles; Charles, in response, displaces responsibility onto his citizens. For instance, when writing about his repulse at Hull in the summer of 1642, when Sir John Hotham denied him entry to the city, Charles calls the event a stroke of "divine vengeance"

(35) upon a sinful nation. He interprets the civil wars as God's judgment upon the nation, even a "reaping" (5) of God's due. Charles prays,

> Our sins have overlaid our hopes; Thou hast taught us to depend on Thy mercies to forgive, not on our purpose to amend.
>
> When Thou hast vindicated thy glory by Thy judgments and hast showed us how unsafe it is to offend Thee upon presumptions afterwards to please Thee, then I trust Thy mercies will restore those blessings to us which we have so much abused as to force Thee to deprive us of them. (5)

The High Court of Justice had branded Charles a "Tyrant, a Traytor, a Murtherer, and a publicke enemy to the Commonwealth of *England*," but in *Eikon Basilike*, it is the nation—not the king—who is to blame for England's troubles.[24] "We have been mutually punished in our unnatural divisions" (152), Charles tells readers, and he advises the young prince of Wales,

> If neither I nor you be ever restored to our rights, but God in His severest justice will punish my subjects with continuance in their sin and suffer them to be deluded with the prosperity of their wickedness, I hope God will give me and you that grace which will teach and enable us to want, as well as to wear, a crown which is not worth taking up or enjoying upon sordid, dishonorable, and irreligious terms. (168–69)

In Charles's interpretation of history, his removal as king was God's judgment upon England. The reason for that judgment was the iniquities of the nation ("their sin" and "their wickedness"), and like Israel of old, England is being chastised into greater godliness.[25] Additionally, by invoking the Last Judgment and imagining the crown Christ would give him then, Charles undermines the High Court's authority to judge him. Warning readers that a national reckoning would soon be at hand, Charles imagines God's "tribunal," where "we must give an account of every evil and idle word" (61), and he suggests that erroneous human judgments would soon be overturned by the infallible judge, Christ.

Throughout *Eikon Basilike*, Charles expresses confidence that at the Last Judgment, he would have a defense attorney who could not lose. Calling the Last Judgment that "unavoidable judgment which shall rejudge what among men is but corruptly decided," he prays to Christ, "Plead my cause and maintain my right, O Thou that sittest in the throne, judging rightly" (13–14). Contrasting the judgment of men with the judgment of God, Charles writes of his enemies, "They have often, indeed, had the better against my side in the field, but never, I believe, at the bar of God's tribunal or their own consciences" (119). Appealing to God's tribunal was also a way of suggesting that his trial was not yet over. Things "corruptly decided" by men, Charles warns, would soon be "rejudge[d]" by Christ. Until then, his conduct as a king was solely his affair.

"The Tryal of Justice, Which Is the Sword of God": Milton Responds in *The Tenure of Kings and Magistrates* and *Eikonoklastes*

While Charles worked to undermine his trial, the High Court of Justice and its supporters insisted that the trial of the king was a divine reckoning visited by God. Milton described it as the sword of God brought to bear on a wayward king who had broken his covenant with the national community. Bradshaw believed as much when he claimed the High Court epitomized the duty of the Commons "to Justice, to God, the Kingdom, and themselves."[26] Bradshaw insisted the court's sentence was corporeal *and* spiritual, and he advised Charles that the sentence upon him should drive him into "a sad consideration concerning [his] eternall condition" in the final days of his life.[27]

Like Bradshaw and Milton, John Cook, the lead prosecutor at Charles's trial, argued that God was present with the judges. Declaring, "The righteous Judge [i.e. Christ], whose judgement is not onely inevitable, but infallible, must shortly judge me," Cook avowed that Charles's guilt had been determined by God before he came to Westminster.[28] "The Prisoner was long since condemned to die by Gods Law," Cook proclaimed, and "this High Court was but to pronounce the Sentence and Judgment written against Him."[29] Cook continued,

> [The] High Court was a Resemblance and Representation of the Great day of Judgment, when the Saints shall judge all worldly powers, and where this judgment will be confirmed and admired, for it was not onely *bonum*, but *bene*; not onely good for the matter, but the maner of proceeding.[30]

Drawing on the scriptural prophecy that "the Saints shall judge the world" (1 Cor. 6:2), Cook estimates that Charles has been thrice condemned: once by God, once by the High Court of Justice, and once again by the saints at the Last Judgment. And like the Last Judgment, Charles's trial by the High Court was not only fair but exact. In its application of the deuteronomic *lex talionis*, the court decreed that only a king's blood could pay for the blood Charles spilled in the wars.[31]

Milton also interpreted Charles's trial as a divine reckoning carried out by a godly community, the nation, which had dethroned an unjust tyrant. However, that national community had been fractured of late, and in *The Tenure of Kings and Magistrates*, published two weeks after Charles's execution, Milton railed against the presbyterian backsliders who no longer had the stomach to try Charles, but instead wanted to "plead for him, pity him, extoll him, protest against those that talk of bringing him to the tryal of Justice, which is the Sword of God, superior to all mortal things."[32] Milton writes that it was God who tried and convicted Charles for his crimes. The High Court's decision was the "sentence of Divine justice" (*CPW* 3:226), not a human one. Charles had a "faire and op'n tryal" (*CPW* 3:237), Milton assures his readers, and the king's disruptive behavior before the High Court was an offense against God. In *Eikonoklastes*, Milton criticizes Charles for his contempt for the court:

> And he who at the Barr stood excepting against the form and manner of his Judicature, and complain'd that he was not heard, neither he nor his Friends shall have that cause now to find fault; being mett and debated with in this op'n and monumental Court of his own erecting; and onely heard uttering his whole mind at large, but answer'd.[33]

Milton complains that Charles not only scorned to be judged but wrongfully took his quarrel to the streets by publishing *Eikon Basilike*. As we discussed in chapter 4, after the king's death, the popularity of the king's book among royalist readers was unprecedented, and families often recorded births and marriage dates in it, as they did only in family Bibles.[34] Milton indicates that *Eikon Basilike* allowed Charles to extend his trial and question the High Court's judgment. By erecting a court of public opinion and allowing readers to judge his case, Charles undermined the divine sentence he had already received.[35]

Milton also uses Charles's trial to discredit the king's pretended piety. Milton points out that at his trial, the king "act[ed] against conscience" when defending himself and his actions, and Milton accuses Charles of constantly using "scruples, exceptions and evasions" (*CPW* 3:430, 597) to exculpate himself, so that whether at his trial or in *Eikon Basilike*, the king will do whatever is necessary to appear innocent. Chief among his dissemblings, Milton claims, are the king's many appeals to the Last Judgment, which Milton says will do him no good. Charles "appeal'd to Gods Tribunal," Milton writes, "and behold God hath judg'd, and don to him in the sight of all men according to the verdict of his own mouth [. . .] God and his judgements have not bin mock'd" (*CPW* 3:381–82). The High Court delivered a divine decree, and like Cook, Milton reads their judgment and the judgment that Charles would receive at the Last Judgment as one and the same. Milton proposes that instead of "appeal[ing] to a high Audit," Charles would have better spent his time learning to "tremble at [God's] judgments" (*CPW* 3:405, 485). In this regard, Charles is no better than Nimrod and Pharaoh (*CPW* 3:466, 509), who also thought themselves beyond the reach of divine wrath, learning too late the truth of their perilous condition and bringing devastation to their nations as a result.

Worst of all, Milton argues, are Charles's prideful attempts to usurp God's judgments, which presume a knowledge of the divine mind that no man possesses. For instance, when debunking Charles's account of his defeat at Holmeby, Milton writes,

> No evil can befall the Parlament or Citty, but he positively interprets it a judgement upon them for his sake; as if the very manuscript of Gods judgements had bin deliverd to his custody and exposition [. . .] to counterfet the hand of God is the boldest of all Forgery: And he, who without warrant but his own fantastic surmise, takes upon him perpetually to unfold the secret and unsearchable Mysteries of high Providence, is likely for the most part to mistake and slander them. (*CPW* 3:563–64)

As with his repulse at Hull, Charles interprets his defeat as God's judgment upon a sinful nation. But Milton, keen to exonerate England of wrong-doing, places the blame squarely back on Charles. Hinting that Charles was not the author of *Eikon Basilike*, Milton links the king's spurious authorship with his spurious eschatology, so that the book's claim to be written by Charles becomes as hollow as the king's claims to know the mind of

God. That last activity is beyond the ken of man, Milton asserts, although one character in *Paradise Lost* would do exactly that, when the Son would submit to the Father's reckoning as the instrument by which fallen community is redeemed.

"The High Court of Injustice": The Restoration Legacy of Charles's Trial

The restoration of monarchy in 1660 sparked renewed public interest in Charles's trial, and royalists voiced opinions too dangerous to print during the Interregnum.[36] No longer the "tryal of Justice" and the "Sword of God," as Milton had described it, the trial of Charles I was renamed "the black tribunall," "Cromwell's bloody slaughter-house," and the "illegal Tryall," while the High Court of Justice became "the High Court of Injustice."[37] Royalists attempted to wrestle judgment back from the parliamentarians, often demonizing the king's judges as irreligious men worthy of the divine sentence of death.[38] The author of *A Hue and Cry After the High Court of Injustice*, for instance, declared, "The divine hand of Gods Justice which in all Ages pursues and overtakes blood-thirsty Traitors and Murtherers, [has] now by a most miraculous way of Providence restored *Englands* old Liberties."[39] Turning the engine of God's judgments back against the regicides, the author ridiculed those who foolishly "flye beyond the seas, thereby thinking to escape that Justice and vengeance which its impossible to escape."[40] Accusations that Charles had usurped God's judgments were countered by the claim that the High Court—not the king—had usurped God's jurisdiction. The author of *The High Court of Justice*, for example, declared that "God ha[d] no hand in these proceedings, nor amongst such Judges" and that the judges had "usurp[ed] to themselves (without any calling from God or the People) more than a Regal, Legal or Parliamentary Authority."[41] The High Court, he claimed, was no better than a court of the Inquisition, since it pretended to an authority over souls that only God possessed.[42]

The tables turned, Charles's unruly behavior at his trial was interpreted anew as the noble bearing of a king who had every right to be indignant at the trumped up charges against him. The author of *The Oglio of Traytors: Including the Illegal Tryall of his late Majesty* transformed Charles's defiance of the High Court into a virtue. Praising Charles, he wrote, "The King was often times observed to smile in indignation, during the reading of the Charge especially at the words Tyrant, TRATOR, MURDERER, and publick enemy to the Common-wealth."[43] Viewed posthumously, Charles's smiling was almost prophetic, since it looked forward to the time when others would smile with him. "Times Wheel is turned round!" a broadside titled *The Tryall of Traytors, or, The Rump in the Pound* proclaimed, and the "black Judges who in Fury / Murd'red their KING" now face the same block.[44] The author invited all England to join in mocking Charles's pretended judges, whose appeals to God's judgment at their own trials brought grins to the faces of many spectators.[45]

One popular account, *Cromwell's Bloody Slaughter-House*, was written by John Gauden, coauthor of *Eikon Basilike*. Borrowing imagery from Revelation, Gauden described God's judgment upon the regicides as an end-time portent. "Shall you escape the righteous judgement of God?" he mocks; "will not God visit you for these things?"[46] He warns readers that these "Hucksters of Justice" are the spawn of the red Dragon and also the "Vials of the wrath of God," which have been poured upon the Earth to plague humanity (Rev. 12:3, 16:1).[47] Invoking the Last Judgment, Gauden uses judicial language when telling the regicides that the people of England, "in the sight of God, to whose just Tribunall we appeal, [. . .] summon [the] stupid and cruel hypocrisie [of the regicides]" to stand trial.[48] He asserts that the injustice of Charles's trial would not be resolved "till God take the matter into his own hands, and plead the cause of the *King* and Kingdome against these proud *Goliahs*."[49] *Eikon Basilike* posited that Charles could only be tried at the Last Judgment, and *Cromwell's Bloody Slaughter-House* ushers that eschatological event into the historical present. The nation's reckoning has begun, Gauden asserts, and Charles's vindication is evident in the mangled bodies dangling from London Bridge.

Satan's Sentence and the Fall into Time

In this highly charged political atmosphere, as royalists exhumed both dead regicides and the dead king's honor, Milton wrote *Paradise Lost*, which is concerned with a crime, criminals, and the judgment laid upon them. The poem reworks Milton's earlier concern for proper responses to God's judgment, as expressed in *The Tenure of Kings and Magistrates* and *Eikonoklastes*, and situates them within an epic framework. Within that framework, and in light of contemporary debates over Charles's trial, Milton theorizes about the healing effects of judgment and postulates, as he had in his early poetry, that ultimate reckoning might redeem a fallen community such as the nation. A Satan-Son dichotomy enables Milton to explore how resistance or submission to judgment respectively divides or unites a community. In that dichotomy, the fallen archangel teaches Milton's readers the ramifications of denying and avoiding reckoning, namely, societal corruption and the outbreak of diseased attitudes of disobedience. In the figure of the Son, however, Milton shows that reckoning's unique capacity for discriminating between right and wrong is greatly desired by the godly, and that seeking out judgment is an addictive activity that can inspire a multitude of obedient people to come.

Amid Restoration debates on the king's trial, Satan's refusal to submit to a reckoning he considers illegal echoed of Charles's refusal to acknowledge the High Court's authority. In actuality, the fall of the rebel angels from Heaven was a divine judgment upon them, as the Son acknowledges when he states, "Therefore to mee thir doom [the Father] hath assig'n'd" (6.817). The Son then drives the angels from Heaven from atop the Father's chariot, complete with flaming wheels and cherubic faces, the same which Ezekiel saw (Ezek. 1:4–24) and which Milton presents as a type of the Last Judgment.[50] Milton writes that the rebel angels "wisht the Mountains now might be again / Thrown on them as a shelter from [the Son's] ire" (6.842–43), which is an allusion to the Last Judgment as described in Revelation, when the wicked say to "the mountaines and rockes, Fall on us, and hide us from the face of him that sitteth on the throne" (Rev. 6:16). Consequently, at the world's beginning, Satan encounters the same judgment he would face at the world's end, but he fails to recognize it as such. Calling the Son a "Potent Victor" (1.95) and saying that "force hath made [the Son] supream / Above his equals" (1.248–49), Satan insists upon seeing the Father's judgment as a mere military contest—a matter of might and brawn, not right and wrong—in which he unfortunately proved less equipped than his opponent. His foolishness in this regard contributes to the poem's critique of "the traditional military heroism of epic," as David Quint calls it, embodied here in the muscle-flexing bruiser Satan.[51] Declaring that he will never "bow and sue for grace / With suppliant knee, and deifie his power" (1.111–12), Satan denies the Father's godhood (since God can hardly be God if he requires deification) and thus his ability, as the angel's superior, to judge Satan.[52]

Satan's sin is not only to deny that he has been judged but also to temporalize God's judgment and ascribe to it a historicity it does not have. Satan's fall from Heaven is a fall into time—that is, a fall away from the Eternal Today and into the *saeculum* of mundane experience—and his thinking about judgment reflects those temporal limitations.[53] Envisioning judgment as moments in time that he can evade, circumvent, or otherwise turn to his advantage, Satan forgets that judgment—as something intrinsic to the divine nature—is coeternal with God. Failing to understand that the judgment upon him is ongoing, and believing that the Father has "spent his shafts," Satan warns Beëlzebub that they should "not slip th' occasion" (1.176, 178) but take advantage of a supposed pause in the Almighty's ire and plot out a future for themselves that is, in actuality, no longer a possibility.[54] Satan even deludes himself into believing he can learn from his fall, claiming that "through experience of this great event [. . .] [the angels are] in foresight much advanc't" (1.118–19) and thus better prepared to face their enemy a second time.[55]

Satan further compounds his sin by teaching other angels to disrespect judgment, as he does. Like a virus, Satan infects the fallen angels with his own attitude of disobedience, and he spreads falsehoods about their fall before anyone can voice an opinion to the contrary. Summoning the fallen angels to arise from the burning lake, he praises them as "Warriers" and calls God "the Conquerour" (1.316, 323), thereby illuminating (even glorifying) the martial aspect of their conflict while downplaying any moral implications. Moreover, Satan teaches the fallen angels that God's judgment upon them (though he refuses to recognize it as such) was an isolated event in history—something safely locked in the past. Urging the angels to assemble quickly before God's "swift pursuers from Heav'n Gates discern / Th' advantage, and descending tread us down" (1.326–27), Satan instills within his followers the notion that they can evade their judge and slip the sentence laid upon them.

Succumbing to their chieftain's rhetoric, the angels deny both God's authority to judge them and the fact that their judgment is ongoing. Moloch describes the angels not as criminals but as "fugitives" who are unjustly confined to a "dark opprobrious Den of shame, / The Prison of his Tyranny" (2.57, 58–59), and he speaks with dread of "the torturing hour" when he and his fellows would be "Call[ed] [. . .] to Penance" (2.91–92). Mimicking Satan's own rhetoric of victimization, Moloch sees the fallen angels as innocent victims before an unjust court that (like the Spanish Inquisition in Milton's own day) would force a confession from blameless persons.

Belial, ever the clever one, rightly recognizes their fall into Hell as "the sentence" (2.208) of God upon them. But inspired by Satan's defiance, he too misunderstands the nature of judgment and imagines that their imprisonment is temporary. "This is now / Our doom," he declares, "which if we can sustain and bear, / Our Supream Foe in time may much remit / His anger, and perhaps thus farr remov'd / Not mind us not offending, satisfi'd / With what is punish't" (2.208–13). The truth, of course, is that God's judgment is both final and eternal, and to change it in some way would be to do the impossible and alter the nature of the divine being.

Worst of all is Mammon, who in the manner of Satan not only disrespects the sentence they have received but fills the angels with the grand illusion that they might usurp God's judgment. Like Moloch, Mammon fears having to appear like a criminal before his judge, and he asks, "With what eyes could we / Stand in his presence humble, and receive / Strict Laws impos'd, to celebrate his Throne / With warbl'd Hymns, and to his Godhead sing / Forc't Halleluiah's[?]" (2.239–43). Rather than accept judgment, Mammon imitates Satan's empty rhetoric of freedom when advocating "Hard liberty before the easie yoke / Of servile Pomp" (2.256–57) and emboldening the angels to continue in their disobedience.

Mammon further proposes that the fallen angels "Imitate" (2.270) God's glory and content themselves with the heavenly kingdom they have constructed in Hell. He remembers the throne Satan erected for himself in the heavenly Northlands, which was made "In imitation of that Mount whereon / *Messiah* was declar'd in sight of Heav'n" (5.764–65), and he admires the "Throne of Royal State" (2.1) upon which Satan now sits. Then enthroned on "golden seat's" (1.796), the fallen angels have become gods unto themselves. Mammon suggests that their best good will come from continuing in this capacity, where they pass "peaceful Counsels" (2.279) like the Father and issue judgments of their own making. Through Mammon's evil proposal, Milton indicates that the very worst response to reckoning is to attempt to usurp God's judgment, as the self-crowned Satan had done in Heaven and in Hell and again once more would do.

Satan's Second Coming

As Mammon's proposal reveals, Satan taught the fallen angels that divine judgment can be usurped. When Satan returns to Hell after corrupting Eve, he enviously recalls his rival's promotion in Heaven, when the Father invited the Son to share his throne and "judge / Bad men and Angels" (3.330–31) at the world's end, and presents himself to the fallen angels like Christ at the Second Coming. In Heaven, the Father tells that at the Last Judgment, the Son "attended gloriously from Heav'n / Shalt in the Sky appeer" (3.323–24), at which the heavenly hosts will break out in jubilation. Upon his return to Hell, Satan seeks to imitate this moment when, appearing from on high and seated on a throne, the archangel dazzles his followers like the sun (or Son) bursting through the clouds. "All amaz'd / At that so sudden blaze" (10.452–53), the angels cower before their lord, but ecstatic at his return, shouts of joy soon fill the hellish air as the angels rush forward and congregate around him, eager to hear news of their redemption.

The redemption of fallen community is indeed what Satan proclaims, but whereas the Son's appearance at the Last Judgment would unite humanity with God, Satan's Second Coming divides the angels. In Heaven, Satan heard the Father foretell that the Son would lead the faithful into a "New Heav'n and Earth, / wherein the just shall dwell / And after all thir tribulations long / See golden days" (3.335–37). Envying the Son's role at this future moment, Satan is eager to play the messiah before his own followers, and he proclaims that he has "returnd / Successful beyond hope, to lead ye forth / Triumphant out of this infernal Pit" (10.462–64). Satan invites the angels to "possess, / As Lords, a spacious World, to our native Heaven / Little inferiour, by my adventure hard / With peril great atchiev'd" (10.466–69), just as the saints were prophesied to inherit an eternal world at Christ's return. The Father explains that at that moment, the saints would join God in eternal society, as Christ would become all in all and humanity would become copartner with divinity. By contrast,

Satan's Second Coming inverts this leveling process and reinforces the existing social hierarchy, rather than collapsing it. As his choice of pronouns indicates, Satan's triumph is his alone, and his return to Hell does not elevate the angels to a higher position but rather effects their further debasement.

As he announces the good news of salvation, Satan again flaunts his disregard for divine justice. Mocking the sentence he received in the Garden as inconsequential, even silly, Satan tells the angels:

> True is, mee also he hath judg'd, or rather
> Mee not, but the brute Serpent in whose shape
> Man I deceav'd: that which to mee belongs,
> Is enmity, which he will put between
> Mee and Mankinde; I am to bruise his heel;
> His Seed, when is not set, shall bruise my head:
> A World who would not purchase with a bruise,
> Or much more grievous pain? Ye have th' account
> Of my performance: What remains, ye Gods,
> But up and enter now into full bliss.
>   (10.494–503)

Satan's pride leads him to think that he tricked God into judging the animal, not himself. Gloating that he has deceived God and mankind, Satan is in fact the one deceived, and the extent of his delusion is evident in his diction. Styling himself a martyr who has hazarded much for his people, Satan offers the angels "th' account" of his victory. In doing so, he unknowingly echoes the Son's words to the Father, "Account mee man" (3.238), and thus unintentionally parodies the Son's offer to sacrifice himself for humanity. But whereas the Son's reckoning was characterized by humility, Satan's is anything but humble, and his "account" becomes a rip-roaring tale of his own ingenuity and guile.

At the Last Judgment, the living would join with the dead to form *ecclesia*, but at Satan's Second Coming, a transformation of flesh leads this diabolical community into further ruin. Scripture prophesies that at the Resurrection, "many of them that sleepe in the dust of the earth shall awake, some to everlasting life, and some to shame *and* everlasting contempt" (Dan. 12:2), and in *Paradise Lost*, the Father tells the Son that at his "dread Tribunal" (the Last Judgment), "The living, and forthwith the cited dead / Of all past Ages to the general Doom / Shall hast'n, such a peal shall rouse thir sleep" (3.326–29). At Satan's Second Coming, a miraculous metamorphosis occurs, but instead of saints donning glorified bodies and ascending to Christ, fallen angels assume the shapes of serpents and fall to the ground. Instead of Christ descending from heaven with "a shout, with the voyce of the Archangel" (1 Thess. 4:16), in Hell the "universal shout and high applause" Satan receives quickly sours into "a dismal universal hiss, the sound / Of public scorn" (10.505, 508–9). In his moment of greatest triumph, when Satan is convinced he has successfully robbed God of his judgments, the weight of his own reckoning brings him low, both figuratively and literally. The Son, in his moment of reckoning, is accounted a suitable sacrifice for humanity's disobedience, but Satan, in a similar moment, is accounted no better than a reptile.

As when he fell into Hell, Satan's sin is again to temporalize judgment and to fail to recognize that God judges not once but always. Thinking the fulfillment of his curse would occur sometime in the future—"when is not set," he tells the angels, that Adam's seed should bruise his head—he imagines that they are unaffected in the present, and he invites his mates to "up and enter now into full bliss." When the angels suddenly transform into serpents, they are tempted with tantalizing fruit:

> oft they assayd,
> Hunger and thirst constraining, drugd as oft,
> With hatefullest disrelish writh'd thir jaws
> With soot and cinders fill'd; so oft they fell
> Into the same illusion, not as Man
> Whom they triumph'd once lapst.
>
> (10.567–72)

The repetitive nature of the angels' torment mocks their inability to understand the enduring nature of the judgment they have received. Again and again, the angels try to taste the fruit, only to have it turn to ashes in their mouths. Unlike Adam and Eve, who "once lapst" and learned from their mistake, the angels are doomed to endless acts of idiocy that reflect the temporal limitations of their fallen imaginations. The "doom" (10.517) handed down to Satan from the Son is, in fact, not for a future time but for *all* time. Christ's sacrifice on the cross, when

Satan would at last be defeated, would be merely one step in a divine process of judgment that has been ongoing from the time the angels first fell from Heaven.

Satan does not realize it, but embarrassing encounters with types of the Last Judgment are a recurring fact of his existence. He has faced a judgment like this before, when the Son drove him from Heaven, and he will face one like it again at the Last Judgment, when the Son will "surprise / The Serpent, Prince of aire, and drag in Chaines / Through all his Realme, and there confounded leave" (12.453–55). Michael tells Adam that on that day, the Son would "be reveald / In glory of the Father, to dissolve / *Satan* with his perverted World" (12.545–47), and the great archangel would be no more. Again and again, Satan faces types of the Last Judgment, only to be forcefully shamed into the humility the Son adopts without hesitation. Although Satan himself never learns the lesson, *Paradise Lost* teaches that God's judgments are perpetual and therefore unavoidable, and that while the wicked fear and shun them, the faithful few seek them out with joy.

"Account Mee Man": The Singular Virtues of the Son

While Satan's denial of his sentence taps into the national memory of Charles's trial, in the figure of the Son, Milton shows his readers what a godly response to divine judgment looks like. The first words spoken by the Son in *Paradise Lost* are an acknowledgment of the Father's role as judge. When the Father decrees that humanity would receive grace but the angels none, the Son responds, "Gracious was that word which clos'd / Thy sovran sentence" (3.144–45). Milton's pun on "sentence" (as both a unit of thought and a juridical decree) illustrates the unique character of God's judgment: in the Father's case, to speak is to judge, since he simply utters truth and his sentence is fact.[56] As the Son acknowledges, the Father is "Judg / Of all things made, and judgest onely right" (3.154–55). Unlike Satan, who both denies the Father's authority to judge him and attempts to usurp that authority, the Son correctly identifies judgment as a fundamental part of who the Father is. Satan misconceives of judgment as the form of the Father's revenge upon him, but the Son understands that judgment will be the vehicle for the Father's grace upon a criminal humanity.

Consequently, rather than skirting judgment as Satan does, the Son seeks it out as the instrument by which a fallen community would be reconciled to God. In humanity's trial at the beginning of book 3, the Son welcomes God's judgments as the prerequisite to grace and further fellowship. When the Father asks for a volunteer to stand condemned in humanity's place, the Son steps forward to die on their behalf:

> Behold mee then, mee for him, life for life
> I offer, on mee let thine anger fall
> Account mee man; I for his sake will leave
> Thy bosom, and this glorie next to thee
> Freely put off, and for him lastly dye
> Well pleas'd, on me let Death wreck all his rage;
>
> (3.236–41)

So thoroughly does the Son believe in the Father's judgments, he is willing to die in order to see them carried out. In Sonnet 19 "When I Consider How My Light is Spent," Milton used biblical parables to imagine reckoning as a tallying of sums, and here in *Paradise Lost* he employs similar imagery to describe the fallen state of humanity, which the Son says is "indebted" to the Father but lacks an "offering meet" (3.235, 234) wherewith to pay for its crimes. Recognizing humanity's great need, the Son tells the Father, "Account mee man." Milton's use of zeugma suggests the financial transaction taking place: the Son is inviting the Father both to "account him" (or reckon with him) and also to "account him man," or consider him humanity's stand-in. This, Milton indicates, is true martyrdom, as one man offers to die for the people he loves.[57] Neither dispersing judgment and diluting its effects, nor usurping God's authority to judge, the Son not only submits to reckoning but also asks that all the Father's rage be consolidated in him, so that he alone should suffer the worst of the punishment to come.

Moreover, the Son's sacrifice on the cross and his future sovereignty at the Last Judgment are depicted as two temporal endpoints in the same juridical process. From the perspective of God's Eternal Today, they appear as one and the same moment. In this regard, judgment is both necessary and salvific, and the juridical law that demands the Son's death is also the

law that enables the Son to lead the faithful into the New Heavens and
New Earth, as the Father tells him:

> When thou attended gloriously from Heav'n
> Shalt in the Sky appeer, and from thee send
> The summoning Arch-Angels to proclaime
> Thy dread Tribunal: forthwith from all Windes
> The living, and forthwith the cited dead
> Of all past Ages to the general Doom
> Shall hast'n, such a peal shall rouse thir sleep.
> Then all thy Saints assembl'd, thou shalt judge
> Bad men and Angels, they arraignd shall sink
> Beneath thy Sentence; Hell her numbers full,
> Thenceforth shall be fore ever shut. Mean while
> The World shall burn, and from her ashes spring
> New Heav'n and Earth, wherein the just shall dwell
> (3.323–35)

Ceasing to be judged, the Son becomes the judge. The Father indicates
that the Son's sacrifice on the cross would not be complete until the Last
Judgment, when those of ages past ("the cited dead") would join the faithful remnant still alive upon the Earth ("the living") to form *ecclesia* and
inherit an endless kingdom. Because the Son has "quitted all to save / A
world from utter loss" (3.307–8), he is rewarded with sovereignty over
this new, eternal world. *Lex talionis*—the law that demanded that "Man
[. . .] Shall satisfy for Man" (3.294–95)—also demands that the Son, who
submitted to judgment to an extent that no one ever has, be recompensed
by ruling such as no one ever will.

As the Son comes to learn, reckoning is an instrument not only for
separation but also for cohesion—that is, for gathering around God those
who had wandered and been lost. Unlike Satan, who is temporally limited
in his thinking, the Son sees judgment as the Father sees it, from God's
"prospect high, / Wherein past, present, future he beholds" (3.77–78).
As a result, the Son understands that his rule at the Last Judgment is the
same as his rule in the present. As Raphael relates to Adam, the Father
addressed the heavenly hosts and declared,

> your Head I him appoint;
> And by my Self have sworn to him shall bow

All knees in Heav'n, and shall confess him Lord:
Under his great Vice-regent Reign abide
United as one individual Soule
For ever happie: him who disobeyes
Mee disobeyes, breaks union, and that day
Cast out from God and blessed vision, falls
Into utter darkness

(5.606–14)

In the Eternal Today of Heaven, all times are now, and the Son's judgment at the Last Judgment only appears to be a singular act, when in fact the Son has been judging all along.[58] Milton conveys this sense of judgment's timelessness by describing an event at the dawn of history through two biblical narratives of the Last Judgment at history's end. One narrative is the parable of the talents, and Milton's reference to "utter darkness" recalls the wicked and slothful servant, who was cast out into "outer darkenesse, [where] there shall be weeping and gnashing of teeth" (Matt. 25:30). The second narrative is Saint Paul's description of humanity's final reckoning, which Milton evokes when the Father states that to the Son "shall bow / All knees in Heav'n." "Wee shall all stand before the Judgement seat of Christ," Paul writes, "For it is written, As I live, saith the Lord, every knee shall bow to mee, and every tongue shall confesse to God. So then every one of us shall give accompt of himselfe to God" (Ro. 14:10–12). Paul's word "accompt" (account) elucidates the complex interplay of textual allusions taking place, since the Son has just asked the Father to "Account mee man" in his own moment of reckoning. Whereas Satan's sin was to teach the fallen angels to disrespect judgment, the Son's virtue is to teach the faithful to submit to God, as he does, and offer their own true account.

By giving his account to the Father, the Son makes himself a model for all the faithful who would come after him, both those within *Paradise Lost* and those in Restoration England. As a faithful remnant, the Son alone decides to remain obedient unto judgment. He suggests how a righteous king who submits to God's reckoning might bring healing to his nation, rather than destruction. The Son also inspires others to do as he did, and from Abdiel choosing to seek out judgment from God's throne to Eve choosing to return to the place of judgment, other figures in Milton's epic intuit the Son's obedience and become faithful remnants in their own moments of reckoning. In the figures of Abdiel and Eve, Milton offers models of what his readers might do when, fallen upon dark days, the righteous are in need of the divine truths only judgment can provide.

"Servant of God, Well Done": Abdiel and Counternationalism

Abdiel is another example of singular virtue in a time of apostasy and a testament to the addictive nature of seeking God's judgments. Alone and unaided, Abdiel steps out from the angelic legions to confront Satan. He had recently witnessed a similar act, when the Son offered himself on behalf of humanity while "all the Heav'nly Quire stood mute" (3.217). Abdiel is, in fact, putting into practice the righteous response to judgment he saw the Son employ, and his opposition toward Satan is fueled by the recognition that Satan intends to usurp God's authority as judge. In the heavenly Northlands, Satan appears atop

> his Royal seat
> High on a Hill, far blazing, as a Mount
> Rais'd on a Mount,
>
> [. . .]
>
> In imitation of that Mount whereon
> *Messiah* was declar'd in sight of Heav'n.
> (5.756–58, 764–65)

The throne infuriates Abdiel, since he recognizes it as an idolatrous mockery of God's throne, from which the Son would preside over *ecclesia* at the Last Judgment. Of all the outrageous and blasphemous things Satan has just said, Abdiel hones in on the archangel's affront to the Son's sovereignty at the Last Judgment. He demands to know how Satan can presume to steal from the Son the moment when all "shall bend the knee, and in that honour due / Confess him rightful King?" (5.817–18). By defending Christ's sovereignty, Abdiel defends the promise of *ecclesia*, which the Father has foretold would one day come to pass.

Abdiel's departure from Satan's troops is a decision to exchange a diabolical community for a godly one. Separated from his fellows, Abdiel rediscovers his true identity when he returns to the celestial city and is greeted with "joy and acclamations loud, that one / That of so many Myriads fall'n, yet one / Returnd not lost" (6.23–25). In his early poetry, Milton used parables to describe the remnant's encounter with judgment, and here, Abdiel's association with the one stray sheep out of ninety-nine illustrates his singular virtue. "The sonne of man is come to save that which was lost," Christ says, and so, "if a man have an hundred sheepe, and one of them be gone astray, doth he not leave the ninetie and nine, and goeth into the mountaines, and seeketh that which is gone astray?" (Matt. 18:11–12). Abdiel's homecoming, then, as the one lost sheep that went astray, is a glorious return to godly community, now that the shepherd has led him back to the flock he abandoned.

At Abdiel's homecoming, the parable of the ninety-nine sheep cooperates with a narrative of the remnant, the parable of the talents, to present Abdiel in the manner of the remnant meeting *ecclesia* at the world's end. Like the faithful servants in the parable, Abdiel is greeted with praise for his labors:

> On to the sacred hill
> They led him high applauded, and present
> Before the seat supream; from whence a voice
> From midst a Golden Cloud thus milde was heard.
> Servant of God, well done, well hast thou fought
> The better fight, who single hast maintaind
> Against revolted multitudes the Cause
> Of Truth, in word mightier then they in Armes;
> And for the testimonie of Truth has born
> Universal reproach, far worse to beare
> Then violence: for this was all thy care
> To stand approv'd in sight of God, though Worlds
> Judg'd thee perverse
>
> (6.25–37)

The white-robed saints congregating around Andrewes in Elegy III, the "sweet Societies" who wash Lycidas's hair, and the "Thousands [who] at

[God's] bidding speed" in Sonnet 19—all these literary types of *ecclesia* find their cognate here in Heaven's "friendly Powers" (6.22), who welcome one righteous person into the kingdom of God. As with the Son, Milton emphasizes Abdiel's singular virtue as the remnant. Yet unlike the Son's reckoning, Abdiel's encounter with a type of the Last Judgment is a rare moment of counternationalism in Milton's corpus. The Son's submission to judgment brings about humanity's reconciliation with God; similarly, Eve's decision (as we shall see) to return to the place where she was judged mends the rift between humanity.

But Abdiel's moment of reckoning is different. Building upon the conceit he developed in Sonnet 19, Milton imagines one individual at the Last Judgment, like the servants in the parable reckoning with their lord. But whereas the parable was a rallying cry for reforming the national community, at the moment of Abdiel's homecoming, the parable serves rather to divide than unite. Abdiel's experience suggests to Milton's readers that one must choose *ecclesia* even if the nation does not. Membership in that universal community must take priority over membership in any particular community. Only by extricating himself from a diabolical community and severing all ties to his compatriots can Abdiel prove his faithfulness and rejoin the godly community he left behind.

Consequently, Abdiel constitutes an altogether different model of faithfulness in *Paradise Lost*, in which obedience to God consists of choosing *ecclesia* over all else. Abdiel's decision to abandon his diabolical community anticipates gospel truths that unless a person abandons all, he or she is not worthy of the kingdom of God. "Whosoever he be of you, that forsaketh not all that he hath, he cannot be my disciple," Christ proclaims, and "I am come to set a man at variance against his father, & the daughter against her mother [. . .] [and] he that loveth father or mother more then me, is not worthy of me" (Luke 14:33; Matt. 10:35, 37). In Abdiel's homecoming, the parable of the ninety-nine sheep and the parable of the talents work in conjunction to show Milton's readers the wondrous reception they, too, might soon receive at the Last Judgment. By following Abdiel's example, they might constitute a remnant, that audience "fit [. . .] though few," who remain faithful until the world's end. Abdiel's homecoming indicates that *ecclesia* is the true reward of the faithful, and unless they are willing to sacrifice everything to attain it, they are unworthy of the service to which they have been called.

"[I] to the Place of Judgment Will Return": Eve and Epic Reconciliation

Not everyone in *Paradise Lost* learns from the Son's example, and when the Son curses humanity in the Garden, Adam immediately tries to displace judgment from himself to another. Adam's prevarications recall Satan's evasions, and in an elaborate display of rhetorical acrobatics, Adam tries to weasel his way out of punishment and says, "O Heav'n! in evil strait this day I stand / Before my Judge, either to undergoe / My self the total Crime, or to accuse / My other self, the partner of my life" (10.125–28). Adam's response to judgment, flowery and grandiose in its rhetorical ornamentation, resembles Satan's tirades, and like the fallen angel, he works to avoid reckoning at all costs. For Adam's intention, of course, is not to intercede for his partner (as the Son would do) but instead to offer Eve up as the unwilling scapegoat for his crimes. Adam knows that his sentence is death, and like Satan, he stubbornly refuses to give an honest account of his actions. In doing so, he estranges himself from the one person—Eve—with whom he can relate, and in its moment of testing, humanity becomes further divided.[59]

Unlike Adam, Eve confesses her crime without excuse and gives her account without delay. Overwhelmed with shame at the charge against her, Eve, "confessing soon, yet not before her Judge / Bold or loquacious, thus abasht repli'd. / The Serpent me beguil'd and I did eate" (10.160–62). Eve's short reply anticipates Christ's teachings on speedy confession: "Agree with thine adversarie quickly," he says, and "if thou bring thy gift to the altar, and there remembrest that thy brother hath ought against thee: Leave there thy gift before the altar, and goe thy way, first be reconciled to thy brother" (Matt. 5:25, 23–24). Significantly, the Son does not interrogate Eve further, as he does Adam. Unlike Adam's response, Eve's response to judgment is deemed acceptable, since it recalls the Son's own reaction to reckoning in Heaven. Unbeknownst to Eve, she has imitated the Son's humility, and her simple confession before her judge—"the Serpent me beguil'd and I did eat"—mirrors the Son's simple confession to the Father, "Account mee man." In this moment of testing, when the epic heroes, pushed to their limits, show their true mettle, it is Eve and not Adam who puts into practice the Son's attitude of immediate and unreserved submission to judgment.

Eve further imitates the Son by recognizing that God's judgment ought to unite humanity, rather than divide it. After the Son's decree, Adam attempts to go off on his own, but Eve wants to mend the rift between them. Seeking him out, she tries to assuage his rage. Adam, however, is ruled by his wrath and shouts, "Out of my sight, thou Serpent"! (10.867). Streaming abuses upon her and turning to leave, Adam is caught off guard when Eve

> at his feet
> Fell humble, and imbracing them, besaught
> His peace, and thus proceeded in her plaint.
> Forsake me not thus, *Adam*, witness Heav'n
> What love sincere, and reverence in my heart
> I beare thee, and unweeting have offended,
> Unhappilie deceav'd; thy suppliant
> I beg, and clasp thy knees; bereave me not,
>
> [. . .]
>
> On me exercise not
> Thy hatred for this miserie befall'n,
> On me alreadie lost, mee then thy self
> More miserable; both have sin'd, but thou
> Against God onely, I against God and thee,
> And to the place of judgment will return,
> There with my cries importune Heaven[.]
>   (10.911–18, 927–33)

Eve's supplication before Adam recalls the Son's supplication in Heaven. Like the Son before the Father, Eve presents herself before Adam as though she is on trial. Milton describes her speech as a "plaint" (a statement delivered in court), and Eve confesses her sin and appeals to Heaven as a witness of her love.[60] In her moment of self-sacrifice, Eve unknowingly echoes the Son when he told the Father, "on mee let thine anger fall; / Account mee man [. . .] on me let Death wreck all his rage." Like the Son, her humility as the passive recipient of judgment is evident even at the grammatical level, and Eve too employs the accusative case when begging her husband, "Forsake me not," "bereave me not," and "On me exercise not / Thy hatred." In Hell, the fallen angels mimicked Satan's disregard for God's judgment, and in Eden, the Son finds his own faithful follower in Eve, who comes to learn as the Son did that judgment is God's means of edifying the faithful.[61]

Eve's idea to return to the place of judgment is borrowed from the *Iliad* and evinces Milton's creative reworking of epic for a Protestant readership.[62] Homer is deeply concerned with the political, social, and moral implications of the gods' judgments, and it is fitting that Milton would turn to him when reinventing epic heroism as submission to divine judgment.[63] Eve's declaration that she will return to the place of reckoning recalls one of the most memorable moments in the *Iliad*: when Priam "the godlike," heart-stricken at the loss of his son, obeys the gods' decree to return to the place of Hector's reckoning and seek out the man who killed his son.[64] When Priam arrives at Achilles's tent, Priam softens the warrior's anger by falling before him as a suppliant and urging him to respect the gods, as he does:

> Priam came in unseen by the other men, and standing near him,
> Caught Achilles's knees in his arms and kissed the terrible,
> Man-slaughtering hands, which had killed so many of his sons.
>
> [. . .]
>
> "But respect the gods, Achilles, and have pity on me,
> Remembering your own father; yet I am more pitiable by far, since
> I have endured what no other mortal man upon Earth has yet endured:
> I extend my hand to the face of the man who slayed my children."
> So he spoke, and stirred up in Achilles an outburst of weeping for his own father;
> Grasping Priam by the hand, he pushed the old man back a little.
> They remembered together: Priam, crouched close
> Before the feet of Achilles, cried for man-slaying Hector;
> But Achilles cried for his own father, and then again
> For Patroclus: the sound of their wailing rushed throughout the house.[65]

Priam's selfless act of prostrating himself before his son's killer enables an unexpected moment of heartfelt reconciliation between these two warring peoples. Moved by Priam's extraordinary humility, Achilles forgets his rage, and both men weep in each other's arms for what they have lost. In a key moment in Homer's epic, when Achilles is at the height of his pride, the Greek suddenly learns that there is a different sort of greatness in life, which is epitomized in the abject king weeping before him.

As the king and the warrior mourn together, they restore a social economy of respect that was shattered by Agamemnon ten years earlier, when the Greek commander took Chryseis as his slave and refused to allow her father to ransom her back.[66] For that crime, Apollo struck the Greeks with a plague that fractured their community and sent soldiers into isolation, thereby symbolizing the social corrosion of Agamemnon's toxic leadership. However, at the end of Homer's epic, the bonds of community have been restored by Priam. By returning to the place of his son's reckoning, Troy's king has fixed that which was broken and wrought reconciliation where before was only hatred.

In Milton's revision of the Homeric episode, Eve channels Priam's submissive attitude toward divine judgment.[67] A moment of reconciliation between two warring kings becomes in *Paradise Lost* a moment of Protestant fellowship, as Adam and Eve mourn together over their sin. Eve's heroism is evident in her ability to teach Adam to respect God's judgment, much as Priam taught Achilles piety. Like Achilles, Adam is full of rage and vitriol, but Eve's pleading before him has a wondrous effect, and "soon his heart relented / Towards her, his life so late and sole delight, / Now at his feet submissive in distress" (10.940–42). Lifting her to her feet, Adam accepts Eve's offer of reconciliation and decides that they should indeed return to the place of judgment together. He asks, "What better can we do, then to the place / Repairing where he judg'd us, prostrate fall / Before him reverent, and there confess / Humbly our faults, and pardon beg[?]" (10.1086–89). Until now, Adam had followed a course similar to Satan in fleeing from judgment, but after Eve's instruction, he learns that judgment is not to be avoided but desired. Eve's kneeling becomes their joint strategy of confession, as they return to the place of judgment, kneel, and pray for forgiveness. Rescuing Adam from the convolutions of his mind—those "evasions vain / And reasonings" (10.829–30) that had ensnared him, just they had ensnared Satan before him—Eve has guided her husband to a holy path visible only to those humble enough to look down and pray.[68]

Eve's decision to return, like Priam, to the place of judgment marks her as another faithful remnant in *Paradise Lost*. Like the Son and Abdiel, Eve moves toward judgment (rather than away from it) and demonstrates her singular virtue in doing so. In Milton's revision of epic, Eve's submission to reckoning becomes a new heroic virtue, and her experience has political implications for Milton's readers in Restoration England. To be truly righteous, as Priam and Eve are, is to obey God even when it is terrifying and illogical to do so. If Eve's experience offers a political lesson, it is that the acts of violent and bloody people engender further acts of violence and rage, but the heroic acts of a faithful few have the power to heal old wounds and bring people closer together (and closer to God) than they were before. For like Priam, Eve is privy to a secret her wrathful partner does not know: grace has the capacity to overcome wrath, and simple acts of kindness are the building blocks of any godly society.

The End of the World and the Beginning of *Ecclesia*

In Milton's Protestant revision of epic, seeking out divine judgment becomes a new heroic virtue. Books 11 and 12 of *Paradise Lost* present a series of faithful remnants who put this new virtue into practice. The wicked communities from which Enoch, Noah, Abraham, and Moses emerge, by contrast, are filled with people who spurn God's judgment. The men of Enoch's generation, for instance, style themselves great conquerors, and they despise Enoch for uttering the "odious Truth, that God would come / To judge them with his Saints" (11.704–5). Noah, too, preaches to his own wicked generation of "Judgments imminent: / But all in vain" (11.725–26), and refusing to repent, their world is abolished by the flood. Additionally, Nimrod is a great hunter of men, and in his "Empire tyrannous," he usurps divine authority by claiming from Heaven a "second Sovrantie" (12.32, 35).[69] And while Moses is a godly man who respects God's authority, Pharaoh as well is a "lawless Tyrant" who denies God and "must be compelld by Signes and Judgements dire" (12.173, 175). Both Nimrod and Pharaoh exhibit an alarming disregard for God's judgments. As a result, their nations end in cataclysmic destruction, as Babel is dismantled, its people scattered, and Egypt is consumed by hail and fire from the sky.

Amid debates over Charles's trial in Restoration England, Milton's message about violence would have resonated with contemporary readers, who likely caught the suggestion that kings of "bloody designe" (as Bradshaw had called Charles at his trial) would be visited by divine judgment.[70] In *The Tenure of Kings and Magistrates*, Milton wrote that Charles was a man "lad'n with all the innocent blood spilt in three Kingdoms" (*CPW* 3:197), and he accused Charles of steering the nation recklessly close to a disastrous end. In *Paradise Lost*, Michael's account of perpetual judgment upon tyrants gestures toward Charles I but also to Charles II and the Last Judgment still to come. The nation, Milton suggests, hangs in a precarious balance between national ruin and national redemption. The actions of a few individuals—like Enoch, Noah, and Moses before them—could tip the scales one way or the other. By offering these models, *Paradise Lost* seeks to create a faithful remnant in Restoration England whose pursuit of the Last Judgment might guarantee England's "*Nationall Honours* and *Rewards*" at Christ's return.

The world-ending episodes in Michael's narrative thus work to dislodge a national history Milton found undesirable, in which tyrants like the Stuarts triumphed, and replace it with a narrative of victorious faithful remnants. Through their obedience, these remnants offer hope to Milton's own nation, and by believing that reckoning would redeem fallen community, they constitute godly examples that Englishmen might follow. One could hardly read of Nimrod and Pharaoh without wondering if England, too, faced a similar impending judgment, and if the despotic ambitions of one man had caused the near ruin of an entire nation.[71] By suggesting as much, *Paradise Lost* undermines both royalist accounts of Charles I as a loving benefactor to his people and royalist praises of Charles II as a fatherly king. Far from enjoying what one royalist writer called "that inexpressible Happiness, which these Kingdoms have received by the glorious Restauration of our Sovereign to His Throne," readers of *Paradise Lost* learn, as Adam learns, that violent kings have violent ends.[72] More important, Milton's epic indicates that while one man's refusal to accept God's judgment had devastating consequences, the actions of a faithful few who submit to judgment might be equally powerful and effect the redemption of an entire community.

The serial judgments in books 11 and 12 epitomize a larger narrative pattern in *Paradise Lost*, in which Milton reads Genesis through Revelation.[73] As Milton tells the story of humanity's beginning through the story of humanity's end, the Last Judgment shapes the poem's ideas of justice, obedience, and humility. Like Christ's declaration in scripture, "I am Alpha and Omega, the beginning and the end" (Rev. 22:13), *Paradise Lost* conflates beginnings and endings to draw the totality of divine judgment into the reader's present, the "I am" of temporal existence.

Milton's method of reading the beginning through the end galvanizes his own historical present with new meaning. *Paradise Lost* is punctuated with types and images of the Last Judgment, and they have the combined effect of reminding Milton's readers that divine judgment is always present. Augustine, living in the cataclysmic end of the ancient world, reassured the faithful that God had not forgotten them and his judgments were still near. *[Deus] nunc iudicat*, he wrote, *et ab humani generis initio iudicavit dimittens de paradiso et a ligno vitae separans primos homines peccati magni perpetratores* (God judges even now, and he has been judging from the beginning of the human race when the first humans were expelled from paradise and separated from the tree of life as perpetrators of a great sin).[74] Recycling this Augustinian truth for his own time, in which God seemed worryingly absent in the aftermath of the wars and the Restoration, *Paradise Lost* teaches Milton's readers that judgment is ever present and God is with them even until the end of the age.

Paradise Lost thus seeks to cultivate within its readers an appreciation for a divine perspective that sees beginnings and endings as one and celebrates the world's end as *ecclesia*'s beginning. Adam's hope in a world to come is also the hope of Milton's reader, who learns alongside Adam that the Last Judgment is England's bridge to the kingdom of God, when Christ would be "all in all" (1 Cor. 15:28) with creation. If Satan's sin is to temporalize judgment, to ascribe to it a historicity it does not have, then the correct response is to recognize that judgment is eternally present, as Adam comes to learn, and that a greater community awaits just around the corner. After the Fall of Man and the Son's judgment upon him, Adam was momentarily reduced, like Satan, to thinking temporally. Contemplating his sentence, Adam wondered, "Is this the end / Of this new glorious World"? (10.720–21). Only later, once he has seen worlds destroyed by judgment and rebuilt by the same, does Adam escape the confines of temporal thinking and learn that beginnings and endings are the same to God. "O goodness infinite[!]" (12.469), Adam proclaims at the last, for Michael's narrative ends with a vision of something with which he is now quite familiar, though he has never seen it: the Last Judgment. To a fallen mind, this end-time event might seem like humanity's end, but Adam knows that it is, in fact, just another glorious beginning.

NOTES

Introduction

1. On the history of these editions, see Dan Malan, *Gustave Doré: Adrift on Dreams of Splendor: A Comprehensive Biography and Bibliography* (St. Louis, MO: Malan Classical Enterprises, 1995), 72–103.

2. *Bible, La Sainte* (Tours: A. Mame et fils, 1866), 920.

3. Milton, *Paradise Lost*, ed. by Robert Vaughan (London: Cassell & Co., 1866), sig. B2r.

4. Blanchard Jerrold, *Life of Gustave Doré: with One Hundred and Thirty-Eight Illustrations from Original Drawings by Doré* (London: W. H. Allen & Co., 1891), 143.

5. Doré was a keen student of perspective, and as a child, he often climbed to the tops of mountains to draw. Jerrold, *Life of Gustave Doré*, 5.

6. Bruce M. Metzger and Michael D. Coogan, eds., *The Oxford Companion to the Bible* (Oxford: Oxford University Press, 1993), s.v. "Church," 121–22.

7. David Loewenstein and Paul Stevens, eds., *Early Modern Nationalism and Milton's England* (Toronto: University of Toronto Press, 2008), 4. On writing the nation as a conflicted endeavor, see also Linda Gregerson, "Milton and the Tragedy of Nations," *PMLA* 129, no. 4 (2014); David Baker, *Between Nations: Shakespeare, Spenser, Marvell and the Question of Britain* (Palo Alto: Stanford University Press, 1997); and Richard Helgerson, *Forms of Nationhood: The Elizabethan Writing of England* (Chicago: University of Chicago Press, 1992).

8. Loewenstein, "Milton's Nationalism and the English Revolution: Strains and Contradictions," in Loewenstein and Stevens, *Early Modern Nationalism*, 25.

9. Benedict Anderson, *Imagined Communities: Reflections on the Origin and Spread of Nationalism* (New York: Verso, 1983), 7.

10. With regard to the politics of the invisible church, I am building in particular upon the argument made by Andrew Escobedo, "The Invisible Nation: Church, State, and Schism in Milton's England," in Loewenstein and Stevens, *Early Modern Nationalism*.

11. John Kerrigan, *Archipelagic English: Literature, History, and Politics 1603–1707* (Oxford: Oxford University Press, 2008), 12. See also Philip Schwyzer and Simon Mealor, eds., *Archipelagic Identities: Literature and Identity in the Atlantic Archipelago, 1550–1800* (Aldershot: Ashgate, 2004); Willy Maley, *Nation, State and Empire in English Renaissance Literature: Shakespeare to Milton* (New York: Palgrave, 2003); and Baker and Maley, eds., *British Identities and English Renaissance Literature* (Cambridge: Cambridge University Press, 2002).

12. Kerrigan, *Archipelagic English*, 12.

13. Jürgen Habermas, *The Postnational Constellation: Political Essays* (Cambridge, MA: MIT Press, 2001), 69–70; and Craig Calhoun, *Nations Matter: Culture, History, and the Cosmopolitan Dream* (New York: Routledge, 2007), 31; see also Calhoun, *Nationalism* (Minneapolis: University of Minnesota P, 1997). On literature and the law of nations, see Christopher N. Warren, *Literature and the Law of Nations, 1580–1680* (Oxford: Oxford University Press, 2015).

14. Anderson, *Imagined Communities*, 7.

15. Robert Boyle, *Occasional Reflections upon Several Subjects* (London: W. Wilson, 1665), sig. Mm5v.

16. Bryan Ball, *A Great Expectation: Eschatological Thought in English Protestantism to 1660* (Leiden: Brill, 1975), 37; see also Jeffrey Jue, *Heaven Upon Earth: Joseph Mede (1586–1638) and the Legacy of Millenarianism* (Dordrecht: Springer, 2006); and Peter Toon, ed., *Puritans, The Millennium and the Future of Israel: Puritan Eschatology 1600 to 1660* (Cambridge: James Clarke & Co. Ltd, 1970).

17. The New Testament refers to the Last Judgment as *hēmera kriseōs* (the Day of Judgment); the Greek word *krisis* (from which our word "crisis" derives) means "a separating, [a] distinguishing" and is cognate to the verb *krinō,-ein*, meaning "to judge" (see *LSJ* s.v. κρίσις,-εως, *n*. A.1 and A.2; see also *OED* s.v. "crisis," *n*.; and *LSJ* s.v. κρίνω,-εῖν, *v*. A.II.4, A.I.1., and A.II.1). The Last Judgment, then, might well be called the Day of Separation or even the Day of Crisis, since it threatens to reorganize humanity into new categories of the faithful and wicked.

18. Rosemond Tuve, *A Reading of George Herbert* (London: Faber & Faber, 1952), 108.

19. Julia Reinhard Lupton, *Citizen-Saints: Shakespeare and Political Theology* (Chicago: University of Chicago Press, 2005), 4.

20. Charles Taylor, *A Secular Age* (Cambridge, MA: Belknap Press of Harvard University Press, 2007), 36.

21. Alister Chapman, John Coffey, and Brad Gregory, eds., *Seeing Things Their Way: Intellectual History and the Return of Religion* (South Bend: University of Notre Dame Press, 2009). For the work of the Cambridge school, see primarily Quentin Skinner, *Hobbes and Republican Liberty* (Cambridge: Cambridge University Press, 2008); Skinner, *Visions of Politics*, 3 vols. (Cambridge: Cambridge University Press, 2002); Skinner, *Liberty before Liberalism* (Cambridge: Cambridge University Press, 1998); J. G. A. Pocock, ed., *The Varieties of British Political Thought, 1500–1800* (Cambridge: Cambridge University Press, 1993); Skinner, *The Foundations of Modern Political Thought*, 2 vols. (Cambridge: Cambridge University Press, 1978); and Pocock, *The Ancient Constitution and the Feudal Law: A Study of*

English Historical Thought in the Seventeenth Century (Cambridge: Cambridge University Press, 1957).

22. Of religious enchantment, Taylor admits, "This is perhaps not the best expression; it seems to evoke light and fairies" (*A Secular Age*, 25).

23. Debora Kuller Shuger, *The Renaissance Bible: Scholarship, Sacrifice, and Subjectivity* (Berkeley: University of California Press, 1994).

24. Luther, *Sermons*, ed. and trans. Eugene Klug (Grand Rapids: Baker, 1996), 2:368. On Luther and the Last Judgment, see Heiko Oberman, *Luther: Man between God and the Devil*, trans. Eileen Walliser-Schwarzbart (New Haven, CT: Yale University Press, 1989).

25. On the Last Judgment as a core doctrine of the Reformation, see Gerhard Sauter, "Protestant Theology," in *The Oxford Handbook of Eschatology*, ed. by Jerry L. Walls (Oxford: Oxford University Press, 2008); and T. F. Torrance, *Kingdom and Church: A Study in the Theology of the Reformation* (Edinburgh: Oliver and Boyd, 1956).

26. Church of England, *The Booke of Common Prayer* (London: Robert Barker, 1604), sig. M5r.

27. Church of England, *The Booke of Common Prayer*, sig. M8v.

28. Lancelot Andrewes, *The Pattern of Catechistical Doctrine* (London: Roger Norton, 1650), sig. Mmmv.

29. On eschatology and the everyday, see David Cressy, *Birth, Marriage, and Death: Ritual, Religion, and Life-Cycle in Tudor and Stuart England* (Oxford: Oxford University Press, 1999); and Eamon Duffy, *The Stripping of the Altars: Traditional Religion in England 1400–1580* (New Haven, CT: Yale University Press, 1992), 299–337.

30. Church of England, *The Booke of Common Prayer*, sig. A2v.

31. Church of England, *The Booke of Common Prayer*, sig. A2v.

32. John Donne, *Sermons*, ed. by George Potter and Evelyn Simpson (Berkeley: University of California Press, 1955), 2:266.

33. See primarily Andrea Brady and Emily Butterworth, eds., *The Uses of the Future in Early Modern Europe* (New York: Routledge, 2010); C. A. Patrides and Joseph Wittreich, eds., *The Apocalypse in English Renaissance Thought and Literature: Patterns, Antecedents, and Repercussions* (Ithaca, NY: Cornell University Press, 1984); and Christopher Hill, *The World Turned Upside Down: Radical Ideas During the English Revolution* (London: Temple Smith, 1972).

34. Nicholas McDowell, *The English Radical Imagination: Culture, Religion, and Revolution, 1630–1660* (Oxford: Clarendon, 2003); David Loewenstein, *Representing Revolution in Milton and His Contemporaries: Religion, Politics, and Polemics in Radical Puritanism* (Cambridge: Cambridge University Press, 2001); Christopher Hill, *Milton and the English Revolution* (New York: Viking, 1978); and Hill, *The World Turned Upside Down*. See also Nigel Smith, *Literature and Revolution in England, 1640–1660* (New Haven, CT: Yale University Press, 1994); and Smith, *Perfection Proclaimed: Language and Literature in English Radical Religion 1640–1660* (Oxford: Oxford University Press, 1989).

35. On the distinction between eschatology and apocalypticism, see Bill T. Arnold, "Old Testament Eschatology and the Rise of Apocalypticism," in Walls, *Oxford Handbook of Eschatology*; John J. Collins, "Apocalyptic Eschatology in the Ancient World," in Walls, *Oxford Handbook of Eschatology*; Collins, ed., "Apocalypse: The Morphology of a Genre," special issue, *Semeia* 14 (1979); and Stanley Frost, *Old Testament Apocalyptic: Its Origins and Growth* (London: Epworth Press, 1952).

36. Anna Trapnel, *Strange and Wonderful Newes from White-Hall* (London, 1654), sig. A3r. On the apocalyptic tradition in England, see Katharine Firth, *The Apocalyptic Tradition*

in Reformation Britain: 1530–1645 (Oxford: Oxford University Press, 1979); and Richard Bauckham, *Tudor Apocalypse: Sixteenth-Century Apocalypticism, Millenarianism, and the English Reformation* (Oxford: Sutton Courtenay, 1978).

37. Trapnel, *Strange and Wonderful*, sig. A3r.

38. Paul Christianson, *Reformers and Babylon: English Apocalyptic Visions from the Reformation to the Eve of the Civil War* (Toronto: University of Toronto Press, 1978).

39. Augustine, *De Civitate Dei*, ed. by Bernard Dombart and Alphonsus Kalb (Turnhout: Brepols, 1955), 20.1. On Augustine's eschatology, see Brian Leftow, *Time and Eternity* (Ithaca, NY: Cornell University Press, 1991), 73–111.

40. On medieval radicals and the Last Judgment, see Bernard McGinn, *The Calabrian Abbot: Joachim of Fiore in the History of Western Thought* (New York: Macmillan, 1985); McGinn, *Visions of the End: Apocalyptic Traditions in the Middle Ages* (New York: Columbia University Press, 1979); Marjorie Reeves, *The Influence of Prophecy in the Later Middle Ages: A Study in Joachimism* (Oxford: Clarendon, 1969); and Norman Cohn, *The Pursuit of the Millennium* (London: Secker and Warburg, 1957).

41. Luther, *Sermons*, 1:47.

42. Luther, *Sermons*, 1:38.

43. On the faithful remnant, see Metzger and Coogan, *Oxford Companion to the Bible*, s.v. "Remnant," 645–46.

44. On Luther's historical eschatology, see Irena Backus, *Reformation Readings of the Apocalypse: Geneva, Zurich, and Wittenberg* (Oxford: Oxford University Press, 2000), 6–11, 113–38.

45. Calvin, *Institutes of the Christian Religion*, ed. and trans. John Allen (Philadelphia: Presbyterian Board of Christian Education, 1936), 3:781.

46. Crawford Gribben, "Early Modern Reformed Eschatology," in *The Oxford Handbook of Early Modern Theology, 1600–1800*, ed. Ulrich L. Lehner, Richard A. Muller, and A. G. Roeber (Oxford: Oxford University Press, 2016); and Heinrich Quistorp, *Calvin's Doctrine of the Last Things*, trans. Harold Knight (Richmond, VA: John Knox Press, 1955).

47. Calvin, *Institutes*, 3:779, 780.

48. Philip Sidney, *The Defence of Poesie* (London: Thomas Crede, 1595), sig. Cv.

49. Frank Kermode, *The Sense of an Ending: Studies in the Theory of Fiction* (Oxford: Oxford University Press, 2000), 8.

50. Ryan Netzley, *Lyric Apocalypse: Milton, Marvell, and the Nature of Events* (New York: Fordham University Press, 2014), 12, 68.

51. Paul Stevens, "The Pre-Secular Politics of *Paradise Lost*," in *The Cambridge Companion to Paradise Lost*, ed. Louis Schwartz (Cambridge: Cambridge University Press, 2014), 96.

52. This point is well made, with regard to nationalism, by David Norbrook, *Writing the English Republic: Poetry, Rhetoric and Politics, 1627–1660* (Cambridge: Cambridge University Press, 1999), 7.

53. Richard Baxter, *The Saints Everlasting Rest* (London, 1662), sig. L2r, British Library, call number 1476.aaa.41.

54. See, for instance, William Flesch, "Narrative, Judgment, and Justice in *Paradise Lost*," in *Milton's Rival Hermeneutics: Reason is but Choosing*, ed. Richard J. DuRocher and Margaret Olofson Thickstun (Pittsburgh: Duquesne University Press, 2012), 143.

55. Luther, *Sermons*, 1:51.

56. Luther, *Sermons*, 1:41.

57. Calvin, *Institutes*, 3:783.

58. Donne, *Sermons*, 4:84.

59. Luther, *Sermons*, 1:49.

60. Giorgio Agamben, *The Time That Remains: A Commentary on the Letter to the Romans*, trans. Patricia Dailey (Palo Alto: Stanford University Press, 2010), 33.

61. Tertullian, *Tertulliani Opera*, ed. by E. Dekkers (Turnhout: Brepols, 1954), *Adversus Marcionem*, 3.24.3.

62. Achsah Guibbory, *Christian Identity, Jews, and Israel in Seventeenth-Century England* (Oxford: Oxford University Press, 2010), 7, 11. See also Andrew Escobedo, *Nationalism and Historical Loss in Renaissance England: Foxe, Dee, Spenser, Milton* (Ithaca, NY: Cornell University Press, 2004); Liah Greenfeld, *Nationalism: Five Roads to Modernity* (Cambridge, MA: Harvard University Press, 1992), 51–54; and Christopher Hill, *The English Bible and the Seventeenth-Century Revolution* (London: Allen Lane, 1993).

63. Eric Nelson, *The Hebrew Republic: Jewish Sources and the Transformation of European Political Thought* (Cambridge, MA: Harvard University Press, 2010), 16.

64. Nelson, *Hebrew Republic*, 14.

65. See Metzger and Coogan, *Oxford Companion to the Bible*, s.v. "Remnant," 645–46.

66. William Perkins, *A Godly and Learned Exposition or Commentarie upon the Three First Chapters of the Revelation* (London, 1606), sig. Iv; and Donne, *The Complete English Poems of John Donne*, ed. C. A. Patrides (London: Dent & Sons Ltd, 1985), Holy Sonnet 7 ln. 8.

67. On counternationalism in the period, see Patrick Cheney, *Marlowe's Counterfeit Profession: Ovid, Spenser, Counter-Nationhood* (Toronto: University of Toronto Press, 1997); and David Quint, *Epic and Empire: Politics and Generic Form from Virgil to Milton* (Princeton, NJ: Princeton University Press, 1993).

1. Milton and the Faithful Remnant

1. On the faithful remnant, see Metzger and Coogan, *The Oxford Companion to the Bible*, s.v. "Remnant," 645–46. Milton's belief that he was living in the end times is explored in Juliet Cummins, ed., *Milton and the Ends of Time* (Cambridge: Cambridge University Press, 2003); C. A. Patrides, "'Something Like Prophetick Strain': Apocalyptic Configurations in Milton," in Patrides and Wittreich, *Apocalypse in English Renaissance Thought and Literature*; and Wittreich, *Visionary Poetics: Milton's Tradition and His Legacy* (San Marino, CA: Huntington Library Press, 1979).

2. John Milton, *Of Reformation Touching Church-Discipline in England*, in CPW 1:616. On the apocalyptic vision in *Of Reformation*, see Thomas N. Corns, *Uncloistered Virtue: English Political Literature, 1640–1660* (Oxford: Clarendon, 1992), 12; and Janel Mueller, "Embodying Glory: The Apocalyptic Strain in Milton's *Of Reformation*," in *Politics, Poetics, and Hermeneutics in Milton's Prose*, ed. David Loewenstein and James Grantham Turner (Cambridge: Cambridge University Press, 1990).

3. Paul Stevens, "Milton's Janus-Faced Nationalism: Soliloquy, Subject, and the Modern Nation State," *Journal of English and Germanic Philology* 100, no. 2 (2001). On tensions in Milton's nationalism, see also Loewenstein and Stevens, *Early Modern Nationalism*; Loewenstein, "Late Milton: Early Modern Nationalist or Patriot?" *Milton Studies* 48 (2008); Rachel J. Trubowitz, "Body Politics in *Paradise Lost*," *PMLA* 121, no. 2 (2006); Stevens, "Milton's Nationalism and the Rights of Memory," in *Imagining Death in Spenser and Milton*, ed. Elizabeth Jane Bellamy, Patrick Cheney, and Michael Schoenfeldt (Basingstoke: Palgrave, 2003); Loewenstein, *Representing Revolution*, 175–291; and Stevens, "Milton's 'Renunciation' of Cromwell: The Problem of Raleigh's Cabinet-Council," *Modern Philology* 98, no. 3 (2001).

4. Milton, *Complete Shorter Poems*, ed. Stella P. Revard (Malden, MA: Blackwell, 2009), "Lycidas," ln. 179; and Sonnet 19 "When I Consider How My Light is Spent," ln. 12. References to Milton's shorter poems are to this edition and are hereafter given in the text.

5. Elizabeth Sauer, *Milton, Toleration, and Nationhood* (Cambridge: Cambridge University Press, 2014), 115. On this unmooring of the nation, see Gregerson, "Milton and the Tragedy of Nations."

6. Catherine Gimelli Martin, "The Enclosed Garden and the Apocalypse: Immanent versus Transcendent Time in Milton and Marvell," in *Milton and the Ends of Time*, ed. by Cummins, 151.

7. On Milton's hope that England would prepare the way for the kingdom of God, see Barbara K. Lewalski, "Milton and the Millennium," in Cummins, *Milton and the Ends of Time*.

8. On Neo-Latin epics on the Gunpowder Plot, see John Hale, "Milton and the Gunpowder Plot: *In Quintum Novembris* Reconsidered," *Humanistica Lovaniensia* 50 (2001); and Estelle Haan, "Milton's *In Quintum Novembris* and the Anglo-Latin Gunpowder Epic," *Humanistica Lovaniensia* 41 (1992).

9. Martin Luther, *Luther's Works*, trans. James Atkinson (Philadelphia: Westminster Press, 1966), *To the Christian Nobility of the German Nation*, 44:138.

10. Milton, *Paradise Lost*, ed. Barbara K. Lewalski (Malden, Mass.: Blackwell, 2007), 11.701. Subsequent references to *Paradise Lost* are to this edition.

11. Stevens, "Milton and National Identity," in *The Oxford Handbook of Milton*, ed. Nicholas McDowell and Nigel Smith (Oxford: Oxford University Press, 2009), 347.

12. Robert Appelbaum, "Milton, the Gunpowder Plot, and the Mythography of Terror," *Modern Language Quarterly* 68, no. 4 (2007).

13. Erich Auerbach, *Mimesis: The Representation of Reality in Western Literature: Fiftieth Anniversary Edition*, ed. Edward W. Said (Princeton, NJ: Princeton University Press, 2003), 3–23.

14. John K. Hale, *Milton's Cambridge Latin: Performing in the Genres 1625–1632* (Tempe, AZ: Arizona Center for Medieval and Renaissance Studies, 2005), 128–29.

15. W. B. Patterson, *King James VI and I and the Reunion of Christendom* (Cambridge: Cambridge University Press, 1997).

16. F. P. Wilson, *The Plague in Shakespeare's London* (Oxford: Clarendon, 1927).

17. On the poisonous air in plague time, see Rebecca Totaro, *Suffering in Paradise: The Bubonic Plague in English Literature from More to Milton* (Pittsburgh: Duquesne University Press, 2005).

18. Ryan Hackenbracht, "The Plague of 1625–26, Apocalyptic Anticipation, and Milton's Elegy III," *Studies in Philology* 108, no. 3 (2011).

19. Luther, *Luther's Works*, ed. Atkinson, "Preface to 1530 Edition of the New Testament," 2.

20. Noam Reisner discusses the erotics of this and other Ovidian allusions in "Obituary and Rapture in Milton's Memorial Latin Poems," in Jones, *Young Milton*.

21. See primarily M. J. Edwards, "The Pilot and the Keys: Milton's *Lycidas* 167–171," *Studies in Philology* 108, no. 4 (2011); James Kelly and Catherine Bray, "The Keys to Milton's 'Two-Handed Engine' in *Lycidas* (1637)," *Milton Quarterly* 44, no. 2 (2010); Neil Forsyth, "'Lycidas': A Wolf in Saint's Clothing," *Critical Inquiry* 35, no. 3 (2009); Stella Revard, "*Lycidas*," in Corns, *A Companion to Milton*; and Lawrence Lipking, "The Genius of the Shore: Lycidas, Adamastor, and the Poetics of Nationalism," *PMLA* 111, no. 2 (1996).

22. For the context of Elegy I, see Stella Revard, *Milton and the Tangles of Neaera's Hair: The Making of the 1645 Poems* (Columbia: University of Missouri Press, 1997), 13–16.

23. On the nation as a remedy for barbarism, see Eric B. Song, *Dominion Undeserved: Milton and the Perils of Creation* (Ithaca, NY: Cornell University Press, 2013).

24. Milton's early writings express his discontent with Cambridge, which he believed failed to educate him properly; see Cedric Brown, "John Milton and Charles Diodati: Reading the Textual Exchanges of Friends," in Jones, *Young Milton*; and Sarah Knight, "Milton and the Idea of the University," in Jones, *Young Milton*.

25. Lewalski, *The Life of John Milton: A Critical Biography* (Malden, MA: Blackwell, 2000), 15.

26. Thomas H. Luxon notes that Milton would use also his friendship with Diodati as the basis for the relationship between Adam and Eve in *Paradise Lost*; in *Single Imperfection: Milton, Marriage and Friendship* (Pittsburgh: Duquesne University Press, 2005), 80–81.

27. Gordon Campbell, "King, Edward (1611/12–1637)," in *ODNB*, par. 3, accessed May 29, 2018, http://www.oxforddnb.com.lib-e2.lib.ttu.edu/view/10.1093/ref:odnb/9780198614128.001.0001/odnb-9780198614128-e-15558?rskey=uiolY2&result=17.

28. Eric C. Brown notes that Milton's depiction of the sea as a consuming force is indebted to Virgil in "Underworld Sailors in Milton's 'Lycidas' and Virgil's *Aeneid*," *Milton Quarterly* 36, no. 1 (2002).

29. The search for the body of the departed, and a desire to inscribe it into the landscape, is part of the elegiac work of mourning; see Peter Sacks, *The English Elegy: Studies in the Genre from Spenser to Yeats* (Baltimore: Johns Hopkins University Press, 1985).

30. See Gary Bouchard, *Colin's Campus: Cambridge Life and the English Eclogue* (Selinsgrove, PA: Susquehanna University Press, 2000), 123–27; Amy Boesky, "The Maternal Shape of Mourning: A Reconsideration of *Lycidas*," *Modern Philology* 95, no. 4 (1998); and Marjorie Nicolson, "Milton's 'Old Damoetas,'" *Modern Language Notes* 41, no. 5 (1926).

31. Thomas Corns provides an overview of Milton's early anti-clericalism in "Milton before *Lycidas*," in *Milton and the Terms of Liberty*, ed. Graham Parry and Joad Raymond (Cambridge: D. S. Brewer, 2002).

32. In its representation of judgment, *Lycidas* borrows from Nebuchadnezzar's dream of reckoning; see John Leonard, "That Two-Handed Engine and the Millennium at the Door," in Jones, *Young Milton*.

33. *OED*, s.v. "engine," *n.* III and 13.a.

34. Joad Raymond, *Milton's Angels: The Early-Modern Imagination* (Oxford: Oxford University Press, 2010), 229–24.

35. On this point, see Revard, "*Lycidas*," 258; and Wittreich, *Visionary Poetics*, 92.

36. On the New Heavens and New Earth in *Lycidas*, see Gordon Teskey, "Dead Shepherd: Milton's *Lycidas*," in *Milton's Rival Hermeneutics: "Reason is But Choosing,"* ed. Richard J. DuRocher and Margaret Thickstun (Pittsburgh: Duquesne University Press, 2012); and M. H. Abrams, "Five Types of Lycidas," in *Milton's Lycidas: The Tradition and the Poem*, ed. C. A. Patrides (Columbia: University of Missouri Press, 1983).

37. On Milton's hopes for national reform in the late 1630s, see Thomas N. Corns, "Milton and the Characteristics of a Free Commonwealth," in *Milton and Republicanism*, ed. David Armitage, Armand Himy, and Quentin Skinner (Cambridge: Cambridge University Press, 1995).

38. On "Lycidas" and the vernacular, see Revard, *Milton and the Tangles of Neaera's Hair*, 203–4.

39. Anna K. Nardo, *Milton's Sonnets and the Ideal Community* (Lincoln: University of Nebraska Press, 1979), 100–136. For the political context of the sonnets to Cromwell, Fairfax, and Vane, see Blair Worden, *Literature and Politics in Cromwellian England: John Milton, Andrew Marvell, Marchamont Nedham* (Oxford: Oxford University Press, 2007), 154–261.

40. William B. Hunter Jr. points out that Milton admired the Waldensians for their ancient faith, in "Milton and the Waldensians," *Studies in English Literature* 11, no. 1 (1971).

41. Elizabeth Sauer, "Tolerationism, the Irish Crisis, and Milton's *On the Late Massacre in Piemont,*'" *Milton Studies* 44 (2005).

42. The end-time imagery in Sonnet 18 is documented by Jay Rudd, "Milton's Sonnet 18 and Psalm 137," *Milton Quarterly* 26, no. 3 (1992); John Knott, "The Biblical Matrix of Milton's 'On the Late Massacre in Piemont,'" *Philological Quarterly* 62, no. 2 (1983); and Kester Svendsen, "Milton's Sonnet on the Massacre in Piedmont," *Shakespeare Bulletin* 20 (1945).

43. Milton, *Paradise Regain'd: A Poem, in Four Books. To which is added Samson Agonistes and Poems upon Several Occasions*, ed. Thomas Newton (London, 1752), 530.

44. See, among others, Angelica Duran, "The Blind Bard, According to John Milton and His Contemporaries," *Mosaic* 46, no. 3 (2013); Tobias Gregory, "Murmur and Reply: Rereading Milton's Sonnet 19," *Milton Studies* 51 (2010); Margaret Thickstun, "Resisting Patience in Milton's Sonnet 19," *Milton Quarterly* 44, no. 3 (2010); David V. Urban, "The Talented Mr. Milton: A Parabolic Laborer and His Identity," *Milton Studies* 43 (2004); and Dayton Haskin, *Milton's Burden of Interpretation* (Philadelphia: University of Pennsylvania Press, 1994).

45. John Shawcross, *John Milton: The Self and the World* (Lexington: University of Kentucky Press, 1993), 73–76, 168–69, 327n13; William Riley Parker, *Milton: A Biography* (Oxford: Clarendon, 1968), 2:1042–43n140; Parker, "The Dates of Milton's Sonnets on Blindness," *PMLA* 73, no. 3 (1958); and Shawcross, "Milton's Sonnet 19: Its Date of Authorship and Its Interpretation," *Notes and Queries* 4 (1957). See also Joseph Pequigney, "Milton's Sonnet XIX Reconsidered," *Texas Studies in Literature and Language* 8, no. 4 (1967). Labeling Parker's nonbiographical reading as "unorthodox" in their *Variorum Commentary*, A. S. P. Woodhouse and Douglas Bush nonetheless confess that biographical interpretations of Sonnet 19 rely upon conjecture—"the state of mind [the poem] expresses" at a theorized moment in Milton's life—rather than hard evidence. Milton, *The Minor Poems*, ed. Woodhouse and Bush, vol. 2 of *A Variorum Commentary on the Poems of John Milton*, ed. Merritt Hughes (New York: Columbia University Press, 1970), 462.

46. On the ordering of Milton's sonnets, see Lewalski, *The Life of John Milton*, 635n68; Milton, *The Major Works*, ed. Stephen Orgel and Jonathan Goldberg (Oxford: Oxford University Press, 1991), 782–83; Maurice Kelley, "Milton's Later Sonnets and the Cambridge Manuscript," *Modern Philology* 54, no. 1 (1956); and James Holly Hanford, "The Arrangement and Dates of Milton's Sonnets," *Modern Philology* 18, no. 9 (1921).

47. On Milton's innovativeness in politicizing this personal genre, see Barbara K. Lewalski, "Contemporary History as Literary Subject: Milton's Sonnets," *Milton Quarterly* 47, no. 4 (2013); R. F. Hall, "Milton's Sonnets and His Contemporaries," in *The Cambridge Companion to Milton*, ed. by Dennis Danielson (Cambridge: Cambridge University Press, 1999); and Nardo, *Milton's Sonnets*, 100–136.

48. Milton, *The Reason of Church-Government Urg'd against Prelaty*, in CPW 1:795.

49. Haskin, *Milton's Burden*, 33; and Ryan Hackenbracht, "Milton and the Parable of the Talents: Nationalism and the Prelacy Controversy in Revolutionary England," *Philological Quarterly* 94, nos. 1–2 (2015).

50. On Milton and the Smectymnuans, see Feisal G. Mohamed, "Milton, Sir Henry Vane, and the Brief but Significant Life of Godly Republicanism," *Huntington Library Quarterly* 76, no. 1 (2013); N. H. Keeble, "Pamphlet Wars," in Dobranski, *Milton in Context*; Neil Forsyth, "The English Church," in Dobranski, *Milton in Context*; Thomas Kranidas, *Milton and the Rhetoric of Zeal* (Pittsburgh: Duquesne University Press, 2005); and Joad Raymond, "The Literature of Controversy," in Corns, *A Companion to Milton*.

51. Edmund Calamy, *Gods Free Mercy to England* (London, 1641/2), sigs. A4v, D3v.

52. Calamy, *Gods Free Mercy*, sigs. A4v, D3v.

53. Stephen Marshall, *Meroz Curse for Not Helping the Lord against the Mightie* (London, 1641), sig. A2r.

54. Marshall, *Meroz Curse*, sigs. A3v–A4r.

55. Marshall, *The Strong Helper or, the Interest, and Power of the Prayers of the Destitute* (London: Richard Cotes, 1645), sig. B2r.

56. Jeffrey Alan Miller, "Milton and the Conformable Puritanism of Richard Stock and Thomas Young," in Jones, *Young Milton*.

57. Thomas Young, *Hopes Incouragement Pointed at in a Sermon* (London, 1643/4), sig. D2r.

58. Young, *Hopes Incouragement*, sig. F2v.

59. Young, *Hopes Incouragement*, sig. F2v.

60. Additionally, Samuel Hartlib, dedicatee of Milton's *Of Education*, used the parable to teach his countrymen that, as they labored on behalf of religion, they built the kingdom of God: "For the very Reformation itself (if truly compleated) will oblige the Nation more effectually, then ever hitherto it hath bin; to mind a further Interest both in the generall Communion of Saints, and in the Universall Kingdom of God: For then Christs saying wil take place in Us, *Luk.* 12.48. *Unto whomsoever much is given, of him shall bee much required; and to whom men have committed much, of him they will aske the more.* Therefore whatever blessing through redress of our Evils in our Reformation shall be attained by Us, or advanced to Us within this State, God will not conferre it upon us, that it should rest there and lye dead as a Talent buried in the ground; but he will expect that we should trade with it, and make it usefull in his service towards All for the enlargement of his Kingdome." *Considerations Tending to the Happy Accomplishment of England's Reformation in Church and State* (London, 1647), sigs. B4r-B4v.

61. Scholars are divided over whether the phrase is an indication of the poem's date of composition or a literary device; on the former, see Campbell, "Milton, John (1608–1674)," in *ODNB*, par. 48, accessed May 29, 2018, http://www.oxforddnb.com.lib-e2.lib.ttu.edu/view/10.1093/ref:odnb/9780198614128.001.0001/odnb-9780198614128-e-18800?rskey=y2ggy2&result=6; on the latter, see Dixon Fiske, "Milton in the Middle of Life: Sonnet XIX," *English Literary History* 41, no. 1 (1974); Lawrence Sasek, "'Ere Half My Days': A Note on Milton's *Sonnet 19*," *Milton Quarterly* 15, no. 1 (1981); Rene Rapin, "Milton's Sonnet XIX," *Notes and Queries* 20 (1973); and Shawcross, "Milton's Sonnet 19."

62. On Milton's use of conscience as a defining characteristic of the nation, see Giuseppina Iacono Lobo, *Writing Conscience and the Nation in Revolutionary England* (Toronto: University of Toronto Press, 2017), 150–84.

63. Victoria Silver observes that the speaker is "telling a story [. . .] about the way he conceives his identity in relation to God's judgment," in "*Lycidas* and the Grammar of Revelation," *English Literary History* 58, no. 4 (1991): 786.

64. David V. Urban, "Talents and Labourers: Parabolic Tension in Milton's Sonnet 19," in *Milton in France*, ed. Christophe Tournu (New York: Peter Lang, 2008).

65. Sharon Achinstein, *Milton and the Revolutionary Reader* (Princeton, NJ: Princeton University Press, 1994), 16.

66. My translation of John 15:4.

2. Postponing the Last Judgment

1. Nicholas D. Jackson, *Hobbes, Bramhall and the Politics of Liberty and Necessity: A Quarrel of the Civil Wars and Interregnum* (Cambridge: Cambridge University Press, 2007).

2. John Bramhall, *Castigations of Mr. Hobbes His Last Animadversions, in The Case Concerning Liberty, and Universal Necessity. With an Appendix Concerning The Catching of Leviathan, Or the Great Whale* (London: E. T., 1658), sigs. Dd7r-Dd8r.

3. Jackson, *Hobbes, Bramhall*; Parkin, *Taming the Leviathan: The Reception of the Political and Religious Ideas of Thomas Hobbes in England, 1640–1700* (Cambridge: Cambridge University Press, 2007); and Martinich, *The Two Gods of Leviathan: Thomas Hobbes on Religion and Politics* (Cambridge: Cambridge University Press, 1992). Other major studies of Hobbes as a religious thinker include George Herbert Wright, *Religion, Politics, and Thomas Hobbes* (Dordrecht: Springer, 2006); Bernard Baumrin, "Hobbes's Christian Commonwealth," *Hobbes Studies* 13 (2000); Patricia Springborg, "Hobbes, Heresy, and the *Historia Ecclesiastica*," *Journal of the History of Ideas* 55, no. 4 (1994); F. C. Hood, *The Divine Politics of Thomas Hobbes: An Interpretation of Leviathan* (Oxford: Clarendon, 1964); and Howard Warrender, *The Political Philosophy of Hobbes: His Theory of Obligation* (Oxford: Clarendon, 1957). On Hobbes as largely secular in his thinking, see for example Jeffrey R. Collins, *The Allegiance of Thomas Hobbes* (Oxford: Oxford University Press, 2005); Skinner, *Liberty before Liberalism*; Skinner, *Reason and Rhetoric in the Philosophy of Thomas Hobbes* (Cambridge: Cambridge University Press, 1996); and Edwin Curley, "'I Durst Not Write So Boldly,' or How to Read Hobbes's Theological-Political Treatise," in *Hobbes e Spinoza*, ed. Emilia Giancotti (Naples: Bibliopolis, 1992). This view was popularized in the early twentieth century by Leo Strauss, *The Political Philosophy of Thomas Hobbes: Its Basis and Its Genesis* (Oxford: Clarendon, 1936).

4. On Hobbes's absolutism and its historical context, see Johann P. Sommerville, "Hobbes and Absolutism," in *The Oxford Handbook of Hobbes*, ed. A. P. Martinich and Kinch Hoekstra (Oxford: Oxford University Press, 2016). Hobbesian sovereignty builds upon a medieval political tradition that associated ruling with regal power (*potestas*) and majesty (*maiestas*); see Conal Condren, "Sovereignty," in *The Oxford Handbook of British Philosophy in the Seventeenth Century*, ed. Peter R. Anstey (Oxford: Oxford University Press, 2013).

5. Hobbes's decision to write *Leviathan* in English was also an attempt to distinguish himself from continental philosophers; see Richard Serjeantson, "Becoming a Philosopher in Seventeenth-Century Britain," in Ansey, *Oxford Handbook of British Philosophy*, 29.

6. Andrew Angel, *Chaos and the Son of Man: The Hebrew Chaoskampf Tradition in the Period 515 BCE to 200 CE* (London: T & T Clark, 2006); Rebecca Watson, *Chaos Uncreated: A Reassessment of the Theme of Chaos in the Hebrew Bible* (Berlin: Walter de Gruyter, 2005); Neil Forsyth, *The Old Enemy: Satan and the Combat Myth* (Princeton, NJ: Princeton University Press, 1987); and Mary Wakeman, *God's Battle with the Monster: A Study in Biblical Imagery* (Leiden: Brill, 1973).

7. Carl Schmitt, *The Leviathan in the State Theory of Thomas Hobbes: Meaning and Failure of a Political Symbol*, trans. George Schwab and Erna Hilfstein (Westport, CT: Greenwood, 1996), 46. On the symbolism of the leviathan, see also Patricia Springborg, "Hobbes's Biblical Beasts: Leviathan and Behemoth," *Political Theory* 23, no. 2 (1995).

8. William Shakespeare, *The Riverside Shakespeare*, ed. G. Blakemore Evans (Boston: Houghton Mifflin, 1997), *Richard II* (2.1.40). Hobbes's antipathy to republicanism is documented by Quentin Skinner, *Hobbes and Republican Liberty*.

9. In addition to the two scholarly camps that identify Hobbes as a religious thinker or a secular one, Richard Tuck offers a third alternative, in which Hobbes anticipates the Deism of the eighteenth-century philosophers; see Tuck, "The Christian Atheism of Thomas Hobbes," in *Atheism from the Reformation to the Enlightenment*, ed. Michael Hunter and David Wootton (Oxford: Clarendon, 1991); and Tuck, *Natural Rights Theories: Their Origin and Development* (Cambridge: Cambridge University Press, 1979).

10. On Abraham Bosse and Hobbes's involvement in the title page's design, see Horst Bredekamp, "Thomas Hobbes's Visual Strategies," in *The Cambridge Companion to Hobbes's "Leviathan,"* ed. Patricia Springborg (Cambridge: Cambridge University Press, 2007); and Bredekamp, *Thomas Hobbes Visuelle Strategien: Der Leviathan, Urbild des modernen Staates; Werkillustrationen und Portraits* (Berlin: Akademie Verlag, 1999), 39–52.

11. Emile Mâle, *The Gothic Image: Religious Art in France of the Thirteenth Century*, trans. Dora Nussey (New York: Harper & Row, 1958), 355–87.

12. Christine Göttler, *Last Things: Art and the Religious Imagination in the Age of Reform* (Turnhout: Brepols, 2010).

13. On Hobbes's *Elements of Law* and its contentious reception, see Noel Malcolm, "Hobbes and Spinoza," in *The Cambridge History of Political Thought 1450–1700*, ed. J. H. Burns (Cambridge: Cambridge University Press, 1991).

14. For an account of the tympanum's iconography, see Alain Erlande-Brandenburg and Caroline Rose, *Notre-Dame de Paris* (New York: Harry N. Abrams, Inc., 1998), 105–10.

15. The arch's significance as a framing device is discussed in Valerie Shrimplin, *Sun-Symbolism and Cosmology in Michelangelo's Last Judgment* (Kirksville, MO: Truman State University Press, 2000), 53. Keith Brown notes that the arch serves a similar function in *Leviathan*'s title page; see Brown, "The Artist of the *Leviathan* Title-Page," *British Library Journal* 4, no. 1 (1978): 26.

16. For an account of the tympanum's iconography, see Sumner McKnight Crosby and Pamela Z. Blum, *The Royal Abbey of Saint-Denis: From Its Beginnings to the Death of Suger, 475–1151* (New Haven, CT: Yale University Press, 1987), 182–87.

17. On the politics of messianism in the seventeenth century, see Richard H. Popkin and Matthew Goldish, eds., *Millenarianism and Messianism in Early Modern European Culture.* Vol. 1. *Jewish Messianism in the Early Modern World* (Dordrecht: Kluwer, 2001).

18. Steven Ozment, *The Serpent and the Lamb: Cranach, Luther, and the Making of the Reformation* (New Haven, CT: Yale University Press, 2010), 39–42, 106–10; David Hotchkiss Price, *Albrecht Dürer's Renaissance: Humanism, Reformation, and the Art of Faith* (Ann Arbor: University of Michigan Press, 2006), 29–65; Frances Carey, *The Apocalypse and the Shape of Things to Come* (Toronto: University of Toronto Press, 1999), 99–114; and Jaroslav Pelikan, *The Reformation of the Bible / The Bible of the Reformation* (New Haven, CT: Yale University Press, 1996), 63–69.

19. S. L. Greenslade, ed., *The Cambridge History of the Bible.* Vol. 3. *The West from the Reformation to the Present Day* (Cambridge: Cambridge University Press, 1963), 94–103, 141–68; and F. F. Bruce, *The English Bible: A History of Translations* (Oxford: Oxford University Press, 1961), 42–112.

20. Hobbes, *Leviathan* (2.17.13). References to Hobbes's text are from *Leviathan: With Selected Variants from the Latin Edition of 1668*, ed. Edwin Curley (Indianapolis: Hackett, 1994), and subsequent references are given in text as part, chapter, and section.

21. On Hobbes and social contract theory, see Victoria Kahn, *Wayward Contracts: The Crisis of Political Obligation in England, 1640–1674* (Princeton, NJ: Princeton University Press, 2004); Deborah Baumgold, *Hobbes's Political Theory* (Cambridge: Cambridge University Press, 1988); Klaus-Michael Kodalle, "Covenant: Hobbes's Philosophy of Religion and His Political System 'More Geometrico,'" in *Hobbes's Science of Natural Justice*, ed. C. Walton and P. J. Johnson (Dordrecht: Nijhoff, 1987); Jean Hampton, *Hobbes and the Social Contract Tradition* (Cambridge: Cambridge University Press, 1986); and Quentin Skinner, "The Ideological Context of Hobbes's Theory of Political Obligation," in *Hobbes and Rousseau: A Collection of Critical Essays*, ed. Maurice Cranston and Richard Peters (Garden City, NY: Doubleday, 1972).

22. On reason as a guiding principle in Hobbes's biblical hermeneutics, see James Farr, "Atomes of Scripture: Hobbes and the Politics of Biblical Interpretation," in *Thomas Hobbes and Political Theory*, ed. Mary G. Dietz (Lawrence: University of Kansas Press, 1990).

23. Ryan Hackenbracht, "Hobbes's Hebraism and the Last Judgement in *Leviathan*," in *Identities in Early Modern English Writing: Religion, Gender, Nation*, ed. Lorna Fitzsimmons (Turnhout: Brepols, 2014); and Nelson, *The Hebrew Republic*.

24. Jewish influence on seventeenth-century political philosophy is discussed in Jeffrey Shoulson, *Fictions of Conversion: Jews, Christians, and Cultures of Change in Early Modern England* (Philadelphia: University of Pennsylvania Press, 2013); Jason P. Rosenblatt, *Renaissance England's Chief Rabbi: John Selden* (Oxford: Oxford University Press, 2006); and Allison Coudert and Shoulson, eds., *Hebraica Veritas? Christian Hebraists and the Study of Judaism in Early Modern Europe* (Philadelphia: University of Pennsylvania Press, 2004).

25. On the tradition of ruling as judging in western history, see Ernst H. Kantorowicz, *The King's Two Bodies: A Study in Medieval Political Theology* (Princeton, NJ: Princeton University Press, 1957), 87–192.

26. Gary Herbert, "Fear of Death and the Foundations of Natural Right in the Philosophy of Thomas Hobbes," *Hobbes Studies* 7 (1994): 56; and Robert Kraynak, *History and Modernity in the Thought of Thomas Hobbes* (Ithaca, NY: Cornell University Press, 1990), 66.

27. On Hobbes's theory of personation, see A. P. Martinich, "Authorization and Representation in Hobbes's *Leviathan*," in Martinich and Hoekstra, *Oxford Handbook of Hobbes*; Franck Lessay, "Hobbes's Covenant Theology and Its Political Implications," in Springborg, *Cambridge Companion to Hobbes's "Leviathan"*; and Quentin Skinner, "Hobbes on Persons, Authors and Representatives," in Springborg, *Cambridge Companion to Hobbes's "Leviathan."*

28. John Deigh, "Political Obligation," in Martinich and Hoekstra, *Oxford Handbook of Hobbes*, 301.

29. Martin Luther, *Luther's Works*, ed. and trans. Pelikan et al., Vol. 22: *Sermons on the Gospel of St. John, Chapters 1–4* (Saint Louis, MO: Concordia Publishing House, 1955–59), 53.

30. Michael Fixler, *Milton and the Kingdoms of God* (Evanston, IL: Northwestern University Press, 1964).

31. See Nelson, *The Hebrew Republic*. On Hobbes's opposition to republicanism, see Skinner, *Hobbes and Republican Liberty*.

32. Hobbes uses the kingdom of God as both a historical kingdom and an abstract ideal; see Naomi Sussmann, "How Many Commonwealths can *Leviathan* Swallow? Covenant, Sovereign and People in Hobbes's Political Theory," *British Journal for the History of Philosophy* 18, no. 4 (2010).

33. Martinich, *The Two Gods of Leviathan*, 262.

34. My thanks to A. P. Martinich for pointing out to me the difference between these two accounts of the Saul narrative.

35. On Hobbes's materialism, see Stephen M. Fallon, *Milton among the Philosophers: Poetry and Materialism in Seventeenth-Century England* (Ithaca, NY: Cornell University Press, 1991); and Thomas Spragens, *The Politics of Motion: The World of Thomas Hobbes* (Lexington: University of Kentucky Press, 1973).

36. J. G. A. Pocock, *Politics, Language, and Time: Essays on Political Thought and History* (New York: Atheneum, 1971), 186.

37. Hobbes is opposed, in particular, to the Calvinist resistance theory popularized in the British Isles by George Buchanan, which resurfaced during the English Revolution; see Sarah Hutton, *British Philosophy in the Seventeenth Century* (Oxford: Oxford University

Press, 2015), 116–18; and Quentin Skinner, *Foundations of Modern Political Thought*, vol. 2, 189–238.

38. See Fallon, *Milton among the Philosophers*; and Pocock, *Politics, Language, and Time*.

39. Jacques Derrida, "No Apocalypse, Not Now (Full Speed Ahead, Seven Missiles, Seven Missives)," *Diacritics* 14, no. 2 (1984): 23.

40. *OED*, s.v. "actually," accessed May 29, 2018, http://www.oed.com.lib-e2.lib.ttu.edu/view/Entry/1980?redirectedFrom=actually#eid.

41. On Hobbes and human reason, see Adrian Blau, "Reason, Deliberation, and the Passions," in Martinich and Hoekstra, *Oxford Handbook of Hobbes*.

42. Parkin, *Taming the Leviathan*, 16. On the reception of *Leviathan*, see also Samuel Mintz, *The Hunting of Leviathan: Seventeenth-Century Reactions to the Materialism and Moral Philosophy of Thomas Hobbes* (Cambridge, MA: Harvard University Press, 1962).

43. On Hobbes and the accusation of atheism, see Alan Cromartie, "The God of Thomas Hobbes," *The Historical Journal* 51, no. 4 (2008); and Nigel Smith, "The Charge of Atheism and the Language of Radical Speculation, 1640–1660," in Hunter and Wootton, *Atheism from the Reformation*.

44. At the time, this accusation was part of a larger debate over Erastianism; see A. P. Martinich, "Interpreting the Religion of Thomas Hobbes: An Exchange: Hobbes's Erastianism and Interpretation," *Journal of the History of Ideas* 70, no. 1 (2009); Johann P. Sommerville, "Hobbes, Selden, Erastianism, and the History of the Jews," in *Hobbes and History*, ed. G. A. J. Rogers and Tom Sorrell (New York: Routledge, 2000); and David Johnston, *The Rhetoric of Leviathan: Thomas Hobbes and the Politics of Cultural Transformation* (Princeton, NJ: Princeton University Press, 1986), 174.

45. Richard Baxter, *Humble Advice: Or the Heads of Those Things Which Were Offered to Many Honourable Members of Parliament* (London, 1654/5), sig. B2r.

46. Baxter, *Humble Advice*, sig. B2r.

47. Filmer, *Observations Concerning the Originall of Government* (London, 1652), sig. Cv.

48. Filmer, *Observations*, sig. C2r.

49. Bramhall, *Castigations*, sig. Gg4v.

50. Bramhall, *Castigations*, sig. Hh6r.

51. Bramhall, *Castigations*, sig. Hh7r.

52. Bramhall, *Castigations*, sig. N5v.

3. Turning Swords into Plowshares

1. Coppe, *A Fiery Flying Roll* (London, 1649/50). References to *A Fiery Flying Roll* are to this copy and are hereafter given in the text by signature mark.

2. Coppe, *A Second Fiery Flying Roule* (London, 1649/50). References to *A Second Fiery Flying Roule* are to this copy and are hereafter given in the text by signature mark.

3. See Prasanta Chakravarty, *"Like Parchment in the Fire": Literature and Radicalism in the English Civil War* (New York: Routledge, 2006); McDowell, *The English Radical Imagination*; Robert Appelbaum, *Literature and Utopian Politics in Seventeenth-Century England* (Cambridge: Cambridge University Press, 2002); and Hill, *The World Turned Upside Down*.

4. John Lilburne, *The Second Part of England's New-Chaines Discovered*, in *The Leveller Tracts 1647–1653*, ed. William Haller and Godfrey Davies (New York: Columbia University Press, 1944), 189. On the Levellers' influence on the Diggers, see Henry Noel Brailsford, *The Levellers and the English Revolution* (London: Cresset, 1961).

5. James Holstun, *Ehud's Dagger: Class Struggle in the English Revolution* (New York: Verso, 2000). Holstun discusses the relationship between economics and utopianism in *A Rational Millennium: Puritan Utopias of Seventeenth-Century England and America* (Oxford: Oxford University Press, 1987).

6. The Digger and Ranter movements were an important step toward popular sovereignty; see Nicholas McDowell, "Ideas of Creation in the Writings of Richard Overton the Leveller and *Paradise Lost*," *Journal of the History of Ideas* 66, no. 1 (2005).

7. Linda Woodbridge, *English Revenge Drama: Money, Resistance, Equality* (Cambridge: Cambridge University Press, 2010); David Hawkes, *Idols of the Marketplace: Idolatry and Commodity Fetishism in English Literature, 1580–1680* (New York: Palgrave, 2001); and Marc Shell, *Money, Language, and Thought: Literary and Philosophical Economies from the Medieval to the Modern Era* (Berkeley: University of California Press, 1982), 1–4, 24–83.

8. Ariel Hessayon notes that although the Diggers were wary of the Ranters, both groups shared "a profound sense of community" based on their belief in the present revelation of spiritual truths; see Hessayon, "Abiezer Coppe and the Ranters," in *The Oxford Handbook of Literature and the English Revolution*, ed. Laura Lunger Knoppers (Oxford: Oxford University Press, 2012), 358.

9. A detailed account of the Cobham events can be found in David Taylor, "Gerrard Winstanley at Cobham," in *Winstanley and the Diggers, 1649–1999*, ed. Andrew Bradstock (London: Frank Cass, 2000).

10. Winstanley, *The Complete Works of Gerrard Winstanley*, ed. Thomas N. Corns, Ann Hughes, and David Loewenstein (Oxford: Oxford University Press, 2009), *The New Law of Righteousness*, 1:508. References to Winstanley's works are to this edition and are hereafter given in the text by volume number and page number.

11. See primarily Thomas N. Corns, "'I Have Writ, I Have Acted, I Have Peace': The Personal and the Political in the Writings of Winstanley and Some Contemporaries," *Prose Studies* 36, no. 1 (2014); Geoff Kennedy, *Diggers, Levellers, and Agrarian Capitalism: Radical Political Thought in Seventeenth-Century England* (Lanham, MD: Lexington Books, 2008); and John Gurney, *Brave Community: The Digger Movement in the English Revolution* (Manchester: Manchester University Press, 2007).

12. Joanna Picciotto, *Labors of Innocence in Early Modern England* (Cambridge, MA: Harvard University Press, 2010), 57.

13. David Loewenstein, "Gerrard Winstanley and the Diggers," in Knoppers, *The Oxford Handbook of Literature and the English Revolution*; Loewenstein, "Digger Writing and Rural Dissent in the English Revolution: Representing England as a Common Treasury," in *The Country and the City Revisited: England and the Politics of Culture, 1550–1850*, ed. Gerald MacLean, Donna Landry, and Joseph P. Ward (Cambridge: Cambridge University Press, 1999); George Shulman, *Radicalism and Reverence: The Political Thought of Gerrard Winstanley* (Berkeley: University of California Press, 1989), 76, 121; and T. Wilson Hayes, *Winstanley the Digger: A Literary Analysis of Radical Ideas in the English Revolution* (Cambridge, MA: Harvard University Press, 1979), 7. The recession itself is described in Steve Hindle, "Dearth and the English Revolution: The Harvest Crisis of 1647–50," *The Economic History Review* 61, no. S1 (2008).

14. The influence of Winstanley's bankruptcy on his commitment to "things in common" is discussed in J. C. Davis and J. D. Alsop, "Winstanley, Gerrard (bap. 1609, d. 1676)," *ODNB*, accessed May 29, 2018, http://www.oxforddnb.com.lib-e2.lib.ttu.edu/view/10.1093/ref:odnb/9780198614128.001.0001/odnb-9780198614128-e-29755?rskey=xECLKw&result=1; Alsop, "Gerrard Winstanley: What Do We Know of his Life?" in Bradstock, *Winstanley and the Diggers*; and Alsop, s.v. "Gerrard Winstanley," in *Biographical Dictionary of British Radicals in the Seventeenth Century*, ed. Richard Greaves and Robert Zaller (Brighton: Harvester, 1982–84).

15. On the centrality of soil to Winstanley's utopianism, see Loewenstein, "Gerrard Winstanley and the Diggers," 329.

16. On the Digger communities as new Edens, see John Rogers, *The Matter of Revolution: Science, Poetry, and Politics in the Age of Milton* (Ithaca, NY: Cornell University Press, 1996), 39–50.

17. On Winstanley's adaptive typology, see Bradstock, "Theological Aspects of Winstanley's Writings," *Prose Studies* 36, no. 1 (2014); and Bradstock, "Restoring all Things from the Curse: Millenarianism, Alchemy, Science and Politics in the Writings of Gerrard Winstanley," in *The Arts of 17th-Century Science: Representations of the Natural World in European and North American Culture*, ed. Claire Jowitt and Diane Watt (Aldershot: Ashgate, 2002).

18. See Kennedy, *Diggers, Levellers, and Agrarian Capitalism.*

19. Lewis Berens observes that in Winstanley's understanding of history, "[on] the day of Judgement, the good will triumph, Reason will cast out Covetousness, Universal Love will cast out Self Love, meekness will cast out pride, righteousness will cast out unrighteousness: and all men made perfect by the Inward Light." Berens, *The Digger Movement in the Days of the Commonwealth* (London: Simpkin, Marshall, Hamilton, Kent, 1906), 49.

20. On reason as God in Winstanley's theology, see Rob Stacy, "For the Bible Tells Me So: The Scriptural Hermeneutics of Gerrard Winstanley," *Pleiades* 12, no. 2 (1992).

21. As John Coffey observes, the exodus narrative was central to the rhetoric of religious reform; see Coffey, *Exodus and Liberation: Deliverance Politics from John Calvin to Martin Luther King, Jr.* (Oxford: Oxford University Press, 2014), 25–55.

22. Anon., *Two Great Fights in Ireland Neer the City of Dublin* (London, 1649), sig. Av.

23. Anon., *Two Great Fights*, sig. Av.

24. Anon., *Two Great Fights*, sig. Av.

25. Walter Blith, *The English Improver Improved or The Survey of Husbandry Surveyed* (London, 1653), sig. C3r.

26. Marchamont Nedham, *The Case of the Common-Wealth of England, Stated* (London, 1650), sig. M4r.

27. Nedham, *The Case of the Common-Wealth*, sig. M4r.

28. Nedham, *The Case of the Common-Wealth*, sig. M4r.

29. A detailed account of the events of 1649 can be found in John Gurney, "Gerrard Winstanley and the Context of Place," *Prose Studies* 36, no. 1 (2014); Gurney, "'Furious Divells'? The Diggers and their Opponents," in Bradstock, *Winstanley and the Diggers*; and Gurney, "Gerrard Winstanley and the Digger Movement in Walton and Cobham," *The Historical Journal* 37, no. 4 (1994).

30. N. H. Keeble, *The Literary Culture of Nonconformity in Later Seventeenth-Century England* (Athens: University of Georgia Press, 1987), 93.

31. Ann Hughes, "Gerrard Winstanley, News Culture, and Law Reform in the Early 1650s," *Prose Studies* 36, no. 1 (2014): 73.

32. Coppe's idea of a class revolution was closely related to his libertinism; see Jean-Pierre Cavaillé, "'Libertine' and 'Libertinism': Polemic Uses of the Terms in Sixteenth- and Seventeenth-Century English and Scottish Literature," *Journal for Early Modern Cultural Studies* 12, no. 2 (2012).

33. Smith, *Perfection Proclaimed*, 271.

34. Coppe, *Copp's Return to the Wayes of Truth* (London, 1651), sig. B3v. References to *Copp's Return* are to this copy and are hereafter given in the text by signature mark.

35. Coppe, *Some Sweet Sips, of Some Spirituall Wine* (London, 1649), sig. A3v. References to *Some Sweet Sips* are to this copy and are hereafter given in the text by signature mark. The terms "Flesh" and "Spirit" refer to 2 Corinthians 3:6, "For the letter killeth, but the spirit giveth life," which many radicals used to justify their antinomianism.

36. Loewenstein, *Representing Revolution*, 97.

37. The radicals' program of helping the poor was "inherently hostile to national distinction" (265); see Jonathan Scott, *England's Troubles: Seventeenth-Century English Political Instability in European Context* (Cambridge: Cambridge University Press, 2000).

38. Nicholas McDowell, "A Ranter Reconsidered: Abiezer Coppe and Civil War Stereotypes," *Seventeenth Century* 12, no. 2 (1997).

39. Coppe's claims to divinity are discussed in Robert Kenny, "'In These Last Days': The Strange Work of Abiezer Coppe," *Seventeenth Century* 13, no. 2 (1998).

40. Anna Trapnel, *The Cry of a Stone*, ed. Hilary Hinds (Tempe: Arizona Center for Medieval and Renaissance Studies, 2000), 45.

41. The Ranters also believed their confusing language was evidence of their divine calling; see Andrew Bradstock, *Radical Religion in Cromwell's England: A Concise History from the English Civil War to the End of the Commonwealth* (London: I. B. Tauris & Co Ltd, 2011), 88.

42. *OED*, s.v. "scandalous" (A.1.a).

43. See Ariel Hessayon, "Coppe, Abiezer (1619–1672?)," *ODNB*, accessed May 29, 2018, http://www.oxforddnb.com.lib-e2.lib.ttu.edu/view/10.1093/ref:odnb/9780198614128. 001.0001/odnb-9780198614128-e-6275?rskey=SacRrK&result=1.

44. Coppe, *A Remonstrance of the Sincere and Zealous Protestation of Abiezer Coppe* (London, 1650/1), sigs. A2r–A2v.

45. Hessayon, "Abiezer Coppe and the Ranters," 355; and Hessayon, *"Gold Tried in the Fire": The Prophet TheaurauJohn Tany and the English Revolution* (Aldershot: Ashgate, 2007), 1–20. Ranter populations have been a topic of debate since J. C. Davis questioned their size and number in *Fear, Myth, and History: The Ranters and the Historians* (Cambridge: Cambridge University Press, 1986).

46. The radicals frequently modeled themselves after the ancient Jewish prophets; see Achsah Guibbory, "England's 'Biblical' Prophets, 1642–60," in *Writing and Religion in England, 1558–1689: Studies in Community-Making and Cultural Memory*, ed. Roger D. Sell and Anthony W. Johnson (Farnham: Ashgate, 2009).

47. On Coppe and the enthusiastic tradition, see Clement Hawes, *Mania and Literary Style: The Rhetoric of Enthusiasm from the Ranters to Christopher Smart* (Cambridge: Cambridge University Press, 1996), 25–100.

4. The Fire and the Scythe

1. Anon., *Gemitus Ecclesiae Cambro-Britannicae: Or, the Candle-Sticks Removed, by the Ejectment of the Ministers of Wales* (London, 1654), sig. A2v.

2. Anon., *Gemitus Ecclesiae*, sig. A3r.

3. Anon., *Gemitus Ecclesiae*, sig. A3r.

4. Kerrigan, *Archipelagic English*, 197. On regional identity during the English Revolution, see Mark Stoyle, "English 'Nationalism,' Celtic Particularism, and the English Civil War," *The Historical Journal* 43, no. 4 (2000); and Robert W. Barrett, *Against All England: Regional Identity and Cheshire Writing, 1195–1656* (South Bend: University of Notre Dame Press, 2009).

5. Henry Vaughan, *The Works of Henry Vaughan*, ed. L. C. Martin (Oxford: Clarendon, 1957), "To My Worthy Friend Master T. Lewes" (ln. 10). References to Henry's works are to this edition and are hereafter given in the text as page number (for prose) or line number (for poetry). On royalist literature during the English Revolution, see Jason McElligott, *Royalism, Print, and Censorship in Revolutionary England* (Woodbridge: Boydell Press, 2007); McElligott and David Smith, eds., *Royalists and Royalism during the English Civil Wars*

(Cambridge: Cambridge University Press, 2007); Robert Wilcher, *The Writing of Royalism, 1628–1660* (Cambridge: Cambridge University Press, 2003); and James Loxley, *Royalism and Poetry in the English Civil Wars: The Drawn Sword* (New York: St. Martin's Press, 1997).

6. On the rise of universalism in the seventeenth century, see D. P. Walker, *The Decline of Hell: Seventeenth-Century Discussions of Eternal Torment* (Chicago: University of Chicago Press, 1964). The Vaughans' universalism was a response to the Welsh millenarianism of men like Llwyd and Powell, which preached the salvation of a select few; see Nigel Smith, "Henry Vaughan and Thomas Vaughan: Welsh Anglicanism, 'Chymick,' and the English Revolution," in *The Oxford Handbook of Literature and the English Revolution*, ed. Laura Lunger Knoppers (Oxford: Oxford University Press, 2012), 416; and Philip West, *Henry Vaughan's Silex Scintillans: Scripture Uses* (Oxford: Oxford University Press, 2001), 196.

7. Jennifer Speake, "Vaughan, Thomas (1621–1666)," *ODNB*, par. 4, accessed May 29, 2018, http://www.oxforddnb.com.lib-e2.lib.ttu.edu/view/10.1093/ref:odnb/9780198614128.001.0001/odnb-9780198614128-e-28148?rskey=vZujUe&result=8.

8. Speake, "Vaughan, Thomas," par. 3.

9. Henry More [Alazonomastix Philalethes], *Observations upon Anthroposophia Theomagica, and Anima Magica Abscondita* (London, 1650), sig. D3v; and Thomas Vaughan, *The Man-Mouse Taken in A Trap, And Tortur'd to Death for Gnawing the Margins of Eugenius Philalethes* (London, 1650), sig. G3r.

10. John Dury, "The Preface upon the Exposition to the Revelation," in *Clavis Apocalyptica: Or, a Prophetical Key*, trans. by Samuel Hartlib (London: William Du Gard, 1651), sig. b2r.

11. On the eschatological aims of mid-century natural philosophy, see Margaret J. Osler, "Robert Boyle on Knowledge of Nature in the Afterlife," in *The Millenarian Turn: Millenarian Contexts of Science, Politics, and Everyday Anglo-American Life in the Seventeenth and Eighteenth Centuries*, ed. James E. Force and Richard H. Popkin (Dordrecht: Kluwer, 2001); and Donald R. Dickson, *The Tessera of Antilia: Utopian Brotherhoods and Secret Societies in the Early Seventeenth Century* (Leiden: Brill, 1998), 145–80.

12. Francis Bacon, *Summi Angliae Cancellarii Instauratio Magna* (London, 1620).

13. Samuel Hartlib, *The Hartlib Papers*, 2nd ed. (Sheffield: Humanities Research Institute, 2002), compact-disc version, letter from Hartlib to Robartes and Waller, dated February 20, 1640/1, ref. 7/43A-B.

14. On Thomas Vaughan, the Hartlib circle, and the Great Instauration, see Mark Greengrass, Michael Leslie, and Timothy Raylor, eds., *Samuel Hartlib and Universal Reformation: Studies in Intellectual Communication* (Cambridge: Cambridge University Press, 1994); and Charles Webster, *The Great Instauration: Science, Medicine and Reform 1626–1660* (London: Gerald Duckworth & Co. Ltd., 1975).

15. Thomas Vaughan, *The Works of Thomas Vaughan*, ed. Arthur Edward Waite (New York: University Books, 1968), *Magia Adamica*, 150. References to Thomas's works are to this edition and are hereafter given in the text.

16. On Thomas and the Rosicrucians, see Michael Srigley, "Thomas Vaughan, the Hartlib Circle and the Rosicrucians," *Scintilla* 6 (2002); and Dickson, *The Tessera of Antilia*, 181–217.

17. Thomas Vaughan, *The Fame and Confession of the Fraternity of R: C: Commonly, of the Rosie Cross* (London, Giles Calvert 1652), sig. A8v, Huntington Library copy no. 600090.

18. The Vaughans' matriculation is described in Brigid Allen, "The Vaughans at Jesus College, Oxford, 1638–48," *Scintilla* 4 (2000).

19. Alchemists were deeply interested in matters of "spiritual alchemy," as Gertrude Hamilton puts it in "Thomas Vaughan and the Divine Art of Alchemy," *Cauda Pavonis: The Hermetic Text Society Newsletter* 4, no. 2 (1985): 1.

20. On materialist philosophy, see Fallon, *Milton among the Philosophers*.

21. LSJ, s.v. ἀποκατάστασις.

22. Origen, *De Principiis*, trans. Rufinus, in *Patrologiae Cursus Completus*, vol. 11, ed. J. P. Migne (Paris, 1857).

23. Anon, *Corpus Hermeticum*, ed. A. D. Nock (Paris: Les Belles Lettres, 2002), 1:87, 88.

24. David Crane observes that the alchemical process "allows nothing to fall outside its boundary," and so death becomes nothing more than "the depositors of sediment in the bottom of the refining vessel." Crane, "The Poetry of Alchemy and the Alchemy of Poetry in the Work of Thomas and Henry Vaughan," *Scintilla* 1 (1997): 116. See also Brian Copenhaver, "Hermes Trismegistus, Proclus, and a Philosophy of Magic," in *Hermeticism and the Renaissance: Intellectual History and the Occult in Early Modern Europe*, ed. by Ingrid Merkel and Allen G. Debus (Washington, DC: Folger Shakespeare Library, 1988).

25. On the context of the debate, see Noel Brann, "The Conflict between Reason and Magic in Seventeenth-Century England: A Case Study of the Vaughan-More Debate," *Huntington Library Quarterly* 43, no. 2 (1980).

26. More, *Observations*, sig. Br.

27. More, *Observations*, sigs. Cr, D3r.

28. More, *Observations*, sig. A4r.

29. More, *Observations*, sigs. B2r, B5r.

30. More, *Observations*, sig. E6r.

31. More, *Observations*, sig. B2r.

32. More, *Observations*, sig. C6r.

33. More, *Observations*, sig. C3v.

34. More, *Observations*, sig. D3v.

35. More, *Observations*, sigs. C6v, G6v.

36. Thomas Vaughan, *The Man-Mouse*, sig. B3v.

37. Vaughan, *The Man-Mouse*, sig. F3r.

38. Vaughan, *The Man-Mouse*, sig. E5r.

39. Vaughan, *The Man-Mouse*, sig. G6v.

40. Vaughan, *The Man-Mouse*, sig. H7r.

41. More, *Enthusiasmus Triumphatus* (London, 1656), sig. A4r.

42. More [Alazonomastix Philalethes], *The Second Lash of Alazonomastix Laid on in Mercie upon that Stubborn Youth Eugenius Philalethes* (London, 1651), sig. B8v.

43. More, *The Second Lash*, sig. Cr.

44. More, *The Second Lash*, sig. H5r.

45. More, *The Second Lash*, sig. G3r.

46. More, *The Second Lash*, sig. H7v.

47. More, *The Second Lash*, sig. I3r.

48. More, *The Second Lash*, sig. I3r.

49. Henry's biographer, F. E. Hutchinson, suggests that Henry was a soldier under Colonel Herbert Price of Brecon Priory until autumn 1645. Hutchinson, *Henry Vaughan: A Life and Interpretation* (Oxford: Clarendon, 1947), 67. John Morrill explains the battle's significance in "Postlude: Between War and Peace, 1651–1662," in *The Civil Wars: A Military History of England, Scotland, and Ireland, 1638–1660*, ed. John Kenyon and Jane Ohlmeyer (Oxford: Oxford University Press, 1998), 306.

50. See Hutchinson, *Henry Vaughan*, 1–20, 254.

51. Adam Fox, "Aubrey, John (1626–1697)," *ODNB*, par. 4, accessed May 29, 2018, http://www.oxforddnb.com.lib-e2.lib.ttu.edu/view/10.1093/ref:odnb/9780198614128.001.0001/odnb-9780198614128-e-886?rskey=3KCF1y&result=2.

52. On the presence of the Welsh countryside in Henry's poetry, Alan Rudrum comments, "One doubts if anyone could stay for even a few days in Scethrog of Talybont [i.e. Skethrock] without realizing how deeply the sound of running water, the quality of light over the hills, and the rapid succession of sunshine, cloud and shower, had informed his imagination." Rudrum, *Henry Vaughan* (Cardiff: University of Wales Press, 1981), 16.

53. On Breconshire's presence in Henry's poetry, see Peter Thomas, "Henry Vaughan, Orpheus, and The Empowerment of Poetry," in *Of Paradise and Light: Essays on Henry Vaughan and John Milton in Honor of Alan Rudrum*, ed. Donald R. Dickson and Holly Faith Nelson (Newark: University of Delaware Press, 2004); and Chris Fitter, "Henry Vaughan's Landscapes of Military Occupation," *Essays in Criticism* 42, no. 2 (1992).

54. Tacitus, *Annals*, ed. George Long (London: Whittaker & Co., 1872), *Ab Excessu Divi Augusti* (12:32), 314.

55. M. Wynn Thomas "'In Occidentem & Tenebras': Putting Henry Vaughan on the Map of Wales," *Scintilla* 2 (1998); Thomas, "'No Englishman': Wales's Henry Vaughan," *Swansea Review* 15 (1995); and Roland Mathias, "In Search of the Silurist," in *Essential Articles for the Study of Henry Vaughan*, ed. Alan Rudrum (Hamden, CT: Archon Books, 1987).

56. On the literary relationship between Herbert and Henry Vaughan, see Jonathan Post, *Henry Vaughan: The Unfolding Vision* (Princeton, NJ: Princeton University Press, 1982).

57. On Herbert's Anglican theology, see Helen Wilcox, "Herbert and Donne," in *The Oxford Handbook of English Literature and Theology*, ed. Andrew W. Hass, David Jasper, and Elisabeth Jay (Oxford: Oxford University Press, 2007), 398–412.

58. Achsah Guibbory, *Ceremony and Community from Herbert to Milton: Literature, Religion, and Cultural Conflict in Seventeenth-Century England* (Cambridge: Cambridge University Press, 1998), 56. On Herbert's appeal to a wide range of readers, see also Helen Wilcox, "In the Temple Precincts: George Herbert and Seventeenth-Century Community-Making," in *Writing and Religion in England, 1558–1689: Studies in Community-Making and Cultural Memory*, ed. Roger D. Sell and Anthony W. Johnson (Farnham: Ashgate, 2009).

59. Henry bears comparison with Robert Herrick, who also used devotional poetry as an instrument of episcopalian resistance to the Commonwealth; see Achsah Guibbory, "Enlarging the Limits of the 'Religious' Lyric: The Case of Herrick's *Hesperides*," in *New Perspectives on the Seventeenth-Century English Religious Lyric*, ed. John Roberts (Columbia: University of Missouri Press, 1994); and Claude Summers, "Herrick, Vaughan, and the Poetry of Anglican Survivalism," in Roberts, *New Perspectives*.

60. William N. West, "Less Well-Wrought Urns: Henry Vaughan and the Decay of the Poetic Monument," *English Literary History* 75, no. 1 (2008): 212.

61. On the details of *Silex Scintillans*'s publication, see William Riley Parker, "Henry Vaughan and His Publishers," *The Library* 20 (1940); and on the title-page art as an emblem of divine judgment, see Graham Parry, *Seventeenth-Century Poetry: The Social Context* (London: Hutchinson Educational, 1985), 101.

62. Gerard Manley Hopkins, *The Letters of Gerard Manley Hopkins to Robert Bridges*, ed. Claude Colleer Abbott (Oxford: Oxford University Press, 1955), 163.

63. On the literary uses of ritual during the English Revolution, see Holly Faith Nelson, "Historical Consciousness and the Politics of Translation in the Psalms of Henry Vaughan," *Studies in Philology* 104, no. 4 (2007); and Lois Potter, *Secret Rites and Secret Writing: Royalist Literature, 1641–1660* (Cambridge: Cambridge University Press, 1989).

64. Marion White Singleton, *God's Courtier: Configuring a Different Grace in George Herbert's Temple* (Cambridge: Cambridge University Press, 1987), 123–33.

65. George Herbert, *The English Poems of George Herbert*, ed. Helen Wilcox (Cambridge: Cambridge University Press, 2007), "Employment (I)," ln. 1–12. References to Herbert's works are to this edition and are hereafter given in the text by line number.

66. *OED*, s.v. "stuff" (I.1).

67. On the political context of "The Proffer," see Alan Rudrum, "Resistance, Collaboration, and Silence: Henry Vaughan and Breconshire Royalism," in *The English Civil Wars in the Literary Imagination*, ed. Claude J. Summers and Ted-Larry Pebworth (Columbia: University of Missouri Press, 1999); and Frederick Rees, "Breckonshire During the Civil War," *Brycheiniog* 8 (1962).

68. See Geraint Jenkins, *The Foundations of Modern Wales, 1642–1780* (Oxford: Clarendon, 1987), 59; and Ann Hughes, "The King, the Parliament, and the Localities during the English Civil War," *Journal of British Studies* 24, no. 2 (1985): 241.

69. On underground religion in revolutionary Wales, see Kenneth Fincham and Stephen Taylor, "Episcopalian Conformity and Nonconformity 1646–1660," in *Royalists and Royalism during the Interregnum*, ed. Jason McElligott and David Smith (Manchester: Manchester University Press, 2010); Philip Jenkins, "Welsh Anglicans and the Interregnum," *Journal of the Historical Society of the Church in Wales* 27 (1990); and Graeme Watson, "The Temple in 'The Night': Henry Vaughan and the Collapse of the Established Church," *Modern Philology* 84, no. 2 (1986).

70. Jeremy Taylor, *Ductor Dubitantium, or The Rule of Conscience* (London: James Flesher, 1660), sig. N4r.

71. Jeremy Taylor, *XXVIII Sermons Preached at Golden Grove* (London: R.N., 1651), "Of Christian Prudence," sig. Y5v.

72. On the ultraroyalist politics of South Wales, see Philip Jenkins, *A History of Modern Wales, 1536–1990* (London: Longman, 1992), 102–44; Jenkins, *The Making of a Ruling Class: The Glamorgan Gentry, 1640–1790* (Cambridge: Cambridge University Press, 1983), 104; Thomas Richards, *A History of the Puritan Movement in Wales: From the Institution of the Church at Llanfaches in 1639 to the Expiry of the Propagation Act in 1653* (London: National Eisteddfod Association, 1920); and John Walker, *An Attempt Towards Recovering an Account of the Numbers and Sufferings of the Clergy [. . .] in the Late Times of the Grand Rebellion* (London: W. S., 1714).

73. Henry wrote poetic tributes to Herbert and Powell that were printed in *Olor Iscanus*: "Venerabili viro, præceptori suo olim & semper Colendissimo M^{ro}. Matthæo Herbert" and "Præstantissimo viro, Thomæ Poëllo in suum de Elementis opticæ libellum." Henry Vaughan, *Works*, ed. Martin, 93.

74. Rudrum, "Resistance, Collaboration, and Silence," 104.

75. Mark A. Kishlansky and John Morrill, "Charles I (1600–1649)," in *ODNB*, par. 102–14, accessed May 29, 2018, http://www.oxforddnb.com.lib-e2.lib.ttu.edu/view/10.1093/ref:odnb/9780198614128.001.0001/odnb-9780198614128-e-5143?rskey=XPPchV&result=3.

76. Anon., *Grace Imprisoned, and Vertue Despised. C. R. in the Isle* (London, 1648).

77. Anon., *A Groane at the Funerall of that Incomparable and Glorious Monarch, Charles the First* (London, 1649), sig. A3v.

78. See Laura Lunger Knoppers, *Politicizing Domesticity from Henrietta Maria to Milton's Eve* (Cambridge: Cambridge University Press, 2011), 86–93.

79. As a closing device, "The Church Militant" was admired and imitated by later seventeenth-century devotional writers; see Adele Davidson, "The Poet as Prophet: Ending *The Temple*," *George Herbert Journal* 35, nos. 1–2 (2012).

80. Raymond A. Anselment, "'The Church Militant': George Herbert and the Metamorphoses of Christian History," *Huntington Library Quarterly* 41, no. 4 (1978).

81. Herbert had personal reasons for sympathizing with the plight of the pilgrims: Sir John Danvers, his stepfather, and Nicholas Ferrar, his friend, were investors in the Virginia Company.

82. Helen Wilcox, "'Religion Stands on Tip-Toe': George Herbert, the New England Poets, and the Transfer of Devotional Modes," in *Shaping the Stuart World, 1603–1714: The Atlantic Connection*, ed. Allan I. Macinnes and Arthur H. Williamson (Leiden: Brill, 2006).

83. Milton, *Paradise Lost*, ed. Lewalski, 11.836.

84. On Henry's universalism, see Diane Kelsey McColley, "Water, Wood, and Stone: The Living Earth in Poems of Vaughan and Milton," in Dickson and Nelson, *Of Paradise and Light*; Alan Rudrum, "For Then the Earth Shall Be All Paradise: Milton, Vaughan and the Neo-Calvinists in the Ecology of the Hereafter," *Scintilla* 4 (2000); Rudrum, "Henry Vaughan, the Liberation of the Creatures, and Seventeenth-Century English Calvinism," *Seventeenth Century Journal* 4, no. 1 (1989); and Rudrum, "Henry Vaughan's 'The Book': A Hermetic Poem," *Journal of the Australasian Universities Language and Literature Association* 16 (1961).

5. The Trial of Charles I and the Redemption of Fallen Community in Milton's *Paradise Lost*

1. On the king's trial as a planned public spectacle, see Clive Holmes, "The Trial and Execution of Charles I," *The Historical Journal* 53, no. 2 (2010); and Mark Kishlansky, "Mission Impossible: Charles I, Oliver Cromwell and the Regicide," *English Historical Review* 125, no. 515 (2010).

2. Samuel Pecke, ed., *A Perfect Diurnall of Some Passages in Parliament [. . .] from Munday the 15. of Janu. till Munday the 22. of Janu. 1648* (London, 1648/9), sig. 13L4v.

3. Anon., *King Charls His Tryal: Or a Perfect Narrative of the Whole Proceedings of the High Court of Justice in the Tryal of the King in Westminster Hall* (London: Peter Cole, 1649), sig. A3r.

4. William L. Sachse offers a helpful account of Charles's prosecutors in "England's 'Black Tribunal': An Analysis of the Regicide Court," *Journal of British Studies* 12, no. 2 (1973).

5. Anon., *King Charls His Tryal*, sig. A3v.

6. Andrew Marvell, *The Poems of Andrew Marvell*, ed. Nigel Smith (Harlow: Pearson, 2007), "An Horatian Ode upon Cromwell's Return from Ireland" (ln. 53). David Loewenstein discusses Milton's irritation at Charles's theatrics in "The King Among the Radicals: Godly Republicans, Levellers, Diggers and Fifth Monarchists," in *The Royal Image: Representations of Charles I*, ed. Thomas N. Corns (Cambridge: Cambridge University Press, 1999).

7. Samuel Pecke, ed., *A Perfect Diurnall of Some Passages in Parliament [. . .] from Munday the 22. of Janu. till Munday the 29. of Janu. 1648* (London, 1648/9), sigs. 13N2v, 13N3r.

8. Pecke, ed., *A Perfect Diurnall, 22. of Janu. till 29. of Janu. 1648*, sig. 13N3r.

9. Pecke, ed., *A Perfect Diurnall, 22. of Janu. till 29. of Janu. 1648*, sig. 13N3r.

10. In order to legitimize the High Court's authority, Parliament passed an ordinance declaring the nation's sovereignty rested with the Commons; see Austin Woolrych, *Britain in Revolution, 1625–1660* (Oxford: Oxford University Press, 2002), 431.

11. Martin Dzelzainis, "'Incendiaries of the State': Charles I and Tyranny," in Corns, *The Royal Image*, 75.

12. Kevin Sharpe, *Image Wars: Kings and Commonwealths in England, 1603–1660* (New Haven, CT: Yale University Press, 2010); see also Sharpe, *Rebranding Rule: The Restoration and Revolution Monarchy, 1660–1714* (New Haven, CT: Yale University Press, 2013). Other major studies on political representation during the English Revolution include Elizabeth Skerpan-Wheeler, "The First 'Royal': Charles I as Celebrity," *PMLA* 126, no. 4 (2011); Mark Knights, *Representation and Misrepresentation in Later Stuart Britain: Partisanship and Political Culture* (Oxford: Oxford University Press, 2005), 3–66; Laura Lunger Knoppers, *Constructing Cromwell: Ceremony, Portrait, and Print, 1645–1661* (Cambridge: Cambridge University Press, 2000); and Corns, *The Royal Image*.

13. David Loewenstein, *"Paradise Lost* and Political Image Wars," *Ben Jonson Journal* 21, no. 2 (2014): 212; Alison A. Chapman, *The Legal Epic: Paradise Lost and the Early Modern Law* (Chicago: University of Chicago Press, 2017), 2.

14. On obedience as the primary heroic virtue of Milton's epic, see Michael Schoenfeldt, "Obedience and Autonomy in *Paradise Lost,*" in *A Companion to Milton,* ed. Thomas N. Corns (Malden, MA: Blackwell, 2003).

15. Loewenstein, *Representing Revolution,* 242–91.

16. On the faithful remnant, see Metzger and Coogan, *The Oxford Companion to the Bible,* s.v. "Remnant," 645–46.

17. In Milton's England, "audience" signified people present at a judicial hearing, and it is indeed through witnessing the trials of the Son, Abdel, and Eve that Milton's readers are encouraged to internalize the attitudes playing out on the page before them; see Stephen B. Dobranski, "Milton's Ideal Readers," in *Milton's Legacy,* ed. Kristin A. Pruitt and Charles W. Durham (Selinsgrove, PA: Susquehanna University Press, 2005), 193.

18. On Milton's national optimism during the Restoration, see Stevens, "Milton and National Identity"; and Stevens, "How Milton's Nationalism Works: Globalization and the Possibilities of Positive Nationalism," in *Early Modern Nationalism and Milton's England,* ed. David Loewenstein and Paul Stevens (Toronto: University of Toronto Press).

19. My sense of Milton's readers as a faithful remnant draws upon Daniel Shore, *Milton and the Art of Rhetoric* (Cambridge: Cambridge University Press, 2012), 21–38; and Achinstein, *Milton and the Revolutionary Reader.*

20. Elizabeth Skerpan-Wheeler, *"Eikon Basilike* and the Rhetoric of Self-Representation," in Corns, *The Royal Image,* 130.

21. Charles I, *Eikon Basilike,* ed. Philip A. Knachel (Ithaca, NY: Cornell University Press, 1966), xii. References to *Eikon Basilike* are to this edition and are hereafter given in the text. On the book's printing and marketing, see Robert Wilcher, *"Eikon Basilike*: The Printing, Composition, Strategy, and Impact of 'The King's Book,'" in *The Oxford Handbook of Literature and the English Revolution,* ed. Laura Lunger Knoppers (Oxford: Oxford University Press, 2012); Kathleen Lynch, "Religious Identity, Stationers' Company Politics, and Three Printers of *Eikon Basilike,*" *PMLA* 101, no. 3 (2007); and Amos Tubb, "Printing the Regicide of Charles I," *History* 89, no. 4 (2004).

22. Charles I, *Eikon Basilike,* ed. Knachel, 188n5.

23. Lois Potter, "The Royal Martyr in the Restoration: National Grief and National Sin," in Corns, *The Royal Image.*

24. Anon., *King Charls His Tryal,* sig. E4v.

25. On Charles's idea of how God intervenes in history, see Richard Ollard, *The Image of the King: Charles I and Charles II* (London: Hodder and Stoughton, 1979), 54.

26. Anon., *King Charls His Tryal,* sig. A2v.

27. Anon., *King Charls His Tryal,* sig. Fv.

28. John Cook, *King Charls His Case: Or, an Appeal to all Rational Men, Concerning His Tryal at the High Court of Justice* (London: Peter Cole, 1649), sig. A2r.

29. Cook, *King Charls His Case,* sig. E3v.

30. Cook, *King Charls His Case,* sig. E4v.

31. Anon., *King Charls His Tryal,* sig. Fv.

32. Milton, *The Tenure of Kings and* Magistrates, in *CPW* 3:193. On Milton and the Presbyterians, see Go Togashi, "Milton and the Presbyterian Opposition, 1649–50: The Engagement Controversy and *The Tenure of Kings and Magistrates,* Second Edition (1649)," *Milton Quarterly* 39, no. 2 (2005): 59–81.

33. Milton, *Eikonoklastes,* in *CPW* 3:341.

34. Knoppers, *Politicizing Domesticity*, 86–93.

35. Richard Helgerson notes that *Eikon Basilike* operated like a regal pageant in that it "made its readers [. . .] want to be subjects." Helgerson, "Milton Reads the King's Book: Print, Performance, and the Making of a Bourgeois Idol," *Criticism* 29, no. 1 (1987): 8.

36. See Andrew Lacey, *The Cult of King Charles the Martyr* (Woodbridge: Boydell Press, 2003), 129–71.

37. Anon., *England's Black Tribunall. Set forth in the Triall of K. Charles, I* (London, 1660), sig. Ar; John Gauden, *Cromwell's Bloody Slaughter-House* (London, 1660), sig. Ar; Anon., *The Oglio of Traytors: Including the Illegal Tryall of His Late Majesty* (London, 1660), sig. Ar; and Anon., *A Hue and Cry after the High Court of Injustice* (London, 1660), sig. Ar.

38. Laura Lunger Knoppers, "'This So Horrid Spectacle': *Samson Agonistes* and the Execution of the Regicides," *English Literary Renaissance* 20, no. 3 (1990).

39. Anon., *A Hue and Cry*, sig. A3r.

40. Anon., *A Hue and Cry*, sig. A3v.

41. Clement Walker, *The High Court of Justice, or Cromvels New Slaughter-House in England* (London, 1660), sigs. E3v, C2r.

42. Walker, *The High Court*, sig. Fv.

43. Anon., *The Oglio of Traytors*, sig. A8v.

44. Anon., *The Tryall of Traytors, or, the Rump in the Pound* (London, 1660), broadside.

45. Anon., *The Tryal of the Pretended Judges* (London, 1660), sig. B2v.

46. Gauden, *Cromwell's Bloody Slaughter-House*, sig. E12v.

47. Gauden, *Cromwell's Bloody Slaughter-House*, sigs. C2r, C10v.

48. Gauden, *Cromwell's Bloody Slaughter-House*, sig. C5v.

49. Gauden, *Cromwell's Bloody Slaughter-House*, sig. B8v.

50. Michael Lieb, *Children of Ezekiel: Aliens, UFOs, The Crisis of Race, and the Advent of End Time* (Durham, NC: Duke University Press, 1998), 29–31.

51. David Quint, *Inside Paradise Lost: Reading the Designs of Milton's Epic* (Princeton, NJ: Princeton University Press, 2014), 41.

52. On Satan's defiance as an act of treason, see Chapman, *The Legal Epic*, 71–84.

53. This point is in contrast to Satan's fall as "a refusal of time," as argued by Amy Boesky, "*Paradise Lost* and the Multiplicities of Time," in Corns, *A Companion to Milton*, 380–92.

54. William Pallister, *Between Worlds: The Rhetorical Universe of Paradise Lost* (Toronto: University of Toronto Press, 2008), 176.

55. On Satan's understanding of time as static, see Valerie Carnes, "Time and Language in Milton's *Paradise Lost*," *English Literary History* 37, no. 4 (1970).

56. Stanley Fish, *Surprised by Sin: The Reader in Paradise Lost* (Berkeley: University of California Press, 1971), 65.

57. On Milton's coopting of Charles's martyrological rhetoric, see Laura Lunger Knoppers, "*Paradise Regained* and the Politics of Martyrdom," *Modern Philology* 90, no. 2 (1992).

58. Samuel Fallon notes the tension between infinity and the "local, temporal expression" (44) demanded by narrative in "Milton's Strange God: Theology and Narrative Form in *Paradise Lost*," *English Literary History* 79, no. 1 (2012).

59. On the Fall as a loss of community, see Guibbory, *Ceremony and Community*, 215–16.

60. *OED*, s.v. "plaint" (3).

61. As Mandy Green observes, Eve's "softness," which is often seen as a mark of her inferiority to Adam, is in fact the quality that sets humanity on the path to spiritual regeneration. Green, *Milton's Ovidian Eve* (Farnham: Ashgate, 2009), 188.

62. On epic's propensity for self-revision, see Alessandro Barchiesi, *Homeric Effects in Vergil's Narrative*, trans. Ilaria Marchesi and Matt Fox (Princeton, NJ: Princeton University Press, 2015); Quint, *Inside Paradise Lost*; Quint, *Epic and Empire*; E. M. W. Tillyard, *The English Epic and Its Background* (London: Chatto and Windus, 1954); and C. S. Lewis, *A Preface to Paradise Lost* (Oxford: Clarendon, 1942).

63. William Allan, "Divine Justice and Cosmic Order in Early Greek Epic," *Journal of Hellenic Studies* 126 (2006).

64. Homer, *Homeri Opera*, ed. David Munro and Thomas Allen (Oxford, 1920), *Iliad* (24.217).

65. Homer, *Homeri Opera*, ed. Munro and Allen, *Iliad* (24.477–79, 503–512).

66. Donna F. Wilson, *Ransom, Revenge, and Heroic Identity in the Iliad* (Cambridge: Cambridge University Press, 2002), 128–30.

67. On the Homeric associations of Milton's Eve, see Gregory Machacek, *Milton and Homer: "Written to Aftertimes"* (Pittsburgh: Duquesne University Press, 2011); Neil Forsyth, *The Satanic Epic* (Princeton, NJ: Princeton University Press, 2003), 239–58.

68. On the similar psychological states of Adam and Satan after their falls, see Anthony Low, "The Fall into Subjectivity: Milton's 'Paradise Within' and 'Abyss of Fears and Horrors,'" in *Reading the Renaissance: Ideas and Idioms from Shakespeare to Milton*, ed. Marc Berley (Pittsburgh, PA: Duquesne University Press, 2003).

69. On Nimrod and tyranny, see Richard Hardin, "Milton's Nimrod," *Milton Quarterly* 22, no. 2 (1998): 38–44.

70. Anon., *King Charls his Tryal*, sig. F2r.

71. Joad Raymond notes that these Old Testament tyrants figured centrally in republican rhetoric of the English Revolution. Raymond, "The King is a Thing," in *Milton and the Terms of Liberty*, ed. Graham Parry and Joad Raymond (Cambridge: D. S. Brewer, 2002), 80–82.

72. John Ogilby, *The Entertainment of His Most Excellent Majestie Charles II, in his Passage through the City of London to his Coronation* (London, 1662), sig. Br.

73. On the cyclical nature of history in books 11 and 12, see Helen Wilcox, "'Is This the End of This New Glorious World?': *Paradise Lost* and the Beginning of the End," *Essays and Studies* 48 (1995).

74. Augustine, *de Civitate Dei*, ed. Dombart and Kalb, 20.1.

BIBLIOGRAPHY

Primary Texts

Andrewes, Lancelot. *The Pattern of Catechistical Doctrine*. London: Roger Norton, 1650.

Anon. *Corpus Hermeticum*. 4 vols. Edited by A. D. Nock. Paris: Les Belles Lettres, 2002.

——. *England's Black Tribunall. Set forth in the Triall of K. Charles, I*. London, 1660.

——. *Gemitus Ecclesiae Cambro-Britannicae: Or, the Candle-Sticks Removed, by the Ejectment of the Ministers of Wales*. London, 1654.

——. *Grace Imprisoned, and Vertue Despised. C. R. in the Isle*. London, 1648.

——. *A Groane at the Funerall of that Incomparable and Glorious Monarch, Charles the First*. London, 1649.

——. *A Hue and Cry after the High Court of Injustice*. London, 1660.

——. *King Charls His Tryal: Or a Perfect Narrative of the Whole Proceedings of the High Court of Justice in the Tryal of the King in Westminster Hall*. London: Peter Cole, 1649.

——. *The Oglio of Traytors: Including the Illegal Tryall of His Late Majesty*. London, 1660.

——. *The Tryal of the Pretended Judges*. London, 1660.

——. *The Tryall of Traytors, or, the Rump in the Pound*. London, 1660.

——. *Two Great Fights in Ireland Neer the City of Dublin*. London, 1649.

Augustine. *De Civitate Dei*. Edited by Bernard Dombart and Alphonsus Kalb. Turnhout: Brepols, 1955.

Bacon, Francis. *Summi Angliae Cancellarii Instauratio Magna*. London, 1620.

Baxter, Richard. *Humble Advice: Or the Heads of Those Things Which Were Offered to Many Honourable Members of Parliament*. London, 1654/5.

——. *The Saints Everlasting Rest*. London, 1662.

Bible, La Sainte. Tours: A. Mame et fils, 1866.

Biblia Sacra Vulgata. Edited by Roger Gryson and Robert Weber. Stuttgart: Deutsche Bibelgesellschaft, 2007.

Blith, Walter. *The English Improver Improved or The Survey of Husbandry Surveyed*. London, 1653.

Boyle, Robert. *Occasional Reflections upon Several Subjects*. London: W. Wilson, 1665.

Bramhall, John. *Castigations of Mr. Hobbes His Last Animadversions, in The Case Concerning Liberty, and Universal Necessity. With an Appendix Concerning The Catching of Leviathan, Or the Great Whale*. London: E. T., 1658.

Calamy, Edmund. *Gods Free Mercy to England*. London, 1641/2.

Calvin, John. *Institutes of the Christian Religion*. 2 vols. Edited and translated by John Allen. Philadelphia: Presbyterian Board of Christian Education, 1936.

Charles I. *Eikon Basilike*. Edited by Philip A. Knachel. Ithaca, NY: Cornell University Press, 1966.

Church of England. *The Booke of Common Prayer*. London: Robert Barker, 1604.

Cook, John. *King Charls His Case: Or, an Appeal to all Rational Men, Concerning His Tryal at the High Court of Justice*. London: Peter Cole, 1649.

Coppe, Abiezer. *Copp's Return to the Wayes of Truth*. London, 1651.

——. *A Fiery Flying Roll*. London, 1649/50.

——. *A Remonstrance of the Sincere and Zealous Protestation of Abiezer Coppe*. London, 1650/1.

——. *A Second Fiery Flying Roule*. London, 1649/50.

——. *Some Sweet Sips, of Some Spirituall Wine*. London, 1649.

Donne, John. *The Complete English Poems of John Donne*. Edited by C. A. Patrides. London: Dent & Sons Ltd, 1985.

——. *Sermons*. 10 vols. Edited by George Potter and Evelyn Simpson. Berkeley: University of California Press, 1955.

Dury, John. "The Preface upon the Exposition to the Revelation." In *Clavis Apocalyptica: Or, a Prophetical Key*. Translated by Samuel Hartlib. London: William Du Gard, 1651.

Filmer, Robert. *Observations Concerning the Originall of Government*. London, 1652.

Gauden, John. *Cromwell's Bloody Slaughter-House*. London, 1660.

Hartlib, Samuel. *Considerations Tending to the Happy Accomplishment of England's Reformation in Church and State*. London, 1647.

——. *The Hartlib Papers*. 2nd ed. Sheffield: Humanities Research Institute, 2002. Compact-disc version.

Herbert, George. *The English Poems of George Herbert*. Edited by Helen Wilcox. Cambridge: Cambridge University Press, 2007.

Hobbes, Thomas. *Leviathan: With Selected Variants from the Latin Edition of 1668.* Edited by Edwin Curley. Indianapolis: Hackett, 1994.

Homer. *Homeri Opera.* 5 vols. Edited by David Munro and Thomas Allen. Oxford: Clarendon, 1920.

Lilburne, John. *The Second Part of England's New-Chaines Discovered.* In *The Leveller Tracts 1647–1653,* edited by William Haller and Godfrey Davies. New York: Columbia University Press, 1944.

Luther, Martin. *Luther's Works.* 55 vols. Edited and translated by Jaroslav Pelikan et al. Saint Louis, MO: Concordia Publishing House, 1955–59.

———. *Luther's Works, vol. 44–47: The Christian in Society.* Edited and translated by James Atkinson. Philadelphia: Fortress Press, 1966–71.

———. *Sermons.* 3 vols. Edited and translated by Eugene Klug. Grand Rapids: Baker, 1996.

Marshall, Stephen. *Meroz Curse for Not Helping the Lord against the Mightie.* London, 1641.

———. *The Strong Helper or, the Interest, and Power of the Prayers of the Destitute.* London: Richard Cotes, 1645.

Marvell, Andrew. *The Poems of Andrew Marvell.* Edited by Nigel Smith. Harlow: Pearson, 2007.

Milton, John. *The Complete Prose Works of John Milton.* Edited by Don M. Wolfe. 8 vols. New Haven, CT: Yale University Press, 1953–82.

———. *Complete Shorter Poems.* Edited by Stella P. Revard. Malden, MA: Blackwell, 2009.

———. *The Major Works.* Edited by Stephen Orgel and Jonathan Goldberg. Oxford: Oxford University Press, 1991.

———. *The Minor Poems.* Edited by A. S. P. Woodhouse and Douglas Bush. Vol. 2 of *A Variorum Commentary on the Poems of John Milton,* edited by Merritt Hughes. New York: Columbia University Press, 1970.

———. *Paradise Lost.* Edited by Barbara K. Lewalski. Malden, MA: Blackwell, 2007.

———. *Paradise Lost.* Edited by Robert Vaughan. London: Cassell & Co., 1866.

———. *Paradise Regain'd: A Poem, in Four Books. To which is added Samson Agonistes and Poems upon Several Occasions.* Edited by Thomas Newton. London, 1752.

More, Henry. *Enthusiasmus Triumphatus.* London, 1656.

———. [Alazonomastix Philalethes]. *Observations upon Anthroposophia Theomagica, and Anima Magica Abscondita.* London, 1650.

———. [Alazonomastix Philalethes]. *The Second Lash of Alazonomastix Laid on in Mercie upon that Stubborn Youth Eugenius Philalethes.* London, 1651.

Nedham, Marchamont. *The Case of the Common-Wealth of England, Stated.* London, 1650.

Ogilby, John. *The Entertainment of His Most Excellent Majestie Charles II, in his Passage through the City of London to his Coronation.* London, 1662.

Origen. *De Principiis.* Translated by Rufinus. *Patrologiae Cursus Completus, vol. 11.* Edited by J. P. Migne. Paris, 1857.

Pecke, Samuel, ed. *A Perfect Diurnall of Some Passages in Parliament [. . .] from Munday the 15. of Janu. till Munday the 22. of Janu. 1648.* London, 1648/9.

——, ed. *A Perfect Diurnall of Some Passages in Parliament [. . .] from Munday the 22. of Janu. till Munday the 29. of Janu. 1648.* London, 1648/9.

Perkins, William. *A Godly and Learned Exposition or Commentarie upon the Three First Chapters of the Revelation.* London, 1606.

Shakespeare, William. *The Riverside Shakespeare.* Edited by G. Blakemore Evans. Boston: Houghton Mifflin, 1997.

Sidney, Philip. *The Defence of Poesie.* London: Thomas Crede, 1595.

Tacitus. *Annals.* Edited by George Long. London: Whittaker & Co., 1872.

Taylor, Jeremy. *XXVIII Sermons Preached at Golden Grove.* London: R.N., 1651.

——. *Ductor Dubitantium, or The Rule of Conscience.* London: James Flesher, 1660.

Tertullian. *Tertulliani Opera.* 2 vols. Edited by E. Dekkers. Turnhout: Brepols, 1954.

Trapnel, Anna. *The Cry of a Stone.* Edited by Hilary Hinds. Tempe: Arizona Center for Medieval and Renaissance Studies, 2000.

——. *Strange and Wonderful Newes from White-Hall.* London, 1654.

Vaughan, Henry. *The Works of Henry Vaughan.* Edited by L. C. Martin. Oxford: Clarendon, 1957.

Vaughan, Thomas. *The Fame and Confession of the Fraternity of R: C: Commonly, of the Rosie Cross.* London: Giles Calvert, 1652.

——. *The Man-Mouse Taken in A Press, And Tortur'd to Death for Gnawing the Margins of Eugenius Philalethes.* London, 1650.

——. *The Works of Thomas Vaughan.* Edited by Arthur Edward Waite. New York: University Books, 1968.

Walker, Clement. *The High Court of Justice, or Cromwels New Slaughter-House in England.* London, 1660.

Walker, John. *An Attempt Towards Recovering an Account of the Numbers and Sufferings of the Clergy [. . .] in the Late Times of the Grand Rebellion.* London: W. S., 1714.

Winstanley, Gerrard. *The Complete Works of Gerrard Winstanley.* 2 vols. Edited by Thomas N. Corns, Ann Hughes, and David Loewenstein. Oxford: Oxford University Press, 2009.

Young, Thomas. *Hopes Incouragement Pointed at in a Sermon.* London, 1643/4.

Secondary Texts

Abrams, M. H. "Five Types of Lycidas." In *Milton's Lycidas: The Tradition and the Poem,* edited by C. A. Patrides, 216–35. Columbia: University of Missouri Press, 1983.

Achinstein, Sharon. *Milton and the Revolutionary Reader.* Princeton, NJ: Princeton University Press, 1994.

Agamben, Giorgio. *The Time That Remains: A Commentary on the Letter to the Romans.* Translated by Patricia Dailey. Palo Alto: Stanford University Press, 2010.

Allan, William. "Divine Justice and Cosmic Order in Early Greek Epic." *Journal of Hellenic Studies* 126 (2006): 1–35.

Allen, Brigid. "The Vaughans at Jesus College, Oxford 1638–48." *Scintilla* 4 (2000): 68–78.

Alsop, J. D. "Gerrard Winstanley: What Do We Know of his Life?" In Bradstock, *Winstanley and the Diggers, 1649–1999*, 19–36.

Anderson, Benedict. *Imagined Communities: Reflections on the Origin and Spread of Nationalism*. New York: Verso, 1983.

Angel, Andrew. *Chaos and the Son of Man: The Hebrew Chaoskampf Tradition in the Period 515 BCE to 200 CE*. London: T & T Clark, 2006.

Anselment, Raymond A. "'The Church Militant': George Herbert and the Metamorphoses of Christian History." *Huntington Library Quarterly* 41, no. 4 (1978): 299–316.

Appelbaum, Robert. *Literature and Utopian Politics in Seventeenth-Century England*. Cambridge: Cambridge University Press, 2002.

——. "Milton, the Gunpowder Plot, and the Mythography of Terror." *Modern Language Quarterly* 68, no. 4 (2007): 461–91.

Arnold, Bill T. "Old Testament Eschatology and the Rise of Apocalypticism." In *The Oxford Handbook of Eschatology*, edited by Jerry L. Walls, 23–39. Oxford: Oxford University Press, 2008.

Auerbach, Erich. *Mimesis: The Representation of Reality in Western Literature: Fiftieth Anniversary Edition*. Edited by Edward W. Said. Princeton, NJ: Princeton University Press, 2003.

Backus, Irena. *Reformation Readings of the Apocalypse: Geneva, Zurich, and Wittenberg*. Oxford: Oxford University Press, 2000.

Baker, David. *Between Nations: Shakespeare, Spenser, Marvell and the Question of Britain*. Palo Alto: Stanford University Press, 1997.

Baker, David, and Willy Maley, eds. *British Identities and English Renaissance Literature*. Cambridge: Cambridge University Press, 2002.

Ball, Bryan. *A Great Expectation: Eschatological Thought in English Protestantism to 1660*. Leiden: Brill, 1975.

Barchiesi, Alessandro. *Homeric Effects in Vergil's Narrative*. Translated by Ilaria Marchesi and Matt Fox. Princeton, NJ: Princeton University Press, 2015.

Barrett, Robert W. *Against All England: Regional Identity and Cheshire Writing, 1195–1656*. South Bend: University of Notre Dame Press, 2009.

Bauckham, Richard. *Tudor Apocalypse: Sixteenth-Century Apocalypticism, Millenarianism, and the English Reformation*. Oxford: Sutton Courtenay, 1978.

Baumgold, Deborah. *Hobbes's Political Theory*. Cambridge: Cambridge University Press, 1988.

Baumrin, Bernard. "Hobbes's Christian Commonwealth." *Hobbes Studies* 13 (2000): 3–11.

Berens, Lewis. *The Digger Movement in the Days of the Commonwealth*. London: Simpkin, Marshall, Hamilton, Kent, 1906.

Blau, Adrian. "Reason, Deliberation, and the Passions." In Martinich and Hoekstra, *The Oxford Handbook of Hobbes*, 195–220.

Boesky, Amy. "The Maternal Shape of Mourning: A Reconsideration of *Lycidas*." *Modern Philology* 95, no. 4 (1998): 463–83.

——. "*Paradise Lost* and the Multiplicities of Time." In Corns, *A Companion to Milton*, 380–92.

Bouchard, Gary. *Colin's Campus: Cambridge Life and the English Eclogue*. Selinsgrove, PA: Susquehanna University Press, 2000.

Brady, Andrea, and Emily Butterworth, eds. *The Uses of the Future in Early Modern Europe*. New York: Routledge, 2010.

Bradstock, Andrew. *Radical Religion in Cromwell's England: A Concise History from the English Civil War to the End of the Commonwealth*. London: I. B. Tauris & Co Ltd., 2011.

——. "Restoring all Things from the Curse: Millenarianism, Alchemy, Science and Politics in the Writings of Gerrard Winstanley." In *The Arts of 17th-Century Science: Representations of the Natural World in European and North American Culture*, edited by Claire Jowitt and Diane Watt, 95–108. Aldershot: Ashgate, 2002.

——. "Theological Aspects of Winstanley's Writings." *Prose Studies* 36, no. 1 (2014): 32–42.

——, ed. *Winstanley and the Diggers, 1649–1999*. London: Frank Cass, 2000.

Brailsford, Henry Noel. *The Levellers and the English Revolution*. London: Cresset, 1961.

Brann, Noel. "The Conflict between Reason and Magic in Seventeenth-Century England: A Case Study of the Vaughan-More Debate." *Huntington Library Quarterly* 43, no. 2 (1980): 103–26.

Bredekamp, Horst. "Thomas Hobbes's Visual Strategies." In *The Cambridge Companion to Hobbes's "Leviathan*," edited by Patricia Springborg, 29–60. Cambridge: Cambridge University Press, 2007.

——. *Thomas Hobbes Visuelle Strategien: Der Leviathan, Urbild des modernen Staates; Werkillustrationen und Portraits*. Berlin: Akademie Verlag, 1999.

Brown, Cedric. "John Milton and Charles Diodati: Reading the Textual Exchanges of Friends." In Jones, *Young Milton*, 107–36.

Brown, Eric C. "Underworld Sailors in Milton's 'Lycidas' and Virgil's *Aeneid*." *Milton Quarterly* 36, no. 1 (2002): 34–45.

Brown, Keith. "The Artist of the *Leviathan* Title-Page." *British Library Journal* 4, no. 1 (1978): 24–36.

Bruce, F. F. *The English Bible: A History of Translations*. Oxford: Oxford University Press, 1961.

Calhoun, Craig. *Nationalism*. Minneapolis: University of Minnesota Press, 1997.

——. *Nations Matter: Culture, History, and the Cosmopolitan Dream*. New York: Routledge, 2007.

Carey, Frances. *The Apocalypse and the Shape of Things to Come*. Toronto: University of Toronto Press, 1999.

Carnes, Valerie. "Time and Language in Milton's *Paradise Lost*." *English Literary History* 37, no. 4 (1970): 517–39.

Cavaillé, Jean-Pierre. "'Libertine' and 'Libertinism': Polemic Uses of the Terms in Sixteenth-and Seventeenth-Century English and Scottish Literature." *Journal for Early Modern Cultural Studies* 12, no. 2 (2012): 12–36.

Chakravarty, Prasanta. "*Like Parchment in the Fire*": Literature and Radicalism in the English Civil War*. New York: Routledge, 2006.

Chapman, Alison A. *The Legal Epic: Paradise Lost and the Early Modern Law*. Chicago: University of Chicago Press, 2017.

Chapman, Alister, John Coffey, and Brad Gregory, eds. *Seeing Things Their Way: Intellectual History and the Return of Religion*. South Bend: University of Notre Dame Press, 2009.

Cheney, Patrick. *Marlowe's Counterfeit Profession: Ovid, Spenser, Counter-Nationhood*. Toronto: University of Toronto Press, 1997.

Christianson, Paul. *Reformers and Babylon: English Apocalyptic Visions from the Reformation to the Eve of the Civil War*. Toronto: University of Toronto Press, 1978.

Cohn, Norman. *The Pursuit of the Millennium*. London: Secker and Warburg, 1957.

Coffey, John. *Exodus and Liberation: Deliverance Politics from John Calvin to Martin Luther King, Jr*. Oxford: Oxford University Press, 2014.

Collins, Jeffrey R. *The Allegiance of Thomas Hobbes*. Oxford: Oxford University Press, 2005.

Collins, John J. "Apocalyptic Eschatology in the Ancient World." In *The Oxford Handbook of Eschatology*, edited by Jerry L. Walls, 40–55. Oxford: Oxford University Press, 2008.

——, ed. "Apocalypse: The Morphology of a Genre." Special issue, *Semeia* 14 (1979).

Condren, Conal. "Sovereignty." In *The Oxford Handbook of British Philosophy in the Seventeenth Century*, edited by Peter R. Anstey, 587–608. Oxford: Oxford University Press, 2013.

Copenhaver, Brian. "Hermes Trismegistus, Proclus, and a Philosophy of Magic." In *Hermeticism and the Renaissance: Intellectual History and the Occult in Early Modern Europe*, edited by Ingrid Merkel and Allen G. Debus, 79–110. Washington, DC: Folger Shakespeare Library, 1988.

Corns, Thomas N, ed. *A Companion to Milton*. Malden, MA: Blackwell, 2003.

——. "'I Have Writ, I Have Acted, I Have Peace': The Personal and the Political in the Writings of Winstanley and Some Contemporaries." *Prose Studies* 36, no. 1 (2014): 43–51.

——. "Milton and the Characteristics of a Free Commonwealth." In *Milton and Republicanism*, edited by David Armitage, Armand Himy, and Quentin Skinner, 25–42. Cambridge: Cambridge University Press, 1995.

——. "Milton before *Lycidas*." In *Milton and the Terms of Liberty*, edited by Graham Parry and Joad Raymond, 23–36. Cambridge: D. S. Brewer, 2002.

——, ed. *The Royal Image: Representations of Charles I*. Cambridge: Cambridge University Press, 1999.

——. *Uncloistered Virtue: English Political Literature, 1640–1660*. Oxford: Clarendon, 1992.

Coudert, Allison, and Jeffrey Shoulson, eds. *Hebraica Veritas? Christian Hebraists and the Study of Judaism in Early Modern Europe*. Philadelphia: University of Pennsylvania Press, 2004.

Crane, David. "The Poetry of Alchemy and the Alchemy of Poetry in the Work of Thomas and Henry Vaughan." *Scintilla* 1 (1997): 115–22.

Cressy, David. *Birth, Marriage, and Death: Ritual, Religion, and Life-Cycle in Tudor and Stuart England*. Oxford: Oxford University Press, 1999.

Cromartie, Alan. "The God of Thomas Hobbes." *The Historical Journal* 51, no. 4 (2008): 857–79.

Crosby, Sumner McKnight, and Pamela Z. Blum. *The Royal Abbey of Saint-Denis: From Its Beginnings to the Death of Suger, 475–1151*. New Haven, CT: Yale University Press, 1987.

Cummins, Juliet, ed. *Milton and the Ends of Time*. Cambridge: Cambridge University Press, 2003.

Curley, Edwin. "'I Durst Not Write So Boldly,' or How to Read Hobbes's Theological-Political Treatise." In *Hobbes e Spinoza*, edited by Emilia Giancotti, 497–593. Naples: Bibliopolis, 1992.

Davidson, Adele. "The Poet as Prophet: Ending *The Temple*." *George Herbert Journal* 35, nos. 1–2 (2012): 1–22.

Davis, J. C. *Fear, Myth, and History: The Ranters and the Historians*. Cambridge: Cambridge University Press, 1986.

Deigh, John. "Political Obligation." In Martinich and Hoekstra, *The Oxford Handbook of Hobbes*, 293–314.

Derrida, Jacques. "No Apocalypse, Not Now (Full Speed Ahead, Seven Missiles, Seven Missives)." *Diacritics* 14, no. 2 (1984): 20–31.

Dickson, Donald R. *The Tessera of Antilia: Utopian Brotherhoods and Secret Societies in the Early Seventeenth Century*. Leiden: Brill, 1998.

Dobranski, Stephen B., ed. *Milton in Context*. Cambridge: Cambridge University Press, 2010.

——. "Milton's Ideal Readers." In *Milton's Legacy*, edited by Kristin A. Pruitt and Charles W. Durham, 191–207. Selinsgrove, PA: Susquehanna University Press, 2005.

Duffy, Eamon. *The Stripping of the Altars: Traditional Religion in England 1400–1580*. New Haven, CT: Yale University Press, 1992.

Duran, Angelica. "The Blind Bard, According to John Milton and His Contemporaries." *Mosaic* 46, no. 3 (2013): 141–57.

Dzelzainis, Martin. "'Incendiaries of the State': Charles I and Tyranny." In Corns, *The Royal Image*, 74–95.

Edwards, M. J. "The Pilot and the Keys: Milton's *Lycidas* 167–171." 108, no. 4 (2011): 605–18.

Erlande-Brandenburg, Alain, and Caroline Rose. *Notre-Dame de Paris*. New York: Harry N. Abrams, Inc., 1998.

Escobedo, Andrew. "The Invisible Nation: Church, State, and Schism in Milton's England." In Loewenstein and Stevens, *Early Modern Nationalism*, 173–201.

——. *Nationalism and Historical Loss in Renaissance England: Foxe, Dee, Spenser, Milton*. Ithaca, NY: Cornell University Press, 2004.

Fallon, Samuel. "Milton's Strange God: Theology and Narrative Form in *Paradise Lost*." *English Literary History* 79, no. 1 (2012): 33–57.

Fallon, Stephen M. *Milton among the Philosophers: Poetry and Materialism in Seventeenth-Century England*. Ithaca, NY: Cornell University Press, 1991.

Farr, James. "Atomes of Scripture: Hobbes and the Politics of Biblical Interpretation." In *Thomas Hobbes and Political Theory*, edited by Mary G. Dietz, 172–96. Lawrence: University of Kansas Press, 1990.

Fincham, Kenneth, and Stephen Taylor. "Episcopalian Conformity and Nonconformity 1646–1660." In *Royalists and Royalism during the Interregnum*, edited by Jason McElligott and David Smith, 18–43. Manchester: Manchester University Press, 2010.

Firth, Katharine. *The Apocalyptic Tradition in Reformation Britain: 1530–1645.* Oxford: Oxford University Press, 1979.

Fish, Stanley. *Surprised by Sin: The Reader in Paradise Lost.* Berkeley: University of California Press, 1971.

Fiske, Dixon. "Milton in the Middle of Life: Sonnet XIX." *English Literary History* 41, no. 1 (1974): 37–49.

Fitter, Chris. "Henry Vaughan's Landscapes of Military Occupation." *Essays in Criticism* 42, no. 2 (1992): 123–47.

Fixler, Michael. *Milton and the Kingdoms of God.* Evanston, IL: Northwestern University Press, 1964.

Flesch, William. "Narrative, Judgment, and Justice in *Paradise Lost.*" In *Milton's Rival Hermeneutics: Reason is but Choosing,* edited by Richard J. DuRocher and Margaret Olofson Thickstun, 135–55. Pittsburgh: Duquesne University Press, 2012.

Forsyth, Neil. "The English Church." In Dobranski, *Milton in Context,* 292–304.

——. "'Lycidas': A Wolf in Saint's Clothing." *Critical Inquiry* 35, no. 3 (2009): 684–702.

——. *The Old Enemy: Satan and the Combat Myth.* Princeton, NJ: Princeton University Press, 1987.

——. *The Satanic Epic.* Princeton, NJ: Princeton University Press, 2003.

Frost, Stanley. *Old Testament Apocalyptic: Its Origins and Growth.* London: Epworth Press, 1952.

Göttler, Christine. *Last Things: Art and the Religious Imagination in the Age of Reform.* Turnhout: Brepols, 2010.

Green, Mandy. *Milton's Ovidian Eve.* Farnham: Ashgate, 2009.

Greenfeld, Liah. *Nationalism: Five Roads to Modernity.* Cambridge, MA: Harvard University Press, 1992.

Greengrass, Mark, Michael Leslie, and Timothy Raylor, eds. *Samuel Hartlib and Universal Reformation: Studies in Intellectual Communication.* Cambridge: Cambridge University Press, 1994.

Greenslade, S. L., ed. *The Cambridge History of the Bible.* Vol. 3. *The West from the Reformation to the Present Day.* Cambridge: Cambridge University Press, 1963.

Gregerson, Linda. "Milton and the Tragedy of Nations." *PMLA* 129, no. 4 (2014): 672–87.

Gregory, Tobias. "Murmur and Reply: Rereading Milton's Sonnet 19." *Milton Studies* 51 (2010): 21–43.

Gribben, Crawford. "Early Modern Reformed Eschatology." In *The Oxford Handbook of Early Modern Theology, 1600–1800,* edited by Ulrich L. Lehner, Richard A. Muller, and A. G. Roeber, 259–72. Oxford: Oxford University Press, 2016.

Guibbory, Achsah. *Ceremony and Community from Herbert to Milton: Literature, Religion, and Cultural Conflict in Seventeenth-Century England.* Cambridge: Cambridge University Press, 1998.

——. *Christian Identity, Jews, and Israel in Seventeenth-Century England.* Oxford: Oxford University Press, 2010.

——. "England's 'Biblical' Prophets, 1642–60." In *Writing and Religion in England, 1558–1689: Studies in Community-Making and Cultural Memory,* edited by Roger D. Sell and Anthony W. Johnson, 305–25. Farnham: Ashgate, 2009.

——. "Enlarging the Limits of the 'Religious' Lyric: The Case of Herrick's *Hesperides*." In *New Perspectives on the Seventeenth-Century English Religious Lyric*, edited by John Roberts, 28–45. Columbia: University of Missouri Press, 1994.

Gurney, John. *Brave Community: The Digger Movement in the English Revolution*. Manchester: Manchester University Press, 2007.

——. "'Furious Divells'? The Diggers and their Opponents." In Bradstock, *Winstanley and the Diggers, 1649–1999*, 73–86.

——. "Gerrard Winstanley and the Context of Place." *Prose Studies* 36, no. 1 (2014): 1–14.

——. "Gerrard Winstanley and the Digger Movement in Walton and Cobham." *The Historical Journal* 37, no. 4 (1994): 775–802.

Haan, Estelle. "Milton's *In Quintum Novembris* and the Anglo-Latin Gunpowder Epic." *Humanistica Lovaniensia* 41 (1992): 221–95.

Habermas, Jürgen. *The Postnational Constellation: Political Essays*. Cambridge, MA: MIT Press, 2001.

Hackenbracht, Ryan. "Hobbes's Hebraism and the Last Judgement in *Leviathan*." In *Identities in Early Modern English Writing: Religion, Gender, Nation*, edited by Lorna Fitzsimmons, 85–115. Turnhout: Brepols, 2014.

——. "Milton and the Parable of the Talents: Nationalism and the Prelacy Controversy in Revolutionary England." *Philological Quarterly* 94, nos. 1–2 (2015): 71–93.

——. "The Plague of 1625–26, Apocalyptic Anticipation, and Milton's Elegy III." *Studies in Philology* 108, no. 3 (2011): 403–38.

Hale, John K. "Milton and the Gunpowder Plot: *In Quintum Novembris* Reconsidered." *Humanistica Lovaniensia* 50 (2001): 351–66.

——. *Milton's Cambridge Latin: Performing in the Genres 1625–1632*. Tempe, AZ: Arizona Center for Medieval and Renaissance Studies, 2005.

Hall, R. F. "Milton's Sonnets and His Contemporaries." In *The Cambridge Companion to Milton*, edited by Dennis Danielson, 98–112. Cambridge: Cambridge University Press, 1999.

Hamilton, Gertrude. "Thomas Vaughan and the Divine Art of Alchemy." *Cauda Pavonis: The Hermetic Text Society Newsletter* 4, no. 2 (1985): 1–3.

Hampton, Jean. *Hobbes and the Social Contract Tradition*. Cambridge: Cambridge University Press, 1986.

Hanford, James Holly. "The Arrangement and Dates of Milton's Sonnets." *Modern Philology* 18, no. 9 (1921): 475–83.

Hardin, Richard. "Milton's Nimrod." *Milton Quarterly* 22, no. 2 (1998): 38–44.

Haskin, Dayton. *Milton's Burden of Interpretation*. Philadelphia: University of Pennsylvania Press, 1994.

Hawes, Clement. *Mania and Literary Style: The Rhetoric of Enthusiasm from the Ranters to Christopher Smart*. Cambridge: Cambridge University Press, 1996.

Hawkes, David. *Idols of the Marketplace: Idolatry and Commodity Fetishism in English Literature, 1580–1680*. New York: Palgrave, 2001.

Hayes, T. Wilson. *Winstanley the Digger: A Literary Analysis of Radical Ideas in the English Revolution*. Cambridge, MA: Harvard University Press, 1979.

Helgerson, Richard. *Forms of Nationhood: The Elizabethan Writing of England*. Chicago: University of Chicago Press, 1992.

——. "Milton Reads the King's Book: Print, Performance, and the Making of a Bourgeois Idol." *Criticism* 29, no. 1 (1987): 1–25.

Herbert, Gary. "Fear of Death and the Foundations of Natural Right in the Philosophy of Thomas Hobbes." *Hobbes Studies* 7 (1994): 56–68.

Hessayon, Ariel. "Abiezer Coppe and the Ranters." In Knoppers, *The Oxford Handbook of Literature and the English Revolution*, 346–74.

——. *"Gold Tried in the Fire": The Prophet TheaurauJohn Tany and the English Revolution*. Aldershot: Ashgate, 2007.

Hill, Christopher. *The English Bible and the Seventeenth-Century Revolution*. London: Allen Lane, 1993.

——. *Milton and the English Revolution*. New York: Viking, 1978.

——. *The World Turned Upside Down: Radical Ideas during the English Revolution*. London: Temple Smith, 1972.

Hindle, Steve. "Dearth and the English Revolution: The Harvest Crisis of 1647–50." *The Economic History Review* 61, no. S1 (2008): 64–98.

Holmes, Clive. "The Trial and Execution of Charles I." *The Historical Journal* 53, no. 2 (2010): 289–16.

Holstun, James. *Ehud's Dagger: Class Struggle in the English Revolution*. New York: Verso, 2000.

——. *A Rational Millennium: Puritan Utopias of Seventeenth-Century England and America*. Oxford: Oxford University Press, 1987.

Hood, F. C. *The Divine Politics of Thomas Hobbes: An Interpretation of Leviathan*. Oxford: Clarendon, 1964.

Hopkins, Gerard Manley. *The Letters of Gerard Manley Hopkins to Robert Bridges*. Edited by Claude Colleer Abbott. Oxford: Oxford University Press, 1955.

Hughes, Ann. "Gerrard Winstanley, News Culture, and Law Reform in the Early 1650s." *Prose Studies* 36, no. 1 (2014): 63–76.

——. "The King, the Parliament, and the Localities during the English Civil War." *Journal of British Studies* 24, no. 2 (1985): 236–63.

Hunter, William B., Jr., "Milton and the Waldensians." *Studies in English Literature* 11, no. 1 (1971): 153–64.

Hutchinson, F. E. *Henry Vaughan: A Life and Interpretation*. Oxford: Clarendon, 1947.

Hutton, Sarah. *British Philosophy in the Seventeenth Century*. Oxford: Oxford University Press, 2015.

Jackson, Nicholas D. *Hobbes, Bramhall and the Politics of Liberty and Necessity: A Quarrel of the Civil Wars and Interregnum*. Cambridge: Cambridge University Press, 2007.

Jenkins, Geraint. *The Foundations of Modern Wales, 1642–1780*. Oxford: Clarendon, 1987.

Jenkins, Philip. *A History of Modern Wales, 1536–1990*. London: Longman, 1992.

——. *The Making of a Ruling Class: The Glamorgan Gentry, 1640–1790*. Cambridge: Cambridge University Press, 1983.

——. "Welsh Anglicans and the Interregnum." *Journal of the Historical Society of the Church in Wales* 27 (1990): 51–59.

Jerrold, Blanchard. *Life of Gustave Doré: with One Hundred and Thirty-Eight Illustrations from Original Drawings by Doré*. London: W. H. Allen & Co., 1891.

Johnston, David. *The Rhetoric of Leviathan: Thomas Hobbes and the Politics of Cultural Transformation*. Princeton, NJ: Princeton University Press, 1986.

Jones, Edward, ed. *Young Milton: The Emerging Author, 1620–1642*. Oxford: Oxford University Press, 2013.

Jue, Jeffrey. *Heaven Upon Earth: Joseph Mede (1586–1638) and the Legacy of Millenarianism*. Dordrecht: Springer, 2006.

Kahn, Victoria. *Wayward Contracts: The Crisis of Political Obligation in England, 1640–74*. Princeton, NJ: Princeton University Press, 2004.

Kantorowicz, Ernst H. *The King's Two Bodies: A Study in Medieval Political Theology*. Princeton, NJ: Princeton University Press, 1957.

Keeble, N. H. *The Literary Culture of Nonconformity in Later Seventeenth-Century England*. Athens: University of Georgia Press, 1987.

——. "Pamphlet Wars." In Dobranski, *Milton in Context*, 429–38.

Kelley, Maurice. "Milton's Later Sonnets and the Cambridge Manuscript." *Modern Philology* 54, no. 1 (1956): 220–25.

Kelly, James, and Catherine Bray. "The Keys to Milton's 'Two-Handed Engine' in *Lycidas* (1637)." *Milton Quarterly* 44, no. 2 (2010): 122–42.

Kennedy, Geoff. *Diggers, Levellers, and Agrarian Capitalism: Radical Political Thought in Seventeenth-Century England*. Lanham, MD: Lexington Books, 2008.

Kenny, Robert. "'In These Last Days': The Strange Work of Abiezer Coppe." *Seventeenth Century* 13, no. 2 (1998): 156–84.

Kermode, Frank. *The Sense of an Ending: Studies in the Theory of Fiction*. Oxford: Oxford University Press, 2000.

Kerrigan, John. *Archipelagic English: Literature, History, and Politics 1603–1707*. Oxford: Oxford University Press, 2008.

Kishlansky, Mark A. "Mission Impossible: Charles I, Oliver Cromwell and the Regicide." *English Historical Review* 125, no. 515 (2010): 844–74.

Knight, Sarah. "Milton and the Idea of the University." In Jones, *Young Milton*, 137–60.

Knights, Mark. *Representation and Misrepresentation in Later Stuart Britain: Partisanship and Political Culture*. Oxford: Oxford University Press, 2005.

Knoppers, Laura Lunger. *Constructing Cromwell: Ceremony, Portrait, and Print, 1645–1661*. Cambridge: Cambridge University Press, 2000.

——, ed. *The Oxford Handbook of Literature and the English Revolution*. Oxford: Oxford University Press, 2012.

——. "*Paradise Regained* and the Politics of Martyrdom." *Modern Philology* 90, no. 2 (1992): 200–219.

——. *Politicizing Domesticity from Henrietta Maria to Milton's Eve*. Cambridge: Cambridge University Press, 2011.

——. "'This So Horrid Spectacle': *Samson Agonistes* and the Execution of the Regicides." *English Literary Renaissance* 20, no. 3 (1990): 487–504.

Knott, John. "The Biblical Matrix of Milton's 'On the Late Massacre in Piemont.'" *Philological Quarterly* 62, no. 2 (1983): 259–63.

Kodalle, Klaus-Michael. "Covenant: Hobbes's Philosophy of Religion and His Political System 'More Geometrico.'" In *Hobbes's Science of Natural Justice*, edited by C. Walton and P. J. Johnson, 223–38. Dordrecht: Nijhoff, 1987.

Kranidas, Thomas. *Milton and the Rhetoric of Zeal*. Pittsburgh: Duquesne University Press, 2005.

Kraynak, Robert. *History and Modernity in the Thought of Thomas Hobbes*. Ithaca, NY: Cornell University Press, 1990.

Lacey, Andrew. *The Cult of King Charles the Martyr*. Woodbridge: Boydell Press, 2003.

Leftow, Brian. *Time and Eternity*. Ithaca, NY: Cornell University Press, 1991.

Leonard, John. "That Two-Handed Engine and the Millennium at the Door." In Jones, *Young Milton*, 252–79.

Lessay, Franck. "Hobbes's Covenant Theology and Its Political Implications." In Springborg, *The Cambridge Companion to Hobbes's "Leviathan,"* 243–70.

Lewalski, Barbara K. "Contemporary History as Literary Subject: Milton's Sonnets." *Milton Quarterly* 47, no. 4 (2013): 220–30.

——. *The Life of John Milton: A Critical Biography*. Malden, MA: Blackwell, 2000.

——. "Milton and the Millennium." In Cummins, *Milton and the Ends of Time*, 13–28.

Lewis, C. S. *A Preface to Paradise Lost*. Oxford: Clarendon, 1942.

Lieb, Michael. *Children of Ezekiel: Aliens, UFOs, The Crisis of Race, and the Advent of End Time*. Durham, NC: Duke University Press, 1998.

Lipking, Lawrence. "The Genius of the Shore: Lycidas, Adamastor, and the Poetics of Nationalism." *PMLA* 111, no. 2 (1996): 205–21.

Lobo, Giuseppina Iacono. *Writing Conscience and the Nation in Revolutionary England*. Toronto: University of Toronto Press, 2017.

Loewenstein, David. "Digger Writing and Rural Dissent in the English Revolution: Representing England as a Common Treasury." In *The Country and the City Revisited: England and the Politics of Culture, 1550–1850*, edited by Gerald MacLean, Donna Landry, and Joseph P. Ward, 74–88. Cambridge: Cambridge University Press, 1999.

——. "Gerrard Winstanley and the Diggers." In Knoppers, *The Oxford Handbook of Literature and the English Revolution*, 327–45.

——. "The King Among the Radicals: Godly Republicans, Levellers, Diggers and Fifth Monarchists." In Corns, *The Royal Image*, 96–121.

——. "Late Milton: Early Modern Nationalist or Patriot?" *Milton Studies* 48 (2008): 53–71.

——. "Milton's Nationalism and the English Revolution: Strains and Contradictions." In Loewenstein and Stevens, *Early Modern Nationalism*, 25–50.

——. "*Paradise Lost* and Political Image Wars." *Ben Jonson Journal* 21, no. 2 (2014): 203–27.

——. *Representing Revolution in Milton and His Contemporaries: Religion, Politics, and Polemics in Radical Puritanism*. Cambridge: Cambridge University Press, 2001.

Loewenstein, David, and Paul Stevens, eds. *Early Modern Nationalism and Milton's England*. Toronto: University of Toronto Press, 2008.

Low, Anthony. "The Fall into Subjectivity: Milton's 'Paradise Within' and 'Abyss of Fears and Horrors.'" In *Reading the Renaissance: Ideas and Idioms from Shakespeare to Milton*, edited by Marc Berley, 205–32. Pittsburgh: Duquesne University Press, 2003.

Loxley, James. *Royalism and Poetry in the English Civil Wars: The Drawn Sword*. New York: St. Martin's Press, 1997.

Lupton, Julia Reinhard. *Citizen-Saints: Shakespeare and Political Theology*. Chicago: University of Chicago Press, 2005.

Luxon, Thomas H. *Single Imperfection: Milton, Marriage and Friendship*. Pittsburgh: Duquesne University Press, 2005.

Lynch, Kathleen. "Religious Identity, Stationers' Company Politics, and Three Printers of *Eikon Basilike*." *PMLA* 101, no. 3 (2007): 285–312.

Machacek, Gregory. *Milton and Homer: "Written to Aftertimes."* Pittsburgh: Duquesne University Press, 2011.

Malan, Dan. *Gustave Doré: Adrift on Dreams of Splendor: A Comprehensive Biography and Bibliography*. St. Louis, MO: Malan Classical Enterprises, 1995.

Malcolm, Noel. "Hobbes and Spinoza." In *The Cambridge History of Political Thought 1450–1700*, edited by J. H. Burns, 530–57. Cambridge: Cambridge University Press, 1991.

Mâle, Emile. *The Gothic Image: Religious Art in France of the Thirteenth Century*. Translated by Dora Nussey. New York: Harper & Row, 1958.

Maley, Willy. *Nation, State and Empire in English Renaissance Literature: Shakespeare to Milton*. New York: Palgrave, 2003.

Martin, Catherine Gimelli. "The Enclosed Garden and the Apocalypse: Immanent versus Transcendent Time in Milton and Marvell." In Cummins, *Milton and the Ends of Time*, 144–69.

Martinich, A. P. "Authorization and Representation in Hobbes's *Leviathan*." In Martinich and Hoekstra, *The Oxford Handbook of Hobbes*, 315–38.

——. "Interpreting the Religion of Thomas Hobbes: An Exchange: Hobbes's Erastianism and Interpretation." *Journal of the History of Ideas* 70, no. 1 (2009): 143–63.

——. *The Two Gods of Leviathan: Thomas Hobbes on Religion and Politics*. Cambridge: Cambridge University Press, 1992.

Martinich, A. P., and Kinch Hoekstra, eds. *The Oxford Handbook of Hobbes*. Oxford: Oxford University Press, 2016.

Mathias, Roland. "In Search of the Silurist." In *Essential Articles for the Study of Henry Vaughan*, edited by Alan Rudrum, 189–214. Hamden, CT: Archon Books, 1987.

McColley, Diane Kelsey. "Water, Wood, and Stone: The Living Earth in Poems of Vaughan and Milton." In *Of Paradise and Light: Essays on Henry Vaughan and John Milton in Honor of Alan Rudrum*, edited by Donald R. Dickson and Holly Faith Nelson, 269–91. Newark, DE: University of Delaware Press, 2004.

McDowell, Nicholas. *The English Radical Imagination: Culture, Religion, and Revolution, 1630–1660*. Oxford: Clarendon, 2003.

——. "Ideas of Creation in the Writings of Richard Overton the Leveller and *Paradise Lost*." *Journal of the History of Ideas* 66, no. 1 (2005): 59–78.

——. "A Ranter Reconsidered: Abiezer Coppe and Civil War Stereotypes." *Seventeenth Century* 12, no. 2 (1997): 173–205.

McElligott, Jason. *Royalism, Print, and Censorship in Revolutionary England.* Woodbridge: Boydell Press, 2007.

McElligott, Jason, and David Smith, eds. *Royalists and Royalism during the English Civil Wars.* Cambridge: Cambridge University Press, 2007.

McGinn, Bernard. *The Calabrian Abbot: Joachim of Fiore in the History of Western Thought.* New York: Macmillan, 1985.

——. *Visions of the End: Apocalyptic Traditions in the Middle Ages.* New York: Columbia University Press, 1979.

Metzger, Bruce M., and Michael D. Coogan, eds. *The Oxford Companion to the Bible.* Oxford: Oxford University Press, 1993.

Miller, Jeffrey Alan. "Milton and the Conformable Puritanism of Richard Stock and Thomas Young." In Jones, *Young Milton,* 72–106.

Mintz, Samuel. *The Hunting of Leviathan: Seventeenth-Century Reactions to the Materialism and Moral Philosophy of Thomas Hobbes.* Cambridge, MA: Harvard University Press, 1962.

Mohamed, Feisal G. "Milton, Sir Henry Vane, and the Brief but Significant Life of Godly Republicanism." *Huntington Library Quarterly* 76, no. 1 (2013): 83–104.

Morrill, John. "Postlude: Between War and Peace, 1651–1662." In *The Civil Wars: A Military History of England, Scotland, and Ireland, 1638–1660,* edited by John Kenyon and Jane Ohlmeyer, 306–28. Oxford: Oxford University Press, 1998.

Mueller, Janel. "Embodying Glory: The Apocalyptic Strain in Milton's *Of Reformation.*" In *Politics, Poetics, and Hermeneutics in Milton's Prose,* edited by David Loewenstein and James Grantham Turner, 9–40. Cambridge: Cambridge University Press, 1990.

Nardo, Anna K. *Milton's Sonnets and the Ideal Community.* Lincoln: University of Nebraska Press, 1979.

Nelson, Eric. *The Hebrew Republic: Jewish Sources and the Transformation of European Political Thought.* Cambridge, MA: Harvard University Press, 2010.

Nelson, Holly Faith. "Historical Consciousness and the Politics of Translation in the Psalms of Henry Vaughan." *Studies in Philology* 104, no. 4 (2007): 501–25.

Netzley, Ryan. *Lyric Apocalypse: Milton, Marvell, and the Nature of Events.* New York: Fordham University Press, 2014.

Nicolson, Marjorie. "Milton's 'Old Damoetas.'" *Modern Language Notes* 41, no. 5 (1926): 293–300.

Norbrook, David. *Writing the English Republic: Poetry, Rhetoric and Politics, 1627–1660.* Cambridge: Cambridge University Press, 1999.

Oberman, Heiko. *Luther: Man between God and the Devil.* Translated by Eileen Walliser-Schwarzbart. New Haven, CT: Yale University Press, 1989.

Ollard, Richard. *The Image of the King: Charles I and Charles II.* London: Hodder and Stoughton, 1979.

Osler, Margaret J. "Robert Boyle on Knowledge of Nature in the Afterlife." In *The Millenarian Turn: Millenarian Contexts of Science, Politics, and Everyday Anglo-American Life in the Seventeenth and Eighteenth Centuries,* edited by James E. Force and Richard H. Popkin, 43–54. Dordrecht: Kluwer, 2001.

Ozment, Steven. *The Serpent and the Lamb: Cranach, Luther, and the Making of the Reformation.* New Haven, CT: Yale University Press, 2010.

Pallister, William. *Between Worlds: The Rhetorical Universe of Paradise Lost.* Toronto: University of Toronto Press, 2008.

Parker, William Riley. "The Dates of Milton's Sonnets on Blindness." *PMLA* 73, no. 3 (1958): 196–200.

——. "Henry Vaughan and His Publishers." *The Library* 20 (1940): 401–6.

——. *Milton: A Biography.* 2 vols. Oxford: Clarendon, 1968.

Parkin, Jon. *Taming the Leviathan: The Reception of the Political and Religious Ideas of Thomas Hobbes in England, 1640–1700.* Cambridge: Cambridge University Press, 2007.

Parry, Graham. *Seventeenth-Century Poetry: The Social Context.* London: Hutchinson Educational, 1985.

Patrides, C. A. "'Something Like Prophetick Strain': Apocalyptic Configurations in Milton." In Patrides and Wittreich, *Apocalypse in English Renaissance Thought and Literature,* 207–39.

Patrides, C. A., and Joseph Wittreich, eds. *The Apocalypse in English Renaissance Thought and Literature: Patterns, Antecedents, and Repercussions.* Ithaca, NY: Cornell University Press, 1984.

Patterson, W. B. *King James VI and I and the Reunion of Christendom.* Cambridge: Cambridge University Press, 1997.

Pelikan, Jaroslav. *The Reformation of the Bible / The Bible of the Reformation.* New Haven, CT: Yale University Press, 1996.

Pequigney, Joseph. "Milton's Sonnet XIX Reconsidered." *Texas Studies in Literature and Language* 8, no. 4 (1967): 485–98.

Picciotto, Joanna. *Labors of Innocence in Early Modern England.* Cambridge, MA: Harvard University Press, 2010.

Price, David Hotchkiss. *Albrecht Dürer's Renaissance: Humanism, Reformation, and the Art of Faith.* Ann Arbor: University of Michigan Press, 2006.

Pocock, J. G. A. *The Ancient Constitution and the Feudal Law: A Study of English Historical Thought in the Seventeenth Century.* Cambridge: Cambridge University Press, 1957.

——. *Politics, Language, and Time: Essays on Political Thought and History.* New York: Atheneum, 1971.

——, ed. *The Varieties of British Political Thought, 1500–1800.* Cambridge: Cambridge University Press, 1993.

Popkin, Richard H., and Matthew Goldish, eds. *Millenarianism and Messianism in Early Modern European Culture.* Vol. 1. *Jewish Messianism in the Early Modern World.* Dordrecht: Kluwer, 2001.

Post, Jonathan. *Henry Vaughan: The Unfolding Vision.* Princeton, NJ: Princeton University Press, 1982.

Potter, Lois. "The Royal Martyr in the Restoration: National Grief and National Sin." In Corns, *The Royal Image,* 240–62.

——. *Secret Rites and Secret Writing: Royalist Literature, 1641–1660.* Cambridge: Cambridge University Press, 1989.

Quint, David. *Epic and Empire: Politics and Generic Form from Virgil to Milton.* Princeton, NJ: Princeton University Press, 1993.

———. *Inside Paradise Lost: Reading the Designs of Milton's Epic*. Princeton, NJ: Princeton University Press, 2014.

Quistorp, Heinrich. *Calvin's Doctrine of the Last Things*. Translated by Harold Knight. Richmond, VA: John Knox Press, 1955.

Rapin, Rene. "Milton's Sonnet XIX." *Notes and Queries* 20 (1973): 380–81.

Raymond, Joad. "The King is a Thing." In *Milton and the Terms of Liberty*, edited by Graham Parry and Joad Raymond, 69–94. Cambridge: D. S. Brewer, 2002.

———. "The Literature of Controversy." In Corns, *A Companion to Milton*, 191–210.

———. *Milton's Angels: The Early-Modern Imagination*. Oxford: Oxford University Press, 2010.

Rees, Frederick. "Breckonshire During the Civil War." *Brycheiniog* 8 (1962): 1–9.

Reeves, Marjorie. *The Influence of Prophecy in the Later Middle Ages: A Study in Joachimism*. Oxford: Clarendon, 1969.

Reisner, Noam. "Obituary and Rapture in Milton's Memorial Latin Poems." In Jones, *Young Milton*, 161–81.

Revard, Stella. "*Lycidas*." In Corns, *A Companion to Milton*, 246–60.

———. *Milton and the Tangles of Neaera's Hair: The Making of the 1645 Poems*. Columbia: University of Missouri Press, 1997.

Richards, Thomas. *A History of the Puritan Movement in Wales: From the Institution of the Church at Llanfaches in 1639 to the Expiry of the Propagation Act in 1653*. London: National Eisteddfod Association, 1920.

Rogers, John. *The Matter of Revolution: Science, Poetry, and Politics in the Age of Milton*. Ithaca, NY: Cornell University Press, 1996.

Rosenblatt, Jason P. *Renaissance England's Chief Rabbi: John Selden*. Oxford: Oxford University Press, 2006.

Rudd, Jay. "Milton's Sonnet 18 and Psalm 137." *Milton Quarterly* 26, no. 3 (1992): 80–81.

Rudrum, Alan. "For Then the Earth Shall Be All Paradise: Milton, Vaughan and the Neo-Calvinists in the Ecology of the Hereafter." *Scintilla* 4 (2000): 39–5.

———. *Henry Vaughan*. Cardiff: University of Wales Press, 1981.

———. "Henry Vaughan, the Liberation of the Creatures, and Seventeenth-Century English Calvinism." *Seventeenth Century Journal* 4, no. 1 (1989): 33–54.

———. "Henry Vaughan's 'The Book': A Hermetic Poem." *Journal of the Australasian Universities Language and Literature Association* 16 (1961): 161–65.

———. "Resistance, Collaboration, and Silence: Henry Vaughan and Breconshire Royalism." In *The English Civil Wars in the Literary Imagination*, edited by Claude J. Summers and Ted-Larry Pebworth, 102–18. Columbia: University of Missouri Press, 1999.

Sachse, William L. "England's 'Black Tribunal': An Analysis of the Regicide Court." *Journal of British Studies* 12, no. 2 (1973): 69–85.

Sacks, Peter. *The English Elegy: Studies in the Genre from Spenser to Yeats*. Baltimore: Johns Hopkins University Press, 1985.

Sasek, Lawrence. "'Ere Half My Days': A Note on Milton's *Sonnet 19*." *Milton Quarterly* 15, no. 1 (1981): 16–18.

Sauer, Elizabeth. *Milton, Toleration, and Nationhood*. Cambridge: Cambridge University Press, 2014.

——. "Tolerationism, the Irish Crisis, and Milton's *On the Late Massacre in Piemont.*" *Milton Studies* 44 (2005): 40–61.

Sauter, Gerhard. "Protestant Theology." In *The Oxford Handbook of Eschatology.* Edited by Jerry L. Walls, 248–62. Oxford: Oxford University Press, 2008.

Schmitt, Carl. *The Leviathan in the State Theory of Thomas Hobbes: Meaning and Failure of a Political Symbol.* Translated by George Schwab and Erna Hilfstein. Westport, CT: Greenwood, 1996.

Schoenfeldt, Michael. "Obedience and Autonomy in *Paradise Lost.*" In Corns, *A Companion to Milton*, 363–79.

Schwyzer, Philip, and Simon Mealor, eds. *Archipelagic Identities: Literature and Identity in the Atlantic Archipelago, 1550–1800.* Aldershot: Ashgate, 2004.

Scott, Jonathan. *England's Troubles: Seventeenth-Century English Political Instability in European Context.* Cambridge: Cambridge University Press, 2000.

Serjeantson, Richard. "Becoming a Philosopher in Seventeenth-Century Britain." In *The Oxford Handbook of British Philosophy in the Seventeenth Century*, edited by Peter R. Anstey, 9–40. Oxford: Oxford University Press, 2013.

Sharpe, Kevin. *Image Wars: Kings and Commonwealths in England, 1603–1660.* New Haven, CT: Yale University Press, 2010.

——. *Rebranding Rule: The Restoration and Revolution Monarchy, 1660–1714.* New Haven, CT: Yale University Press, 2013.

Shawcross, John. *John Milton: The Self and the World.* Lexington: University of Kentucky Press, 1993.

——. "Milton's Sonnet 19: Its Date of Authorship and Its Interpretation." *Notes and Queries* 4 (1957): 442–46.

Shell, Marc. *Money, Language, and Thought: Literary and Philosophical Economies from the Medieval to the Modern Era.* Berkeley: University of California Press, 1982.

Shore, Daniel. *Milton and the Art of Rhetoric.* Cambridge: Cambridge University Press, 2012.

Shoulson, Jeffrey. *Fictions of Conversion: Jews, Christians, and Cultures of Change in Early Modern England.* Philadelphia: University of Pennsylvania Press, 2013.

Shrimplin, Valerie. *Sun-Symbolism and Cosmology in Michelangelo's Last Judgment.* Kirksville, MO: Truman State University Press, 2000.

Shuger, Debora Kuller. *The Renaissance Bible: Scholarship, Sacrifice, and Subjectivity.* Berkeley: University of California Press, 1994.

Shulman, George. *Radicalism and Reverence: The Political Thought of Gerrard Winstanley.* Berkeley: University of California Press, 1989.

Silver, Victoria. "*Lycidas* and the Grammar of Revelation." *English Literary History* 58, no. 4 (1991): 779–808.

Singleton, Marion White. *God's Courtier: Configuring a Different Grace in George Herbert's Temple.* Cambridge: Cambridge University Press, 1987.

Skerpan-Wheeler, Elizabeth. "*Eikon Basilike* and the Rhetoric of Self-Representation." In Corns, *The Royal Image*, 122–140.

——. "The First 'Royal': Charles I as Celebrity." *PMLA* 126, no. 4 (2011): 912–34.

Skinner, Quentin. *The Foundations of Modern Political Thought.* 2 vols. Cambridge: Cambridge University Press, 1978.

——. *Hobbes and Republican Liberty*. Cambridge: Cambridge University Press, 2008.

——. "Hobbes on Persons, Authors and Representatives." In Springborg, *The Cambridge Companion to Hobbes's "Leviathan,"* 157–80.

——. "The Ideological Context of Hobbes's Theory of Political Obligation." In *Hobbes and Rousseau: A Collection of Critical Essays*, edited by Maurice Cranston and Richard Peters, 109–42. Garden City, NY: Doubleday, 1972.

——. *Liberty before Liberalism*. Cambridge: Cambridge University Press, 1998.

——. *Reason and Rhetoric in the Philosophy of Thomas Hobbes*. Cambridge: Cambridge University Press, 1996.

——. *Visions of Politics*. 3 vols. Cambridge: Cambridge University Press, 2002.

Smith, Nigel. "The Charge of Atheism and the Language of Radical Speculation, 1640–1660." In *Atheism from the Reformation to the Enlightenment*, edited by Michael Hunter and David Wootton, 131–58. Oxford: Clarendon, 1992.

——. "Henry Vaughan and Thomas Vaughan: Welsh Anglicanism, 'Chymick,' and the English Revolution." In Knoppers, *The Oxford Handbook of Literature and the English Revolution*, 409–24.

——. *Literature and Revolution in England, 1640–1660*. New Haven, CT: Yale University Press, 1994.

——. *Perfection Proclaimed: Language and Literature in English Radical Religion 1640–1660*. Oxford: Oxford University Press, 1989.

Sommerville, Johann P. "Hobbes and Absolutism." In Martinich and Hoekstra, *The Oxford Handbook of Hobbes*, 378–96.

——. "Hobbes, Selden, Erastianism, and the History of the Jews." In *Hobbes and History*, edited by G. A. J. Rogers and Tom Sorrell, 160–88. New York: Routledge, 2000.

Song, Eric B. *Dominion Undeserved: Milton and the Perils of Creation*. Ithaca, NY: Cornell University Press, 2013.

Spragens, Thomas. *The Politics of Motion: The World of Thomas Hobbes*. Lexington: University of Kentucky Press, 1973.

Springborg, Patricia. "Hobbes, Heresy, and the *Historia Ecclesiastica*." *Journal of the History of Ideas* 55, no. 4 (1994): 553–71.

——. "Hobbes's Biblical Beasts: Leviathan and Behemoth." *Political Theory* 23, no. 2 (1995): 353–75.

Srigley, Michael. "Thomas Vaughan, the Hartlib Circle and the Rosicrucians." *Scintilla* 6 (2002): 31–54.

Stacy, Rob. "For the Bible Tells Me So: The Scriptural Hermeneutics of Gerrard Winstanley." *Pleiades* 12, no. 2 (1992): 76–84.

Stevens, Paul. "How Milton's Nationalism Works: Globalization and the Possibilities of Positive Nationalism." In Loewenstein and Stevens, *Early Modern Nationalism*, 273–301.

——. "Milton and National Identity." In *The Oxford Handbook of Milton*, edited by Nicholas McDowell and Nigel Smith, 342–63. Oxford: Oxford University Press, 2009.

——. "Milton's Janus-Faced Nationalism: Soliloquy, Subject, and the Modern Nation State." *Journal of English and Germanic Philology* 100, no. 2 (2001): 247–68.

——. "Milton's Nationalism and the Rights of Memory." In *Imagining Death in Spenser and Milton*, edited by Elizabeth Bellamy, Patrick Cheney, and Michael Schoenfeldt, 171–84. Basingstoke: Palgrave, 2003.

——. "Milton's 'Renunciation' of Cromwell: The Problem of Raleigh's Cabinet-Council." *Modern Philology* 98, no. 3 (2001): 363–92.

——. "The Pre-Secular Politics of *Paradise Lost*." In *The Cambridge Companion to Paradise Lost*, edited by Louis Schwartz, 94–108. Cambridge: Cambridge University Press, 2014.

Stoyle, Mark. "English 'Nationalism,' Celtic Particularism, and the English Civil War." *The Historical Journal* 43, no. 4 (2000): 1113–28.

Strauss, Leo. *The Political Philosophy of Hobbes: Its Basis and Its Genesis*. Oxford: Clarendon, 1936.

Summers, Claude. "Herrick, Vaughan, and the Poetry of Anglican Survivalism." In *New Perspectives on the Seventeenth-Century English Religious Lyric*, edited by John Roberts, 46–74. Columbia: University of Missouri Press, 1994.

Sussmann, Naomi. "How Many Commonwealths can *Leviathan* Swallow? Covenant, Sovereign and People in Hobbes's Political Theory." *British Journal for the History of Philosophy* 18, no. 4 (2010): 575–96.

Svendsen, Kester. "Milton's Sonnet on the Massacre in Piedmont." *Shakespeare Bulletin* 20 (1945): 147–55.

Taylor, Charles. *A Secular Age*. Cambridge, MA: Belknap Press of Harvard University Press, 2007.

Taylor, David. "Gerrard Winstanley at Cobham." In Bradstock, *Winstanley and the Diggers, 1649–1999*, 37–41.

Teskey, Gordon. "Dead Shepherd: Milton's *Lycidas*." In *Milton's Rival Hermeneutics: "Reason is But Choosing,"* edited by Richard J. DuRocher and Margaret Thickstun, 31–56. Pittsburgh: Duquesne University Press, 2012.

Thickstun, Margaret. "Resisting Patience in Milton's Sonnet 19." *Milton Quarterly* 44, no. 3 (2010): 168–80.

Thomas, M. Wynn. "'In Occidentem & Tenebras': Putting Henry Vaughan on the Map of Wales." *Scintilla* 2 (1998): 7–24.

——. "'No Englishman': Wales's Henry Vaughan," *Swansea Review* 15 (1995): 1–19.

Thomas, Peter. "Henry Vaughan, Orpheus, and The Empowerment of Poetry." In *Of Paradise and Light: Essays on Henry Vaughan and John Milton in Honor of Alan Rudrum*, edited by Donald R. Dickson and Holly Faith Nelson, 218–49. Newark: University of Delaware Press, 2004.

Tillyard, E. M. W. *The English Epic and Its Background*. London: Chatto and Windus, 1954.

Togashi, Go. "Milton and the Presbyterian Opposition, 1649–50: The Engagement Controversy and *The Tenure of Kings and Magistrates*, Second Edition (1649)." *Milton Quarterly* 39, no. 2 (2005): 59–81.

Toon, Peter, ed. *Puritans, The Millennium and the Future of Israel: Puritan Eschatology 1600 to 1660*. Cambridge: James Clarke & Co. Ltd, 1970.

Torrance, T. F. *Kingdom and Church: A Study in the Theology of the Reformation*. Edinburgh: Oliver and Boyd, 1956.

Totaro, Rebecca. *Suffering in Paradise: The Bubonic Plague in English Literature from More to Milton*. Pittsburgh: Duquesne University Press, 2005.

Trubowitz, Rachel J. "Body Politics in *Paradise Lost*." *PMLA* 121, no. 2 (2006): 388–404.

Tubb, Amos. "Printing the Regicide of Charles I." *History* 89, no. 4 (2004): 500–524.

Tuck, Richard. "The Christian Atheism of Thomas Hobbes." In Hunter and Wootton, *Atheism from the Reformation*, 111–30.

——. *Natural Rights Theories: Their Origin and Development*. Cambridge: Cambridge University Press, 1979.

Tuve, Rosemond. *A Reading of George Herbert*. London: Faber & Faber, 1952.

Urban, David V. "The Talented Mr. Milton: A Parabolic Laborer and His Identity." *Milton Studies* 43 (2004): 1–18.

——. "Talents and Labourers: Parabolic Tension in Milton's Sonnet 19." In *Milton in France*, edited by Christophe Tournu, 61–71. New York: Peter Lang, 2008.

Wakeman, Mary. *God's Battle with the Monster: A Study in Biblical Imagery*. Leiden: Brill, 1973.

Walker, D. P. *The Decline of Hell: Seventeenth-Century Discussions of Eternal Torment*. Chicago: University of Chicago Press, 1964.

Warren, Christopher N. *Literature and the Law of Nations, 1580–1680*. Oxford: Oxford University Press, 2015.

Warrender, Howard. *The Political Philosophy of Hobbes: His Theory of Obligation*. Oxford: Clarendon, 1957.

Watson, Graeme. "The Temple in 'The Night': Henry Vaughan and the Collapse of the Established Church." *Modern Philology* 84, no. 2 (1986): 144–61.

Watson, Rebecca. *Chaos Uncreated: A Reassessment of the Theme of Chaos in the Hebrew Bible*. Berlin: Walter de Gruyter, 2005.

Webster, Charles. *The Great Instauration: Science, Medicine and Reform 1626–1660*. London: Gerald Duckworth & Co. Ltd., 1975.

West, Philip. *Henry Vaughan's Silex Scintillans: Scripture Uses*. Oxford: Oxford University Press, 2001.

West, William N. "Less Well-Wrought Urns: Henry Vaughan and the Decay of the Poetic Monument." *English Literary History* 75, no. 1 (2008): 197–217.

Wilcher, Robert. "*Eikon Basilike*: The Printing, Composition, Strategy, and Impact of 'The King's Book.'" In Knoppers, *The Oxford Handbook of Literature and the English Revolution*, 289–308.

——. *The Writing of Royalism, 1628–1660*. Cambridge: Cambridge University Press, 2003.

Wilcox, Helen. "Herbert and Donne." In *The Oxford Handbook of English Literature and Theology*, edited by Andrew W. Hass, David Jasper, and Elisabeth Jay, 398–412. Oxford: Oxford University Press, 2007.

——. "In the Temple Precincts: George Herbert and Seventeenth-Century Community-Making." In *Writing and Religion in England, 1558–1689: Studies in Community-Making and Cultural Memory*, edited by Roger D. Sell and Anthony W. Johnson, 253–72. Farnham: Ashgate, 2009.

——. "'Is This the End of This New Glorious World?': *Paradise Lost* and the Beginning of the End." *Essays and Studies* 48 (1995): 1–15.

———. "'Religion Stands on Tip-Toe': George Herbert, the New England Poets, and the Transfer of Devotional Modes." In *Shaping the Stuart World, 1603–1714: The Atlantic Connection*, edited by Allan I. Macinnes and Arthur H. Williamson, 147–74. Leiden: Brill, 2006.

Wilson, Donna F. *Ransom, Revenge, and Heroic Identity in the Iliad*. Cambridge: Cambridge University Press, 2002.

Wilson, F. P. *The Plague in Shakespeare's London*. Oxford: Clarendon, 1927.

Wittreich, Joseph. *Visionary Poetics: Milton's Tradition and His Legacy*. San Marino, CA: Huntington Library, 1979.

Woodbridge, Linda. *English Revenge Drama: Money, Resistance, Equality*. Cambridge: Cambridge University Press, 2010.

Woolrych, Austin. *Britain in Revolution, 1625–1660*. Oxford: Oxford University Press, 2002.

Worden, Blair. *Literature and Politics in Cromwellian England: John Milton, Andrew Marvell, Marchamont Nedham*. Oxford: Oxford University Press, 2007.

Wright, George Herbert. *Religion, Politics, and Thomas Hobbes*. Dordrecht: Springer, 2006.

Index